DISCOVERING ROBIN HOOD

Dedicated to my wonderful niece, Mya Driver

The waies, through which my weary steps I guyde,
In this research of old antiquity,
Are so exceeding spacious and wyde,
And sprinkled with such sweet variety,
Of all that pleasant is to eare or eye,
That I nigh ravish with rare thoughts delight,
My tedious travail doe forget thereby.

Inscription on the title page of
Joseph Ritson's *Memoirs of the Celts* (1827) from
Edmund Spenser's *The Faerie Queene* (1590-96)

DISCOVERING ROBIN HOOD

The Life of Joseph Ritson - Gentleman, Scholar and Revolutionary

STEPHEN BASDEO

PEN & SWORD
HISTORY

AN IMPRINT OF PEN & SWORD BOOKS LTD.
YORKSHIRE - PHILADELPHIA

First published in Great Britain in 2021 by
PEN AND SWORD HISTORY
An imprint of
Pen & Sword Books Ltd
Yorkshire - Philadelphia

ISBN: 978 1 52677 781 2

Typeset in Times New Roman 11.5/14 by
SJmagic DESIGN SERVICES, India.
Printed and bound by CPI Group (UK) Ltd, Croydon, CR0 4YY

Pen & Sword Books Ltd incorporates the Imprints of Pen & Sword Books
Archaeology, Atlas, Aviation, Battleground, Discovery, Family History, History,
Maritime, Military, Naval, Politics, Railways, Select, Transport, True Crime,
Fiction, Frontline Books, Leo Cooper, Praetorian Press, Seaforth Publishing,
Wharncliffe and White Owl.

For a complete list of Pen & Sword titles please contact
PEN & SWORD BOOKS LIMITED
47 Church Street, Barnsley, South Yorkshire, S70 2AS, England
E-mail: enquiries@pen-and-sword.co.uk
Website: www.pen-and-sword.co.uk

Or
PEN AND SWORD BOOKS
1950 Lawrence Rd, Havertown, PA 19083, USA
E-mail: Uspen-and-sword@casematepublishers.com
Website: www.penandswordbooks.com

Contents

Acknowledgements

My first encounter with Joseph Ritson came in August 2014 while I was cobbling together a PhD research proposal on Robin Hood. I came across Allen Wright's *Bold Outlaw* website and found out that the most influential Robin Hood book in the modern era was written by Ritson. As I did further research into Ritson's life and works, I could not help but like and admire him. His political philosophy seemed to accord with my own. He was a republican (a UK republican, not an American one) and Ritson seemed to be interested in the same things that I was: Robin Hood and all things medieval. I ordered reprints of Ritson's *Robin Hood* book (I since managed to get hold, at great cost to myself, a 1795 first edition, and I expect my advance from a previous Pen and Sword book, *Wat Tyler*, is what paid for it). I was captivated by his acerbic wit, his remarkable skills as a historian, and, most importantly, his portrayal of England's most famous outlaw. Ritson struck me as a William Hartnell/'first Doctor Who' kind of guy. After that I think I became something of an evangelist for Ritson; papers on him were given at several conferences; at home Ritson became something of a household name in my family (with one half of my family on the mother's side being from County Durham, as Ritson was, he seemed all the more special to me). I toyed with naming my cat Ritson, although in the end I opted for Robin. In view of my cat's irascible temperament however, perhaps I should have named him Ritson after all. So, I too hope to inspire some interest in this somewhat forgotten man—among general readers, at least—and if I succeed in doing that, my work will not have been in vain.

In virtually every publication I have ever produced, I have always given thanks to Professor Paul Hardwick, Professor Rosemary Mitchell, and Dr Alaric Hall. These people supervised my PhD thesis on post-medieval Robin Hood texts, and they witnessed first-hand the growing enthusiasm with which I learnt about Joseph Ritson. I thank them again—they truly are the best! Likewise, my thanks go to some other scholars: Prof Alex Kaufman, Dr Valerie B. Johnson, Dr Lesley Coote, Allen Wright, Dr Mike Evans, Prof Lorrain Stock, Prof Mikee Deloney, Dr Rebecca Nesvet, Dr Koenraed Claes, Dr Mark Truesdale (a good friend who, when he stays at mine, we generally get drunk and watch bad Robin Hood movies), and finally (at the time of writing the soon-to-be doctor) Rachael Gillibrand—these guys have given me advice countless times on my writing, so many thanks go to them! Another note of thanks goes to someone I do not know personally but who has recently written an excellent PhD thesis on Joseph Ritson: Genevieve Theodora McNutt. Without this, which made interesting new arguments about Ritson's life and scholarship, this book would have been much the poorer. It is encouraging to know that it is not just me and a few eccentric Robin Hood scholars who are still interested in Ritson. Theodora McNutt, if you ever do read this book—thank you!

I would also like to thank the wonderful Dr Owen Holland and the guys at the William Morris Society for allowing me to republish an essay from their journal in this volume on Ritson's influence on Morris, that famous artist, designer, and visionary socialist, in the latter's novel *A Dream of John Ball* (1888). Thanks in this respect also go to the two anonymous readers on the original *Journal of William Morris Studies* article who offered me very constructive advice.

Thanks are also due to the staff at the Beinecke Library, Yale University. They have many of Ritson's unpublished letters in their repositories and, me being in Leeds and the letters being in New Haven, Connecticut, they kindly scanned the materials they had and sent them to me.

Some parts of this book have been adapted from various blog posts and shorter articles I've written over the years, as well as from one or two obscure academic books which are now out of print, so it's nice to see some work reappearing.

My family always gets a special mention in any of my books: my parents, Deborah and Joseph Basdeo, who supported me throughout my education, my sister Jamila, her husband Andrew, and their children, Mya—to whom this book is dedicated—and Alexa, who deserve a big kiss (the next book will be inscribed to Alexa!) Likewise my friends, Richard Neesam, Chris Williams, and Sam Dowling – love all three of you! There is another person too, to whom I owe a great debt: Alison Bowers, a former manager of mine who, when I was a young BA student, was kind enough to schedule my working hours around my university lectures—it is unlikely that I'd have done as well in my studies were it not for her and I'm eternally grateful! My friend and commissioning editor, Jon Wright, and the other wonderful people at Pen and Sword like Aileen Pringle and Laura Hirst. This is the fourth book I have written for them and I am very grateful to them for taking a chance on me back in 2016 when they contracted me to write *Wat Tyler*. Jonathan: thank you for letting me write a book on Ritson—I did not think he would be saleable for anyone! (he may yet prove not to be of course). The production staff are always helpful: a special thanks to Laura for being so understanding of my hasty and panicky last-minute proof changes. And finally my editor, Barnaby Blacker—thanks for all of your help over the years, not just on this book but on two previous projects as well!

Unless otherwise stated, all images are from my own collection. However, a special note of thanks must go to the wonderful people at the Wellcome Collection and the British Library. These institutions have made many of their images freely available. The free and easy dissemination of knowledge is something which the subject of this book would have applauded.

Chronology

Tables Shewing the Chief Moments in Joseph Ritson's Life

Date	Events in Joseph Ritson's life, his family, his friends, as well as notable events in the history of the Robin Hood legend.
1752	**Joseph Ritson, born on 2 October.**
1755	**Ritson's sister Jane born on 12 August but dies in infancy.** Samuel Johnson publishes *Dictionary of the English Language.*
1758	Birth of John Pinkerton, later one of Ritson's rival antiquaries.
1762	John Wilkes founds a radical newspaper: *The North Briton.* Richard Hurd: *Letters on Chivalry and Romance.*
1764	Horace Walpole: *The Castle of Otranto.*
1770	**Ritson makes the acquaintance of Thomas Holcroft, John Cunningham and William Shield.**
1771	**According to B.H. Bronson, Ritson published two poems in *The Literary Register*. Begins working as an apprentice in the firm of Mr Ralph Bradley, a conveyancer in Stockton.**
1772	**'Versees Addressed to the Ladies of Stockton' is published in the *Newcastle Miscellany*. Ritson also reads Bernard Mandeville's *The Fable of the Bees* and resolves thereafter never to eat meat again.**
1773	**Visits Edinburgh to consult MSS in the Advocates' Library.** Boston 'Tea Party' in the American Colonies.
1774	**Reputedly wrote a song that was later included in a light opera written by his friend, the composer Mr Shield.** Thomas Jefferson: *A Summary View of the Rights of British America.* Thomas Warton: *The History of English Poetry.*

1775   **Ritson moves to London to take up position as a clerk in the firm of Messrs Masterman and Lloyd.**

1776   **Publishes *Modes of Trying Peers*.**
Beginning of the American Revolutionary War.
Thomas Paine publishes *Common Sense*. Edward Gibbon publishes *The Decline and Fall of the Roman Empire*, vol. 1. Adam Smith publishes *The Wealth of Nations*.

1777   **Ritson's father dies (exact date unknown).**

1778   **Ritson privately publishes *Tables Shewing the Descent of the Crown of England*.**
Spain and France, allied with the American colonies, declare war on Britain.

1780   **Removes to 8 Holborn Court, Gray's Inn. Begins own conveyancing practice. Ritson appears in Thomas Holcroft's novel Alwyn; or, *The Gentleman Comedian* as a character named Mr Handford. Ritson's mother dies on 22 November.**
Gordon Riots in London.

1781   **Ritson publishes *The Stockton Jubilee*.**

1783   Society of Antiquaries incorporated.

1784   **Enrolled as a law student at the beginning of Easter term. Publishes *The Bishoprick Garland; or, The Durham Minstrel* and *Gammer Gurton's Garland*. Also publishes a letter signed 'Anti-Scot' in *The Gentleman's Magazine*.**
Leonard MacNally's *Robin Hood: A New Musical Entertainment* premieres in London.

1785   **John Thompson, Ritson's tutor at Stockton's Unitarian School, retires to Northumberland. Ritson publishes *The Spartan Manual*.**
J. Cawdell publishes *Miscellaneous Poems*, containing a poem which mocked Ritson.
Birth of Thomas Love Peacock, author of *Maid Marian*.

1786   **Appointment as High Bailiff for the Liberty of the Savoy made permanent.**
Robert Burns: *Poems, Chiefly in the Scottish Dialect*.

1788   **Publishes *The Yorkshire Garland* and *The Quip Modest*.**

1789 **Ritson is called to the Bar at the beginning of Easter term.
Also publishes *A Digest of the Proceedings of the Court Leet
of the Manor and Liberty of the Savoy*.**
William Blake: *Songs of Innocence*.
Louis XVI convenes the Estates General on 5 May, marking
the beginning of the French Revolution.

1790 **Ritson publishes *Ancient Songs from the Time of King
Henry the Third to the Revolution*.**
Edmund Burke: *Reflections on the Revolution in France*.

1791 **Ritson spends summer and early Autumn in Paris.
Publishes *Pieces of Ancient Popular Poetry, The Office of
Constable*, and *The Jurisdiction of the Court Leet*.**
Thomas Paine publishes *The Rights of Man*.
Robert Southey writes *Harold; or, the Castle of Morford*,
the first Robin Hood novel.

1792 **Publishes *Cursory Criticisms on the Edition of Shakespeare
Published by Edmond Malone* and *The North Country
Chorister*.**
Mary Wollstonecraft: *A Vindication of the Rights of Woman*.

1793 **Ritson begins to feel that he is 'being watched' by the
authorities. Ann Ritson (sister) dies in April. Makes his
first investment on the stock exchange. Ritson briefly
adopts the French Revolutionary Calendar in his letters
and begins calling like-minded associates 'Citizen'.
Publishes *The English Anthology* and *The Northumberland
Garland*.**
Execution of Louis XVI and the beginning of the Terror in France.

1794 **Publishes *Scotish Song*.**
Sedition trials of Thomas Hardy, John Thelwall, and John
Horne Tooke.
**Thomas Percy publishes a new edition of *Reliques of
Ancient English Poetry* and silently incorporates Ritson's
suggestions.**

1795 **Ritson publishes *Robin Hood: A Collection of All the
Ancient Poems, Songs, and Ballads*.**
Treasonable Practices and Seditious Meetings Acts passed.

1798   William Pitt introduces the 'temporary' income tax on 4 December.

1799   French Consulate established with Napoleon as First Consul.

1802   **Ritson suffers 'fit of apoplexy'. Loses money on stock exchange and declares he is 'utterly ruined'. Publishes *Bibliographia Poetica, An Essay on Abstinence from Animal Food*, and *Ancient Engleish Metrical Romancees*.**

1803   **Suffers another bout of 'paralysis of the brain'; visits Bath to cure himself; later suffers another fit, barricades himself in his room at Gray's Inn; is removed and confined in Sir Jonathan Miles's house, where he dies on 23 September.**
       War between Britain and France begins again.

1804   ***Practical Points; or, Maxims in Conveyancing* is published from a MS in Ritson's unpublished papers.**

1810   ***Northern Garlands* published, being a compilation of *The Bishoprick Garland, The Newcastle Nightingale, The Yorkshire Garland*, and *The North-Country Chorister*.**

1813   **Percy Shelley's reading of Ritson's *Animal Food* inspires some remarks in the poet's *Queen Mab*.**

1816   **Walter Scott publishes *The Antiquary*, in which Ritson is referenced.**

1818   John Keats: 'Robin Hood: To a Friend'.

1819   **Walter Scott publishes *Ivanhoe*, based in part on his reading of Ritson's *Robin Hood*.**
       Anonymous: *Robin Hood: A Tale of the Olden Time*.

1820   **New edition of *Robin Hood* published, dedicated to Sir Walter Scott.**

1821   **Publication of Ritson's *Caledonian Muse* by Robert Triphook.**

1822   **Thomas Love Peacock publishes *Maid Marian*, based upon Peacock's reading of Ritson's *Robin Hood*.**
       First piece of Animal Rights Legislation passed by parliament.

1823   **New edition of *Robin Hood* published, dedicated to Sir Walter Scott.**

1824   **_Life of King Arthur_ published from a MS in Ritson's unpublished papers.**
RSPCA established.

1827   **_Memoirs of the Celts_ published from a MS in Ritson's unpublished papers.**

1828   **_Annals of Caledonians, Picts, and Scots_ published a MS in Ritson's unpublished papers.**

1829   **James Maidment publishes _Letters of Joseph Ritson, Esq. to Mr. George Paton_.**
Establishment of the Metropolitan Police.

1831   **_Fairy Tales_ is published from a MS in Ritson's unpublished papers.**

       New edition of Ritson's _Robin Hood_ published.

1833   **Joseph Frank publishes _Letters of Joseph Ritson, Esq._**

Introduction

'Though it May Fail to Satisfy, May Possibly Serve to Amuse': General Prologue

Joseph Ritson will be familiar to very few readers in our modern era. He was not a statesman and neither was he a great poet or novelist. He was a conveyancer—a rather dry job in any era—and, from what can be gleaned from his surviving correspondence, a bookworm. Yet his life is worthy of note for several reasons. He was an eyewitness to major events in London, such as the Gordon Riots in 1780. He sojourned in Paris for several months in 1791 at the height of the French Revolution where he was captivated with the revolutionaries'

aims and became 'a disciple of [Thomas] Paine', a leading intellectual in both the American and French Revolutions.[1] Finally, it was Ritson's love of old books and manuscripts which ensured the survival of the legend of Robin Hood for posterity. Through his portrayal of Robin Hood, Ritson has left his mark upon every novel, play, television series and film ever produced which has retold the story of England's famous outlaw.

The principal materials for Ritson's life are the many letters which he wrote to friends and acquaintances. After Ritson's death, these were collected from various sources by his nephew, Joseph Frank, and used by Nicholas Harris to write the first biography of Ritson in the 1830s. Letter writing was of the utmost importance to the social, cultural, and intellectual life of eighteenth-century England and, more widely, to the whole of Enlightenment Europe. Historians, literary critics, philosophers, and poets would discuss various intellectual and artistic matters through the medium of their letters. Ritson conversed with many like-minded literary acquaintances on some quite niche subjects, such as the meaning of a Middle English word or a Latin phrase. Letter writing was considered an art.[2] Manuals such as *The Complete Letter Writer; or, Polite English Secretary* (1772) and *The New and Complete English Letter Writer* (1780) were printed with a view to giving people 'directions for writing letters in an easy and proper manner'.[3] Letters likewise were integral to the successful functioning of a business; the eighteenth century was known as a 'polite and *commercial*' era in which Britain expanded its trade not only in Europe but across the world. Private correspondence obviously helped family members and friends keep in touch with each other, especially when one member may have moved far from home in search of work, as Ritson did when he moved to London.

Letter writing may have been important but the postal service was not always brilliant depending on where a person was sending a letter. During the reign of James II, a pre-paid penny post was established by William Dockwra for the capital. This was a revolutionary act when, before Dockwra, the recipient of a letter and not the sender was the one who usually had to pay the postage costs. Unfortunately this service could only be taken advantage of if you lived in London—the capital was divided into several districts which each had its own sorting office, and the messengers would deliver post up to twelve times a day. Sending a letter to someone in another city was a different matter. Letters could be sent via a post-boy and this service was fairly inexpensive. But as they travelled alone on foot on country roads during day and night—from one 'post' to the next in a relay system—many were robbed by highwaymen. The lads were also poorly paid, which meant that sending money with them was risky. Parcels could be sent by the Royal Mail who contracted merchants—whose coach drivers were often armed—travelling to a particular destination, although their fees were not regulated and it could be expensive to send just one letter. For security, it made sense to send letters along with parcels on these coaches. This is probably why many of the letters which Ritson both sent to people and received were usually accompanied with a package of some description, usually books and other trifles. To take just one example, we find Ritson begin one letter to his nephew by saying:

> Young fellow,
> In the constant, Captain Terry [a nickname which he gave his nephew], is a small box of books (directed to your mother) of which I hope you will take great care and make a good use.[4]

Ritson often sent one parcel to a contact back in Stockton which would contain several letters addressed to other friends and associates, to be distributed by the recipient. This is why there are several letters addressed to different people written on the same day. It was only in 1784 that someone decided enough was enough: the postal service had to be reformed and made more reliable. It was John Palmer (1742–1818), a theatre owner and entrepreneur, who suggested that a network of state-run mail coaches should operate up and down the country and carry both letters and parcels for a standard fixed price. It seems like common sense now, but Palmer is lauded as an innovator all the same. The onus for paying postage costs still fell to the letter's recipient. It would not be until the Victorian era when postal stamps could be affixed to a letter by the sender, that the recipient would be relieved of pecuniary disadvantage. It was these practical considerations which Ritson would have had to consider before he sent a letter.

That we have letters for Ritson at all is a boon to anyone researching his life and times; the letters for a number of literary greats from the eighteenth century do survive, but letters of people of more humble means such as Ritson often do not. Private correspondence has its own peculiar set of advantages and disadvantages for the biographer however.[5] One advantage of studying an individual's private correspondence lies in the fact that historians can acquire an understanding of how someone reacted to a certain life event, say the death of a family member or interactions with siblings, and thereby infer what kind of personality they had, which often contrasts with their conscious 'self-representation' when writing in more formal and public documents. As one eighteenth-century writer remarked: 'there is nothing discovers the true temper of a person so much as his letters.'[6] This is especially the case with Ritson, whose criticisms of fellow scholars' errors were perceived by contemporaries as less than cordial in his published works but he was warm-hearted towards his friends and family in his letters.

Certain details of Ritson's life will be patchy even though we have letters which have survived. The key term in that last sentence is 'which have survived'. There are many gaps. The first and most obvious gap in our knowledge, when basing a biography upon letters written *by* a particular person, is that oftentimes we do not have the letter which was first written *to* them. We read in a letter from Ritson to his friend Mr Wadeson in November 1783 that 'I am much obliged by your kind favour of the 15th instant.'[7] In another letter that Ritson wrote to his friend Mr Walker on 4 November 1789, he opened with the following words: 'I received your interesting letter of the 4th of September, during my stay in the country.'[8] While Ritson's nephew, Frank, has bequeathed to us an invaluable collection of all the letters he could find which Ritson had written to various acquaintances, he did not include the letters which were written to Ritson. We have no way of knowing for sure what the contents of the 'interesting letter' were that Ritson received in September 1789; Ritson's nephew either never bothered to track it down or, if he did manage to find it, did not think to include the letter in the published collection. Other gaps in our knowledge of Ritson's life include those long periods when no letters were seemingly written at all. The first letter recorded in the published *Letters of Joseph Ritson, Esq.* was to Mr George Allan, dated 26 August 1776. The second letter printed immediately after that is one addressed to Ritson's father, who was also named Joseph, which is dated 3 March 1777. That is an almost eight-month gap in correspondence but, in a world where letters were one of the primary modes of communication between people, it is unlikely that Ritson wrote *nothing* in that time. As to whether he continued any correspondence in that time, however, we remain none-the-wiser.

Regarding the minutiae of daily life, activities, and interactions with others, letters can be a double-edged sword. This is most apparent in regard to friendships: letters which survive can often *overemphasise* the connections between two individuals whose acquaintance may have been slight, or who were good friends but who, in an era in which travelling to other cities was long and costly, rarely saw each other. Yet at least we have a record of such friendships and acquaintances. On the other hand, the connections that Ritson made with his work colleagues in London, or his neighbours when he was living at 8 Holborn Court, will forever escape us. Ritson certainly enjoyed an alcoholic beverage, preferring wine and ale but disdaining brandy.[9] Eighteenth-century London boasted many taverns and coffeehouses (where alcohol was also sold); it is inconceivable to think that he did not avail himself of the services of one of London's many drinking establishments—yet these activities, if they occurred, would hardly have been anything to 'write home about'. For example, Ritson mentioned nothing in his letters about his friendship with a fellow attorney named John Britton, who used to visit Ritson at his home regularly. We only know of this interaction, however, from Britton's autobiography published in the Victorian era.[10] An analogy may be made to modern times here: we may send messages to people from personal email addresses who we know only a little, or indeed not very well at all, while we may never email our best friends. After all, if we want to speak to our good friends, we can simply phone or send them a text message—a type of communication which leaves no trace at all—or meet them in person. Social media has made the problem worse, for the communication between individuals is fleeting and whatever is said between friends and individuals on any of the major platforms will likely be deleted from the server after a few months or years. Historians of the future may very well have less to work with than we have today with eighteenth-century figures.

To a certain extent, we can fill some of the gaps in our knowledge of Ritson's life by referring to the many books he published and the articles which he wrote in literary magazines. Often in the prefaces to certain works, Ritson lets his political ideology shine through in his interpretations of old texts, as he does in *Robin Hood*. Other publications are interesting for their own sake; for example, *An Essay on Abstinence from Animal Food as a Moral Duty* (1802), with its advocacy of a near-vegan diet, was unusual in an age when meat eating was viewed as a patriotic act. Nevertheless, we will never get the *full* story of his life. When it comes to discussing the lack of detailed biographical sources available to anyone writing about a historical figure, however, we might do well to take a quote from Ritson himself. Having gathered his materials for a biography of Robin Hood in 1795, and realising that few materials survive and that there were many gaps in his knowledge, he exclaimed,

> The reader must, therefore, be contented with such a detail, however scanty or imperfect, as a zealous pursuit of the subject enables one to give; and which, though it may fail to satisfy, may possibly serve to amuse.[11]

Of his sources Ritson ended by saying that out of everything he could find, 'some there were good, some middling, and some bad; but yet they were the best that could be had.'[12]

When anyone sets out to write a book for the general reader such as this one, it is always completed by having studied the works of previous scholars who have worked on the subject. One researcher in particular who has recently investigated Ritson's work is Genevieve Theodora McNutt who recently completed a brilliant PhD thesis on Ritson's central role in the publication of early and Middle English literature. McNutt's thesis makes the following remark about Ritson's appearance in historical and literary scholarship: 'Since his death, Joseph Ritson's life and legacy have been contested. Scholarship on Ritson has been cumulative, each successive account built upon, directly or indirectly, some subset of the previous work.'[13] One of McNutt's points in her wide-ranging thesis highlights how Ritson was able to market his works not only as truthful and historically accurate, when compared to the shoddy work of his literary contemporaries such as Thomas Percy, but also to write for a variety of readers—learned scholars as well as general readers could make sense of and enjoy Ritson's productions. In the process, Ritson contributed to the nineteenth-century medieval revival. To McNutt's use of the word 'cumulative' I would also add 'scattered'. It is striking that, although Ritson's work still forms a key resource for many modern-day literary critics, folk song scholars, historians, and medievalists, and although his works are cited in many of their footnotes, there have been no book-length biographies of this eccentric scholar since Bronson's brilliant, but now exceedingly rare, *Joseph Ritson: Scholar-at-Arms* (1939).

It would obviously be a rather pointless undertaking to simply reproduce his letters in full, given that editions of them can be found in select libraries and archives across the United Kingdom and the United States. It would probably make for tedious reading as well. Many of his letters contain interesting discussions on various points of medieval and early modern textual criticism, others contain the mundane details of his everyday life. The approach I have pursued is one which tells of Ritson's 'life and times'. As an eyewitness to riots in London and the French Revolution, his letters offer a fascinating insight as to how one man from a relatively humble background became caught up in the major events of the epoch. This is also a thematic study, and is arranged, as the title of this work suggests, into three main themes: professional life, historical research, and political thought. This may seem a strange approach for a biography, which readers usually expect to be set out chronologically, but it will avoid unnecessary repetition of various subjects. It would make little sense, for example, to discuss Ritson's views on masculinity and politeness briefly from comments in 1787, then skip over to some of his historical research for a few chapters, before returning to some remarks he made in 1795 on what he thought the duties of a gentleman should be. In light of this, however, a chronology of his life in context with contemporary events is placed at the beginning of this book. Luckily in Ritson's case the themes of 'gentleman', 'scholar', and 'revolutionary' are somewhat chronological anyway: he first set himself up in business, then devoted more time to antiquarian pursuits, before finally becoming a revolutionary in his old age.

After the discussion of his early life, there are individual chapters on Ritson as a gentleman, which charts his rise through the legal profession and appointments to various offices such as that of High Bailiff of the Liberty of the Savoy. After this follows a discussion of Ritson the scholar and his research into Middle English literature. After this follows the retelling of Ritson's sojourn in Paris and 'radicalisation' after becoming enthralled with the ideals of the French Revolution, from whence we proceed to a discussion of Ritson's *magnum opus*, the book which has had a major but uncredited influence on popular culture even into the twenty-first century: *Robin Hood: A Collection of All the Ancient Poems, Songs, and Ballads* (1795). The sixth chapter sees Ritson in the latter years of his life until his death, while the final chapter examines his legacy and posthumous portrayals in literature, tracing his influence upon writers, socialist activists such as William Morris, and filmmakers. Finally, nestled away in an appendix, there is Ritson's biography of Robin Hood, a selection of his poetry, and a brief biography of Ritson's successor, John Mathew Gutch, who followed in Ritson's footsteps by compiling an anthology of Robin Hood ballads.

I wanted to write this book because, briefly, in the eighteenth and early nineteenth centuries, Ritson was a household name and I wanted to bring him to public notice once more—hence this being a book for the general reader written by a popular history publisher and not a niche academic monograph—and also to dispel the idea, current among many historians of late eighteenth-century English culture, that he was an austere and often cruel individual. This is a reputation which has unfairly dogged Ritson since the early twentieth century. Furthermore, while Bronson's biography was an amazing piece of scholarship for its time, there have been numerous advances in historical scholarship since the 1930s which will go some way to helping us set Ritson's social and scholarly activities more firmly in their historical, intellectual, and cultural context. So in this biography, as opposed to those which have gone before, there are discussions of Ritson's many references to 'politeness' in his letters—which as we will see was a key term in eighteenth-century culture—as well as expanding a little more upon Ritson's views of colonialism and race. This book, then, tells the life of Joseph Ritson: gentleman, scholar, and revolutionary.

Chapter 1

'The Delicious Moments which the Idea of this Once-Loved Place brings to my Recollection': Joseph Ritson's Early Life in Stockton-on-Tees

Between 1724 and 1727, the novelist, satirist, some-time soldier, and spy, Daniel Defoe, undertook a journey throughout England and Scotland. He wrote about the places he visited, his writings upon which were later published as *A Tour Through the Whole Island of Great Britain*. After passing the northern boundary of Yorkshire, he came to Stockton, a town 'of no great note; but ... greatly increased of late years, especially the first, by being the chiefest place in the North Riding of York ... for the shipping off [of] lead, and butter for London.'[14] He might have stayed longer but he realised that 'I had to go, and that I must not stop at small matters', and swiftly travelled on to Durham.[15]

The village of Stockton had been granted borough status by Hugh de Puiset, Bishop of Durham, in 1189. A borough was originally a self-governing walled town. When a place was granted this status, its inhabitants, including some of the richer peasants, could have a say in the appointment of local officials. Councils of local notables—comprising noblemen, merchants and even some rich peasants—could pass by-laws (laws which do not require an Act of Parliament) to deal with local issues. The borough electors could also deal with local petty crime and debt in their own courts, although serious crime was still dealt with by the crown. And farmers and craftsmen did not need the permission of the local lord of the manor to trade their wares on the open market.[16] By the thirteenth century, the serfs in Stockton were freed and the town became a small commercial hub, helped by its proximity to the river Tees, from where merchants exported wool, wine, and other commodities to places in England and Europe. Stockton remained a small mercantile town until the time of Defoe's visit. The wider area outside the town became a prosperous farming district. According to Sir George Bowes, writing in the sixteenth century, Stockton was 'the best country for corn'.[17]

In spite of the town's burgeoning commercial sector in the late medieval and early modern period, the population remained relatively stable over the succeeding centuries and the place never boasted more than perhaps 3,000 inhabitants by the time Defoe arrived. Nevertheless, anyone who visited the town later in the eighteenth century would have seen for themselves that Stockton-on-Tees was undergoing much improvement. In 1735, at the centre of 'a wide and handsome street called High Street, said to be the widest in England and nearly half a mile long' a 'picturesque town-hall or town-house' was built.[18] In 1744, when local officials of this modernising town were conducting their business in a brand new neoclassical building, there was no need for them to be sentimental about the crumbling medieval toll booth which had stood in the town centre since time immemorial. They decided that the toll booth had to go. In its place, on the northern side of the town hall, a grand and neat-looking piazza was put in its place. The construction of the piazza also necessitated the removal of the medieval king's cross in the centre of the town. This was replaced with a Doric column which still stands today. Also in the centre of the town a new theatre was built in 1766. Stockton was becoming a polite and commercial place. Thus, when one of the town's residents, Benjamin Pye, wrote a poem in praise of Stockton during the late 1780s, he could boast that

> Our shews proclaim a thriving town,
> And fortnight days to admiration,
> To see Stockton improve so soon,
> Daily to her commendation.
>
> Our spacious streets each stranger views,
> And fairly gives his approbation,
> Stockton's the place that I do choose,
> So great is Stockton's commendation.
>
> Our gardens, orchards, river, plains,
> All join to raise our contemplation,
> While hand in hand we others join,
> In singing Stockton's commendation.
>
> Our merchants cast a noble shew,
> Rich goods as any in the nation,
> Great is their trade with high and low,
> Makes them sing Stockton's commendation.
>
> All trades shall flourish now I see,
> In their several occupations;
> And all our song it shall be,
> Stockton's lasting commendation.[19]

Further improvements followed to ensure that this increasingly modern town was a pleasant place to live. Trades which for centuries had been conducted in the town centre were relegated to its outskirts—notably the butchers. During the medieval and early modern period, most animals would have been transported 'on the hoof' to the shambles in the town centre and there slaughtered in the middle of the market square. It was not the most pleasant sight for ladies and gentleman to see, and some of the leading cultural figures in the eighteenth century were voicing their disapproval of what they saw as the barbaric practices of the trade. To take one example, Alexander Pope wrote,

> I know nothing more shocking or horrid than the prospect of [butchers'] kitchens covered with blood, and filled with the cries of creatures expiring in tortures … bestrewed with the scattered heads and mangled limbs of his victims.[20]

The stench of dead flesh and the sight of discarded animal carcasses had no place in the newly-refurbished town centre—'barbaric' trades had to be kept 'out of sight and out of mind'.[21]

It was in this up and coming town on 2 October 1752 that Joseph Ritson senior and his wife Jane *née* Gibson, in a tenement in Wheat Sheaf Yard in Stockton-on-Tees,[22] welcomed into the world a new addition to their family. Jane gave birth to a boy, whom she and her husband decided to call Joseph, after the father. Although the family had some distant relations in Westmoreland who owned what is reputed to have been some fairly substantial landholdings,[23] Ritson the elder's family origins were humble. The father was descended from an old but poor yeoman family from Hackthorpe in Cumbria. The term 'yeoman' first emerged

Stockton-on-Tees in 1785. (British Library)

4

in medieval England as a marker of social rank being the title that was given to a servant in a knight's entourage.[24] By the sixteenth century its meaning had evolved: the term came to signify a small landowner who, of lesser rank than the gentry, usually owned a small amount of property and might even be able to vote in parliamentary elections if he owned freehold property worth over 40 shillings.[25] As a young lad, the father had been apprenticed to a Stockton tobacco merchant and carried on a side-trade in carpentry to make ends meet.[26] There was money to be made in the tobacco industry: it was a fashionable substance which many people consumed, believing that it calmed the nerves and healed toothache. In short, it was 'the great panacea'.[27] Had Ritson the elder stayed in this business, he might not have faced financial difficulties later in life. Instead of remaining in the tobacco industry, Ritson's father began working for Mr Robinson, a corn merchant in Stockton.

It was in Mr Robinson's employ that the elder Ritson met his future wife, Jane Gibson. By all accounts Jane was a sweet and affectionate, although uneducated, peasant woman who was a servant in Robinson's household. While she was working for Mr Robinson, Jane would probably still have had to help out on her family's farm while undertaking her second job as a domestic servant. Peasant women like Jane undertook a variety of second jobs—even if the amount they were able to earn was not high at all—not only in domestic service but also in taverns, workshops, and light industry to contribute to the family budget.[28] Peasant families were often poor but held either the lease, copyhold, or freehold of a small plot of land from a local magnate, which they farmed for subsistence while selling surplus in the market. It may surprise readers to learn that people as late as the eighteenth century were designated as 'peasants', for it is usually a term associated with medieval England rather than the 'modern' era of the Georgian kings. A peasant is someone who, along with their family members, cultivates crops on small landholdings and owes rent in either money or services to a local lord and landowner.[29] Jane's family were not serfs. Although 'serf' and 'peasant' are often conflated in modern popular culture, serfs were unfree farm labourers, indentured to the local lord, who could not own or lease property. They had to perform labour services for the lord of manner and could not move to another parish without the permission of their lord. Serfdom had virtually disappeared in England by the sixteenth century, but the peasantry as a class who worked on the land remained.

While the eighteenth century was the great age of mercantile capitalism, with London growing into a modern commercial city and joint-stock companies such as the East India Company driving the expansion of Britain's Empire, older economic and social structures persisted in more remote places. This was especially the case in the rural north of England and Scotland, where certain families such as Jane's were still bound to the land. As Alice Chandler explains, even as late as the 1820s many people's way of life was still thoroughly 'medieval':

> In a sense, the middle ages had never died … Although the enclosure acts had criss-crossed the English countryside with hedgerows and dotted it with flocks of sheep, Chaucer's plowman would have found England's rural life very familiar. The tools and produce of agriculture had scarcely changed for centuries; the old country customs and festivals were only slowly dying out; and the whir of the spinning-wheel had just begun to grow silent.[30]

(Other medieval customs survived too, especially in the punishments meted out to offenders: in 1809, Jenny Pipes was the last woman sentenced to the ducking stool; public whippings in Edinburgh continued until the 1820s; and the last person to be punished with a spell in the pillory was Peter James Bossy in 1830). Peasant women were usually depicted in contemporary literature as people who, although very poor, were goodness and purity personified, untouched by the corruption of the town, much like the 'poor innocent' Fanny Goodwill in Henry Fielding's *Joseph Andrews* (1742).[31] Jane Gibson seems to have fitted this stereotype well. When she married Joseph Ritson senior, a man who tried his hand at multiple trades to make ends meet, she was hardly doing so for the money.[32]

Very little information on Jane and Joseph's lives survives beyond what is written in their son's letters. At some point early in Ritson's life, the whole family moved to a house in Silver Street, Stockton. The father, having worked for a corn merchant, must have assumed that he too could make it big in the agricultural sector, so he purchased some land and started up a business farming and selling corn. Business must have briefly flourished at some point, for the Ritsons appear to have *owned* the house in Silver Street and it passed into Joseph Ritson's ownership on his father's death. But it was not all plain sailing: unfortunately for Ritson the elder, the economic status of yeoman farmers declined drastically in the eighteenth century. Their businesses were often too small to compete with wealthier property owners who were buying up land for commercial purposes, and they had to contend with merchants who paid them late. Ritson the elder would run into financial difficulties when Robinson refused to pay him for the crops he had sold to them. Whole families often found themselves facing serious financial difficulties. The Ritsons also kept cows and sold milk from their house in Silver Street—the family probably could not live by grain alone. The life of a yeoman farmer and his family was not an easy one.

Joseph Ritson the younger—the main subject of this book, whom we shall hereafter call simply Ritson—was not an only child. He had an older sister named Anne, born in 1749. Ritson was especially close to her in later life. Joseph and Jane's marriage was actually done in a hurry—they were married on 22 May 1749 and Anne was born on 15 June.[33] As was often the case, a woman who got married in a rush suffered aspersions on her character by local gossips. Some of Jane's 'friends' in Stockton called her 'flighty' and implied that 'she was easily won by her husband'.[34] Jane's immediate family loved her however, and that is ultimately all that matters. The Ritsons had another son who died in infancy whom they named Christopher after the great grandfather, Christopher Ritson (d. 1703). Several of the Ritsons' children after Joseph, named Christopher, John, Sarah, and Elizabeth, were to suffer the same fate. This was an era of high infant mortality. While much research into historical infant mortality rates has focused on London, a city which published Bills of Mortality, the picture in rural areas before 1837, when better records began to be kept, is not as clear. For the country as a whole, it is probable that a fifth of all children died before their first birthday and one in three died before reaching the age of five.[35] Parents might often wait to see if their child survived those critical first few months before baptising them. However, if a child died before they were baptised, they could not receive a burial service; they might be 'put into the ground' in the churchyard, but no record of their death and burial would be kept. Many children, therefore, in the words of R.E. Jones, 'died unbaptized and lost to the historical record'.[36] Official figures recording the death rate per baptism from before 1837 often give quite a low picture of infant mortality in rural areas, but it

John Wesley preaching to a congregation. Wesley came to Stockton-on-Tees in the mid-eighteenth century and converted many. Joseph Ritson despised them however, and commanded them never to come to his house. (British Library)

is not the whole picture. This was the case with Joseph Ritson's brothers and sisters who died in infancy; there are no birth, baptismal or burial records for Christopher, John, Sarah, or Elizabeth. If Ritson's nephew had not included a footnote to the letters telling us about these siblings, then they would, like so many infants who died before their time, be lost to history.[37] Joseph and Anne, and two later children named Elizabeth and Jane (the latter two whom Ritson barely mentions in his letters), were the Ritsons' only children who survived into adulthood.[38]

Had all of the children survived, the Ritson family would have been a large one. There are several reasons why people opted for large families in this era. Part of a woman's 'duty', so it was thought, was to bear a child for her husband in accordance with the Bible's commandment at Genesis 1:28: 'Be fruitful and multiply. Fill the earth and govern it.' Children would also be needed to contribute to the family economy. They were viewed almost as mini-adults. Children in poorer households would be set to work as soon as they were able. Moreover, there was very little in the way of birth control apart from total abstinence and *coitus interruptus*.

It was probably from social and economic necessity, rather than religious obedience, that the Ritsons opted for a large family. The family was not a religious one. Joseph Ritson, the son, grew up with utter contempt for Anglicanism and Catholicism, and in later life he became a professed atheist. He even refused to give to any charitable causes for the maintenance of deceased clergy's widows in Durham, as one who knew him explained:

> I met him once … and, being for that year Steward for the Charity instituted at Durham for the benefit of Widows and Orphans of the Clergy, I ventured to ask him for a benefaction, as I knew he had property in the County. He snarled furiously, and I was afraid would have bit too; but he answered, with less wit and acrimony than I expected, "The Drones in the Cathedral at Durham ought to maintain their own brats!"[39]

Ritson also despised the Methodists. This denomination was founded when Charles Wesley and his brother John founded the Holy Club at Oxford in 1729. Their aims were to live in a closer manner to the way Jesus taught, so they made sure to receive the sacraments every week and minister to the poor and the sick. The two founders went on several speaking tours throughout the country and even in the American colonies. John Wesley first arrived in Stockton-on-Tees in 1748, where he spoke to what was, according to one contemporary observer, 'a very large and very rude congregation' who became enthralled with his teachings, so much so that when Wesley visited again three years later, the congregation had grown substantially.[40] The Methodists went around preaching in public spaces and in people's houses to spread their gospel. The Wesleys' journals are full of accounts, such as the following which occurred in January 1749 at Knowle in the West Midlands where 'I began preaching directly, in the yard of an inn, to a few gaping, staring people … They increased apace, and were tolerably attentive.'[41] The people of Knowle may have proved ready recipients for the Wesleys' message but they were not welcome in Ritson's home: in later life he wrote to his nephew and said, rather exasperatedly, 'I had been informed of a great many Methodists coming about the house in order to sing, pray.'[42] His use of the term 'Methodist' was actually a slur; their detractors called them by that term because of the 'methods' by which they practised their faith; only by the latter part of the period did the Methodists, who eventually separated from the Church of England, reappropriate the term as a badge of honour. Ritson's reaction was to tell the head of the local Methodist congregation in Stockton that 'none of them should be admitted in future'.[43] That seemed to be the end of the matter—while Ritson had high-minded morals, religion never played a major part in his life. Some of his later literary works manifest clear anti-clerical sentiments. The church—broadly defined—and its representatives were nothing but 'clerical drones and pious locusts'.[44]

Whether Ritson ever helped his father with the family business in his early life is not recorded but it is likely that he did. As we have seen, whatever the family business might be, children of poorer rural families were required, from a young age, to assist their parents in running it: children helped in shops, on farms, and in the family business.[45] One of the best things that the Ritsons did for their son was to ensure that he received a basic education—the Education Act (1870), which mandated compulsory basic education for all children, was a long way off. There was a local grammar school in Stockton which opened in 1758 but this may have been too expensive for the family to send young Ritson to because the fees were 10/6d per quarter—approximately the equivalent of a week's wages for a skilled labourer. Instead Joseph was sent to a local Unitarian church school in the centre of Stockton, at 56 High Street, run by the Reverend John Thompson.[46]

Thompson encouraged young Ritson in his academic pursuits. Ritson found it difficult to get along with the other boys at school and much preferred the company of the girls, and of course his books. It was in these formative years that Ritson's love of history and literature became apparent, and he devoured books. One of his favourites was Miguel de Cervantes's *Don Quixote*, a Spanish-language romance originally published in two parts in 1605 and 1615. It was, declared Ritson, 'one of the best books ever written'.[47] Cervantes's seriocomic tale tells the story of an old Spanish grandee, Alonso Quixano, who has read so many medieval romances that it has turned him somewhat mad. He therefore dons a makeshift suit of armour and decides to become a knight-errant. With his trusty squire, the peasant Sancho Panza, whom Alonso has corralled into joining him on his knight's quest, the pair ride into battle against fearsome giants (which are nothing but windmills) and they

Illustration by Gustave Doré of Don Quixote de la Mancha. *Don Quixote*, published in two parts in 1605 and 1615, was reprinted numerous times in England during the eighteenth century and was one of Joseph Ritson's favourite books.

attempt to rescue beautiful damsels from castles (in reality a maid from a provincial inn). The novel was a big hit with readers in England after Sir Thomas Shelton published his translation in 1612. Between 1700 and 1740, six new editions of this translation were issued from British publishers.[48]

It would, in fact, have been relatively easy for a young lad like Ritson, from the north of England, to become well-versed in the century's great literary works. He could read and write because of his schooling, and Scotland and the north of England more generally boasted a very high level of literacy among people of all classes. Weavers, farmers, apprentices and factory hands, as Jonathan Rose's research has shown, avidly read poetry, novels, and translations of the classics.[49] With the abolition of perpetual copyright in 1774 printers realised that they could make a pretty penny by publishing cheaper copies of older works whose authors had died. As they did not have an author to pay, their books could reach a wider audience by being sold at a lower price. Thus from the 1780s onwards, an 'old canon' of literature emerged, composed of the works of dead seventeenth- and eighteenth-century writers such as Joseph Addison, Richard Steele, Thomas Gray, John Milton, and Alexander Pope—Ritson referred to all of these at some point in his letters.[50]

Ritson especially liked ballads. The study of early modern English ballads was to become the focus of his literary career in later life. A ballad is a song which tells a story. Almost since the dawn of printing in England, publishers knew that printed copies of poems and song lyrics would be popular with audiences from all social classes. The printed versions of these songs were known as 'broadsides': single sheets of paper which sold for a penny or less with the lyrics of a song printed on them. Along with broadsides, there were also chapbooks, which were small octavo pamphlets of between 8 and 24 pages which were either songs or short prose romances—a 'romance', according to Samuel Johnson, signified a 'a military fable of the middle ages; a tale of wild adventure in war in love', and was not a love story.[51] Stories of British worthies, such as Robin Hood, King Arthur, Guy of Warwick, or Tom Thumb, were a prominent feature of chapbook sellers' repertoires. Others included rhymes, such as the rather morbid 'Ballad of the Two Children in the Wood' in which an uncle murders his niece and nephew in the forest to get his hands on their inheritance:

The fellow that did take in hand
These children for to kill
Was for a robbery judged to die,
As was God's blessed will.[52]

According to Joseph Addison, this song was, bizarrely, 'one of the darling songs of the common people, and has been the delight of most Englishmen in some part of their age'.[53]

Two of Ritson's personal childhood favourites were 'The Ballad of Chevy Chase', of which there are several variants,[54] and a simpler one, obviously aimed specifically at children, entitled 'The Melody of Mother Goose'.[55] 'Chevy Chase' retells the events of the Battle of

An early nineteenth-century engraving by J. Romney of a group of orphans singing from a broadside ballad in the street (note the paper from which one child is singing). Broadside ballads were enjoyed by all classes of people in the eighteenth century and by the latter part of the period became the subject of historical research. (Wellcome Collection)

Otterburn in 1388—a border skirmish between the English nobleman Henry 'Hotspur' Percy (1364–1403) and the Scottish noble James, Earl of Douglas (1358–88).[56] Historical ballads rarely made an effort to be historically accurate however: in 'Chevy Chase' we find that Percy is killed in battle[57] (Percy was merely captured at the Battle of Otterburn). Whatever the historical accuracy of the tale, it was still a good, entertaining, rousing song that families such as the Ritsons might enjoy by the fireside late on an evening after the business of the day was concluded. Some of the books and ballads which Ritson read he treasured until later in life and bequeathed to his young nephew, Joseph Frank (Frank). The extract below is typical of several letters that Ritson exchanged with him:

> I have sent you a few books &c. such as I was most entertained with, and instructed by, when I was at your own age; and I hope they will answer as good a purpose, if not better to yourself. Let me tell you, that the oftener you read them, the better you will understand them: and the more you take care of them, the better I shall like you hereafter. It will be the only method to procure others when you are tired of these.[58]

Ritson was trying to inculcate in his nephew the same love of literature which he developed when he was young. Judging by their exchanges in later life, when the pair exchanged various thoughts on obscure literary topics, Ritson succeeded in his endeavour.

After receiving basic schooling, which lasted until around the age of 11, it was usual for boys to be apprenticed to someone to learn a trade. The Elizabethan Statute of Artificers, which remained in force until 1819, decreed that everyone had a *duty* to work and mandated that the sons of the poorer classes should be apprenticed to a trade. An apprenticeship to a trade was viewed as one the best means of ensuring that young boys stayed out of trouble and fashioning them into productive members of society. Apprenticeships usually lasted for seven years and were served in two stages: in the early years the indentured boy worked for free, or perhaps a *very* small allowance, while learning his master's trade and receiving bed and board; in the second half, he would repay his master's investment by working for below-the-market wages.[59] Ritson was apprenticed to the legal profession, entering the conveyancing firm of the Ritsons' family friend Mr Raisbeck, who was Mr Robinson's son-in-law.[60] How long Ritson stayed with the Raisbeck firm is unclear, but by the age of 19 he was working in the offices of Mr Ralph Bradley (1712–88), a conveyancer based in Stockton. In terms of the quality of legal training available, Ritson could not have asked for any better employer than Mr Bradley. Bradley was born to a poor labouring family in Greatham,[61] a village about twelve miles from Stockton-on-Tees. He was sent to London to work as a lawyer's apprentice, was admitted to Gray's Inn and was subsequently called to the bar. London life was not to his liking however, and he returned to Stockton by the mid-eighteenth century to strike out on his own as a conveyancer. His business thrived: at his death he left over £50,000. Life certainly treated Bradley well; although no image of him survives, we know

A CHAPMAN.
From " The Cries and Habits of the City of London,' by M. Lauron, 1709.

An engraving of a 'chapman' from the eighteenth century. These people, predominantly from the poorer classes, would tour the country and sell not only chapbooks but various articles (note his tray containing all manner of small goods).

From the frontispiece to John Ashton's *Chapbooks of the Eighteenth Century* (1882).

from Ritson's writings that he was a rather corpulent fellow, fond of pudding.[62] Bradley ran what nowadays might be called a legal consultancy. It is said by those who worked under him that whenever the paperwork for any case came before him he would read it through thoroughly, and, by spending time in legal archives and libraries, annotated the case notes with every point of law which could have an impact on the matter. Barristers and conveyancers from all over the country wrote to him for advice whenever they had a query about a complicated legal matter because of his thorough legal knowledge. The very studious

THE

FABLE

OF THE

BEES:

O R,

Private Vices
Publick Benefits.

L O N D O N
Printed for J. RoBERTS, near the Oxford Arms in *Warwick Lane*, 1714.

Mandeville's *Fable of the Bees* (1714).
Reading this book when he was about 19
convinced Ritson to become a vegetarian.

and research-orientated manner of working in Bradley's firm, therefore, is probably the place from where Ritson acquired his similar approach to the study of historical texts, which benefitted him later in his career as a historian and literary critic; Ritson would have been taught the importance of seeking out texts and reading them thoroughly, while the drafting of legal texts, such as deeds, required accuracy in every detail.[63]

The daily drudgery of Ritson's legal work by no means dulled his passion for learning and reading. As well as famous literary works he also read philosophical treatises. Around the age of 19, he read a book which was to have a profound impact on his daily life: Bernard Mandeville's *The Fable of The Bees: or, Private Vices, Publick Benefits* (1705). Mandeville's book explored humans' relationship with the environment, society, and the economy. One particular passage struck Ritson. In true eighteenth-century style, it is rather long-winded, but is worth quoting in full:

> I know that Reason excites our Compassion but faintly, and therefore I would not wonder how Men should so little commiserate such imperfect Creatures as Cray fish, Oysters, Cockles, and indeed all Fish in general: As they are mute, and their inward Formation, as well as outward Figure, vastly different from ours, they express themselves unintelligibly to us, and therefore 'tis not strange that their Grief should not affect our Understanding, which it cannot reach; for nothing stirs us to Pity so effectually, as when

the Symptome of Misery strike immediately upon our Senses, and I have seen People mov'd at the Noise a live Lobster makes upon the Spit, that could have kill'd half a dozen Fowls with Pleasure. But in such perfect Animals as Sheep and Oxen, in whom the Heart, the Brain and Nerves differ so little from ours, and in whom the Separation of the Spirits from the Blood, the Organs of Sense, and consequently Feeling itself, are the same as they are in Human Creatures, I can't imagine how a Man not hardened in Blood and Massacre, is able to see a violent Death, and the Pangs of it, without concern. In answer to this, most People will think it sufficient to say, that all Things being allow'd to be made for the Service of Man, there can be no Cruelty in putting Creatures to the use they were design'd for; but I have heard Men make this Reply, whilst their Nature within them has reproach'd them with the Falshood of the Assertion. There is of all the Multitude not one Man in ten but what will own, (if he was not brought up in a Slaughter-house) that of all Trades he could never have been a Butcher; and I question whether ever any body so much as kill'd a Chicken without Reluctancy the first time. Some People are not to be perswaded to taste of any Creatures they have daily seen and been acquainted with, whilst they were alive; others extend their scruple no further than to their own Poultry, and refuse to eat what they fed and took care of themselves, yet all of them will feed heartily and without Remorse on Beef, Mutton and Fowls, when they are bought in the Market. In this behaviour, methinks, there appears something like a consciousness of Guilt, it looks as if they endeavor'd to save themselves from the Imputation of a Crime (which they know sticks somewhere) by removing the cause of it as far as they can from themselves; and I can discover in it some strong remains of Primitive Pity and Innocence, which all the arbitrary Power of Custom, and the violence of Luxury, have not yet been able to conquer. What I build upon I shall be told is a folly that Wise Men are not guilty of: I own it; but whilst it proceeds from a real Passion inherent in our Nature, it is sufficient to demonstrate that we

17

are born with a Repugnancy to the killing, and consequently the eating of Animals; for it is impossible that a natural Appetite should ever prompt us to act, or desire others to do, what we have an aversion to, be it as foolish as it will. It is only man, mischievous man, that can make death a sport. Nature taught your stomach to crave nothing but vegetables; but your violent fondness to change, and greater eagerness after novelties, have prompted you to the destruction of animals without justice or necessity, perverted your nature and warped your appetites which way soever your pride or luxury have called them.[64]

Ritson resolved never to eat meat again, and thereafter subsisted on a diet of milk and vegetables. Many times in his letters did he rail against the eating of 'animal food ... a barbarous and horrible manner of living'.[65] His decision to refrain from eating meat after reading *The Fable of the Bees* was a bold step. Meat eating was seen as a patriotic activity in the period when Ritson was growing up; a diet of beef allegedly made the English a tough, hardy race and would prevent them from becoming effeminate like the French, with whom the British had been at war several times throughout the century. Henry Fielding linked patriotism and beef eating in a song he wrote entitled 'The Roast Beef of Old England'.[66] Ritson's lifelong friend, the novelist and playwright Thomas Holcroft—whom Ritson met at Stockton-on-Tees as part of Mr Bates's travelling theatre company—simply attributed these strange dietary habits to Ritson's eccentricities, and Holcroft was not above occasionally lightly mocking Ritson for his vegetarianism.[67] The only time Ritson came close to eating animal flesh after the age of 19 was when he was visiting an inn; no other food was available other than some potatoes which had been roasted in dripping. Ritson ate eggs, because he reasoned that no creature was being deprived of life, and it was pointless to object to eating a pudding just because it had been made with eggs.[68] While Ritson vigorously defended his vegetarian diet in his private letters to friends and family we should not deduce from this that he was unreasonable in pushing his ideology onto others. Ritson's sister Anne followed him in abstaining from meat. During one of many bouts of a recurring, although unknown, illness her doctor advised her to eat meat. She refused initially, until Ritson urged her to follow the doctor's orders:

> I understand that you are advised to drink wine and eat animal food, both which, it seems, you refuse, wherein I think you are very much to blame. Wine is so perfectly innocent that I cannot see why you should have the least object to it; and though I look upon animal food as a thing prohibited by the moral law, to persons in good health, yet I neither can nor ought to retain the same opinion of it when it becomes, or is thought, necessary to the preservation of human life.[69]

Clearly Ritson had a balanced attitude towards meat eating—the local doctor knew best and his sister should follow his instructions when it was a matter of life or death.

There was also a practical reason for Ritson's abstention from animal food: chronic toothache. Ritson told his young nephew, 'I have, ever since I remember, been tormented with the tooth-ache, the most violent pain

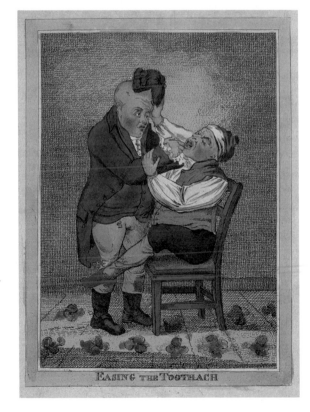

Joseph Ritson suffered all his life from chronic toothache and had many of his teeth removed. This illustration from c.1806 of a tooth-drawer extracting a tooth from a patient who is in such pain that he pulls the tooth-drawer's wig off, is drawn in the style of James Gillray. (Wellcome Collection)

EASING the TOOTHACH

one can possibly experience.'[70] Toothache has plagued mankind since the beginning of time. Many famous figures from English history spent a lifetime in agony due to toothache. Elizabeth I was one such person who continually suffered from 'the Distemper', as did many English noblemen of her time.[71] Once someone was struck with toothache, it was sure to reoccur throughout their life. Treatments for the pain ranged from ineffectual folk remedies to the downright bizarre. One might prepare a *balsamus traumaticus* of crushed crayfish eyes and chalk, or perhaps go to the doctor to be bled or receive an enema, and thereby set one's humours into balance again.[72] Thomas De Quincey, born in 1785, who later chronicled his descent into opium addiction, revealed that his habit began with him initially seeking a remedy for toothache. He spoke of it as 'that terrific curse … hardly a household in Europe being clear of it, each, in turn, having some one chamber intermittently echoing the groans extorted by this cruel torture'.[73] If worst came to worst, people might ask a local tooth-drawer or, failing that, a blacksmith to pull out the offending tooth—it was a lucrative side-business for blacksmiths—although this was a last resort.[74] Ritson resorted to this last resort frequently: by the time he was but 29 years old, he had had almost every single tooth removed from his mouth. He remarked to his nephew that

The Newcastle-based *Literary Register*. Joseph Ritson contributed several poems to this magazine. They were never very good however, and Ritson probably realised that his talents were best employed in researching the poetical works of long-dead authors rather than writing poetry himself.

he never replaced any of the teeth that he had removed because that was an expensive procedure. Our picture of Ritson in later life, then, must be one of a fairly malnourished-looking man with a few badly rotten teeth. It was better, he reasoned, for him to maintain a soft diet of milk and vegetables rather than meat, and to never drink sweetened tea. Every morning Ritson would wash his mouth out with spring water to keep his breath fresh.[75]

During the early 1770s Ritson began writing poetry. This was probably due to his acquaintance with the itinerant actor and poet John Cunningham (1729–73), who performed a season of plays with a travelling theatre company under the management of a Mr Bates, at Stockton-on-Tees in 1770. The acquaintance soon turned to friendship— the pair often enjoyed drinking at the Black Dog public house, and Ritson solicited Cunningham's advice on his poetry, both in person and later through correspondence.[76] Cunningham was an average poet— Samuel Johnson said that Cunningham's compositions 'place him in no contemptible line'. In a later poetical anthology, Ritson included four of Cunningham's works, which was perhaps his own way of honouring his friend, who died a few years later. Ritson's first poem was published in *The Literary Register* in March 1771 and signed simply as 'R'. Ritson never claimed this poem, as far as we know. Indeed no mention of the poem in question—titled 'The Late Mrs Todd of Stockton'—appears in the first bibliography of Ritson's works by Joseph Haslewood published in 1824. The reason that Ritson's former biographer attributes this poem to our Ritson is because the style is similar to Ritson's. The 'R' definitely follows the convention of the time, where authors made contributions to magazines only by writing their initials and without taking full credit. The poem honoured, as its title suggests, a lady from Stockton-on-Tees, and it is clear that Ritson's youthful readings of ballads, poems, and plays inspired him:

Ye nymphs and swains, that haunt the rural grove,
To tell in soothing strains soft tales of love;
Ye tuneful nines to this sad place repair,
Join with sigh and mingle tear with tear.
And tell the world CLARINDA is no more:
She's now no more who once had ev'ry charm,
The eye to please, the social breast to warm;

> Whose winning nature and obliging mien,
> Attracted all, by all with pleasure seen;
> Whose shape, complexion, and whose beauteous face
> Excell'd all others of the female race.[77]

Bronson, having attributed this poem to Ritson, passed completely over it as being of no literary merit.[78] The fact that Ritson—if indeed he wrote it—went on at length about Mrs Todd's many charms, makes one suspect that she was perhaps a childhood sweetheart. He likens Mrs Todd to Clarinda from Edmund Spenser's *The Faerie Queene* (1590–96). *The Faerie Queene* is an allegorical poem in which several virtuous medieval knights go on a quest in the realm of the legendary Gloriana—for which we read Queen Elizabeth I—who is a descendent of Titania, the Queen of the Fairies. Spenser's poem had been reprinted on numerous occasions by the time Ritson was born—many editions were available, ranging from expensive hardback editions of the full poem down to penny chapbooks containing short summaries.[79] Engravers were always sure to make a profit on their pictures of key scenes from the poem, further cementing Spenser's reputation as one of England's finest gothic poets.[80] In Spenser's poem, Clarinda is the ambassador of the Amazons. She is sent to procure the knight Artegall's hand in marriage for her mistress, Radigand, the Queen of the Amazons. However, Clarinda ends up falling in love with Artegall and attempts to woo him for herself. If Todd was one of Ritson's youthful sweethearts, perhaps she had married someone else, had given birth to a child, and subsequently passed away. It is hard to imagine Ritson writing such a poem for someone who was just another local notable with whom he was only casually acquainted.

According to Bronson, Ritson made a second attempt at being a poet. 'My Cousin's Tale' was published in October of the same year in *The Literary Register*:

> There is a town upon the T—,
> Which once was famous for its ale,
> Where houses daily do increase,
> And where my cousin now doth dwell:
> (My cousin is a girl that's pretty,
> And good, and witty.)[81]

EDMUND SPENSER,
AUTHOR OF "THE FAERIE QUEEN."

THE FAERIE
QVEENE.

Difpofed into twelue bookes,

Fashioning

XII. Morall vertues.

LONDON
Printed for VVilliam Ponfonbie.
1596.
m. 47.

Above and right: The poet Edmund Spenser, author of *The Faerie Queene* (1590–96). Joseph Ritson made several allusions to this epic and rather fanciful poem in his early poetical works (British Library and Folger Shakespeare Library)

The poem goes on to recount some of the local legends surrounding Stockton, such as that of a giant who lived in the nearby castle, and of a lad called Jack who slew him. Jacobites also make an appearance in the poem, while the final part praises the ladies of Stockton. The poem is attributed by Bronson to Ritson because it is signed 'H.N.' According to Bronson, this means Josep[H] Ritso[N] and 'it is highly characteristic of him in its interest in and knowledge of local history and tradition'.[82] Yet we must exercise some caution here, for there must have been plenty of people interested in local history from the north of England, and what is more, the poem was subtitled as having been written 'By a Gentleman'. Ritson in 1771 was by no means a gentleman in the eighteenth-century sense of the word and could not in any way make a meaningful pretence to being one. He was only

19 years old, had not completed his legal training, and was not yet financially independent. In a footnote, Bronson admitted that

> Ritson's authorship of these pieces ['Mrs Todd of Stockton' and 'My Cousin's Tale'] cannot be proved. To argue the matter would take more space than the subject deserves. I will content myself with saying that, although doubt is admissible as to the epigrams on the elegy, Ritson's authorship of 'My Cousin's Tale' seems to me almost unquestionable. The internal evidence by itself is sufficiently convincing, and external evidence points strongly in the same direction. Some of the latter will appear *post*.[83]

Bronson never did publish an academic paper outlining his reasons for thinking Ritson wrote the poems, but 'internal evidence' here refers to the fact that the poet praises the ladies of Stockton—which Ritson would do at length in another poem—as well as its Jacobite sympathies and its anti-religious sentiments. Whoever H.N. was, it is *highly likely* that it may have been written by Ritson, but we must entertain the possiblility that it could have been the production of another aspirant writer.

However Ritson was *definitely* the author of 'Versees Addressed to the Ladies of Stockton' ('versees' is not a typographical error but one of Ritson's own peculiar misspellings), which was first printed in the *The Literary Register* in 1772. While posterity is ever grateful for Ritson's diligent archival work and early transcriptions of primary sources, it was perhaps for the best that he did not pursue a career as a poet. Some parts are worth reprinting here because Ritson evidently tried to incorporate as many literary allusions as he could from the books he had read:

> Accept, ye fair, the tribute of my praise,
> And deign a smile upon my humble lays;
> For your applause i strike the tuneless lyre,
> And strive to raise within the poets fire:
> In hobbleing verse your charms attempt to sing;
> Your charms adorn'd with ever blooming spring.
>
> Ye female critics, read, sans spleen, my song,
> Nor deem it or too languid, or too long;

For your applause i write, your frowns I fear;
Hence, fellows! Hence! Your judgment's nothing here.
Let not harsh censure my poor rhimes asperse,
But with the subject dignify the verse.[84]

Where Tees in sweet meanders slowly glides,
And gentlely murmuring rolls his easy tides,
There stands a town, with peace and plenty crown'd,
For wit, for wealth, and loyal sons renown'd;
Far famed for dames, wife, charitable, chaste,
And first in beautys annals ever place'd.

In every age has STOCKTON been revere'd,
Her sons have always been belove'd and fear'd.
When, 'gainst the hardy legions of the North,
Brave Percy led his youthful warriors forth,
Her valiant deeds let history proclaim,
And Cheviot hills record the fatal name.
Her nymphs, erst wont to trip the verdant groves,
Seem'd sisters to the Gracees and the Loves.[85]

Ritson was proud of his heritage; this poem not only extols the virtues of Stockton's ladies but also the greatness of its own local history. The mention of the valiant deeds of 'brave Percy' were clearly influenced by his youthful readings of the 'Ballad of Chevy Chase'. Ritson's readings of Shakespeare are evident even in this early poem because he equated one Stockton lady with Titania herself:

With thee, TITANIA, does the muse advance,
The leader thou in this uncouple'd dance;
Thy prudent maxims, and thy manners sage,
To us seem wonderous, far above thine age;
Thy infant buds, like bees about thee swarm,
Thyself their empress, shielding them from harm;
Of treacherous man warn'd in each dayly task,
Though, spite of thee, he'll soon be all they ask,
To thee the riseing generation bows,
Accept our homage, nor our praise refuse.[86]

Titania got her first 'big break' in Shakespeare's *A Midsummer Night's Dream*. The bard took the name from Ovid's *Metamorphoses* where it is said that she was given the name because she was a descendent of the Titans. As she tells us in *A Midsummer Night's Dream*:

> I am a spirit of no common rate.
> The summer still doth tend upon my state.[87]

Titania is a powerful woman who rules over the seasons. She is also a highly sexualised character—portrayals of her in art and literature after Shakespeare's day often depict her naked.[88] Where Ritson mentioned other famous female literary characters in his 'Versees', in footnotes he mentioned the names of the actual Stockton women to whom he was referring. Titania referred to a certain Miss Dixon. Olivia, from Shakespeare's *Twelfth Night* (c. 1602), referred to Miss Bunting; Daphne, one of the Greek nymphs, referred to another lady of Stockton named Peggy Lamb.[89] Ritson does not appear to have ever had any success with the ladies whom he mentioned in the 'Versees'. In November 1772 a short poem written by 'Sophia' to 'Mr J— R—n of Stockton' praised Ritson's poetical skills but reprimanded him for daring to publish such a set of verses and warned him that he did not stand a chance with her because 'She thinks thou'rt poor'.[90] Whether the other women took it as a compliment being included in what was such a badly-written poem is anyone's guess. As a historian and literary critic who analysed poems, he would become brilliant. As a poet, he had much to learn.

When Ritson was 21 years old, he set off on foot on his first research trip to Edinburgh. He was overjoyed at being granted access to Holyrood Palace's Advocate's Library and spent much of the time reading old Scottish poems and ballads and transcribing them for his own collection, many of which would form the basis of his later published song collections. It is not known whether at this early stage Ritson had any plans to publish the transcripts of the old ballads which he collected and in all likelihood they may simply have been for the purpose of private enjoyment because 'people often wrote down, for their own private use, various poems and songs that they had heard perhaps at work, in the streets, or at festivals'.[91] It was at Edinburgh that he learned two valuable life lessons. The first was to ensure that, if undertaking a pedestrian trip then it helps to have a good pair of walking boots—Ritson had to get

Drawn Eng.d & Pub.d by J & H.S.Storer Chapel Street, Pentonville, March 1.1819.

PARLIAMENT HOUSE.
from the Cowgate.

Edinburgh in the eighteenth century. Ritson travelled there on his first research trip when he was 21 years old. (Wellcome Collection)

his mended, a process that was not cheap in the age before the mass production of boots. The second was that, if you are visiting somewhere new and staying in an inn, then you should make sure to keep enough money behind to pay the reckoning rather than spend it all on books. Ritson did not have enough money at the end of his trip and a fellow traveller had to lend him some money so he could pay up. Such occurrences were by no means infrequent—travellers sometimes ran out of money. Fielding makes a few comic scenes out of a similar scenario in *Joseph Andrews*. Some inn owners were understandably eager to prosecute guests who had no means of paying their bill. Court records from the eighteenth century contain several such cases. In 1722, a man named Samuel Molton attempted to abscond without paying his bill; he was subsequently arrested and sentenced to death.[92] Luckily for Ritson, however, his life was not to cut short on the gallows on account of being a few shillings down on his hotel bill!

His politics at this early stage were of a very different colour to the causes he would become an advocate for in later life: Ritson was a Jacobite. As a young man in Stockton-on-Tees, he viewed the Stuarts as the 'true' British royal line. The last Stuart king, James II, had been ousted from the throne during the Glorious Revolution of 1688 on account of his Catholic beliefs. Parliamentarians invited the Dutch William of Orange and his wife Mary to rule as joint monarchs in James's stead. Their rule would be legitimate because Mary was James's daughter, but had been raised as a protestant. William and Mary died without issue and the crowns of England and Scotland passed first to William's protestant sister-in-law, Anne, the last Stuart monarch without issue. After Anne's death, the crown of the recently united Kingdom of Great Britain passed to George of Hanover, who became George I in 1714. Two unsuccessful rebellions were launched to reclaim the Kingdom of Great Britain for the Stuarts in 1715 and again in 1745. Many Tory statesmen, and people particularly in Scotland and the North of England, supported the Jacobite cause. In the second Jacobite Rebellion of 1745 led by Charles Stuart, officials in London feared that whole towns in northern England had gone over to the Jacobite cause. Manchester, for example, raised a force of 300 men for it. The counties of Northumberland and Durham were likewise viewed as dens of 'Popery and Jacobitism' by officials in London: 'half of the population', wrote one observer, 'is of the papist faith and the other half are well-disposed towards it.'[93] This description was not far from the truth. Many of the local worthies toasted 'the King over the Water' at dinner parties. We should not overestimate, however, the degree of support that the Jacobites enjoyed. Many people's attachment to 'the king over the water' was merely sentimental, for they were less willing to participate in open rebellion. This was also the case with many Catholics who, although their rights would be improved if Britain had another Catholic king (at this point they could not vote in national or local elections or attend university), would lose everything if they were

PRINCE CHARLES STUART (THE YOUNG PRETENDER). FROM AN AUTHENTIC PORTRAIT.

Bonnie Prince Charlie, the Jacobite Pretender. In his youth Joseph Ritson was a supporter of the Jacobite cause.

implicated in any way in treasonous activities. Many Catholics 'bent over backwards to show their goodwill to the Government, swearing endless oaths of loyalty and voluntarily giving up their weapons and horses.'[94] Unlike the citizens of Manchester, the people of the Durham and Northumberland never raised any regiments of soldiers to fight for the Jacobite cause.

In Ritson's view, the Hanoverian kings, George I, George II, and George III, were nothing but usurpers. At age 26, Ritson privately published *Tables Shewing the Descent of the Crown of England* which traced the lineal descent of the 'true crown' of England from the Saxon king, Edgar the Great, right down to Bonnie Prince Charlie. Ritson styles the latter as Charles III. As for William of Orange, he was nothing but an *invader*:

> William III. (prince of Orange) invaded England, under an invitation from some of the discontented nobility, with a pretence of redressing certain misunderstandings between King James and his subjects; and having obliged the King (whose eldest daughter he had married) to abdicate the Realm, and by his own writs convened an assembly consisting of some of the peers, the lord mayor, the aldermen, and common council of London, and the whiggish members of the exclusion parliaments:—These men alone, without possessing the least shadow of authority from the law, government, or constitution, or from the people in general, in the name of the whole English nation, presented him and his princess with the royal diadem on Ash-Wednesday, February 13th, 1688!!!—A proceeding as replete with treachery, inhumanity, and justice, as ever disgraced the annals of a civilized country.[95]

Ritson declined to publish *The Descent of the Crown of England* for the public because he feared that doing so would affect his prospects in the legal profession. He need not have been too worried however; by the time he published his broadside, Jacobitism was virtually dead as a political force. Instead we might class Ritson as a 'romantic' Jacobite, inspired by having heard stories of soldiers led by a gallant leader traversing the English and Scottish countryside to win back the throne

THE DECLARATION OF INDEPENDENCE.

The leading men of the American Revolution. Ritson, as many people in Britain did at this time, seems to have disapproved of the rebellion in the American colonies and cheered 'His Majesty's late signal successes' in the war during the 1770s. This was in spite of his seeming aversion to the ruling Hanoverian dynasty.

for the true monarch. It was like a story taken straight from one of the early modern 'heroic ballads' of which Ritson was fond.

In *The Descent of the Crown of England*, Ritson signed himself as 'A TRUE BRITON'.[96] He may have been a romantic supporter of the Stuarts but he counted himself as a patriot when it came to foreign affairs and had little sympathy for those who would rebel against the British nation itself. He disapproved of the American rebels who were fighting a war to break free from British rule. Ritson's letters during the American War of Independence refer to George III with implicit respect as 'His Majesty', and he extolled 'the late signal successes of His Majesty's arms in America and the West Indies; and since it has pleased god to put us into such a hopeful way, god send he may continue it'.[97] Ritson was not unusual in his support for king and country against the American colonists. As John W. Derry argues, very few opposition MPs doubted the British parliament's right to legislate for the colonies and while many in England regretted the outbreak of war with their Atlantic cousins, contemporary British newspapers and pamphlets contained many criticisms of the Americans. Samuel Johnson famously asked, 'why do we hear the loudest yelps for liberty from the drivers of negroes?'[98] That was of course a snipe at the fact that America's economy depended upon that most disgusting trade, whereas slavery in England had been illegal under since the Somerset Case in 1772 (although the trade continued until 1807 and slavery was not fully abolished in the British Empire until 1833).[99] Johnson further argued that although the Americans viewed the taxes imposed upon them as 'tyrannical', they were necessary. Johnson further reasoned that 'if the subject refuses to obey, it is the duty of authority to use compulsion'.[100] More popular expressions of support for George III in England occurred throughout the country in 1776. When news reached England of the colonists' defeat at Long Island, people in Leeds, Manchester, Bristol, York, and Halifax celebrated in the streets and burnt effigies of George Washington, John Adams, John Hancock, and Arthur Lee.[101] Ritson's letters do contain several snipes at politicians from both the major parties of the day, the Whigs and the Tories, but in spite of his Jacobitism, he took his nation's side in foreign conflicts.

For a man who, as time progressed, became a fervent democrat, Ritson said very little about the rights or wrongs of imperialism. He was a man of his time after all, and empires were a fact of life: Britain, France, Portugal, Spain, the Ottomans and Austria all had empires. One of Ritson's friends from Stockton, Ralph Hoar, went to serve with the 52nd Madras Regiment—the soldiers of the crown having been sent there in the 1780s to buttress the rule of the British East India Company. In a letter to Hoar, written in verse, Ritson expressed the hope that 'Indias [sic] burning soil' might 'repay with wealth' Hoar's 'martial toil'.[102] While a British soldier's pay was very low indeed, it was expected that both the upper and lower ranks of the army in India would return from the subcontinent as rich men due to the fact that prize money from conquests, or what we might more properly call 'loot', was often distributed among the soldiers. The higher a man was in the army, the more prize money he received. The conqueror of Bengal, Robert Clive (1725–74), started his career as a lowly clerk in the East India Company, had then risen through the army's ranks, and through the various campaigns in which he took part amassed a fortune of £300,000. Walter Scott in *The Surgeon's Daughter* (1827) remarked how these returning 'adventurers' often left their country poor but reappeared after a number of years 'surrounded by Oriental wealth and Oriental luxury, which dimmed even the splendour of the most wealthy of the British nobility'.[103] Ritson expected this would be the case and had few reservations that people should make money out of imperial ventures.

Ritson imagined the subcontinent in what the literary critic Edward Said would describe as classic 'Orientalist' terms: it was a place of wonder, of danger and of exciting adventures to those who would seek their fortune:

> Shall I not hear your wond'rous tales
> Of heav'n-high hills, and hell-like vales,
> Rough quarries, rocks, wide-spreading trees,
> Whole armies that enshade with ease;
> Of antres vast, of deserts wild,
> Young Arabs keen, old Bramins mild;
> Of accidents by flood and field,
> Of Nabobs you have made to yield;
> Of Moplas fierce your hand has tam'd,
> And monsters that your sword has maim'd;
> Of hair-breadth scapes i'th' deadly breach;
> How you were sold, and how got free,
> And portance in your history;
> Of battle, siege, disast'rous chances;
> Of murder, famine, death, despair,
> And all the horrours of the war?[104]

Ritson exoticized the people of East and evidently thought that the Indians' skin colour made them dangerous or menacing due to the fact that they could 'enshade' themselves with ease. Yet he expected that the British army would make any of those 'Nabobs'—an English corruption of the term 'Nawab', signifying an Indian ruler—'yield' to them. Ritson does not, however, seem to have shared some of his contemporaries' overt racial prejudices against Indians—as far as we are aware.

Besides writing poetry, visiting libraries, and publishing short broadsides, little is known of what Ritson did for leisure during his years in Stockton. Occasional details shine through in letters from later in his life when he reminisces over 'old times'. Upon having reviewed a first

33

A late eighteenth-century illustration of a British residence in Madras, India. Joseph Ritson's close friend, Mr Ralph Hoar, served in India with the 52nd Madras Regiment. (British Library)

draft of Thomas Langdale's *History of Northallerton* (1791) before its publication, he wrote to his lifelong friend Mr Wadeson that reading of 'the old borough' had stirred up many romantic memories of his childhood:

> You have probably forgot the delicious moments which the idea of this once-loved place brings to my recollection. Can you remember, for instance, our drinking gin and water at Appleton Wiske, while you and the weaver sung 'Despairing Beside a Clear Stream'? Ah! My good friend, if we could but turn the clock back![105]

Appleton Wiske is, as the crow flies, thirteen miles from Stockton, so it would have been a good few hours' walk each way—doable in one day certainly, though probably longer on the way back if the company had imbibed quantities of gin. Set to the haunting tune of 'Grim King of the Ghosts', 'Despairing Beside a Clear Stream' is a pastoral song in which a poor lovesick shepherd named Colin laments the unfaithfulness of his betrothed:

Then to her new love let her go,
And deck her in golden array,
Be finest at ev'ry fine show,
And frolick it all the long day:
While Colin forgotten and gone,
No more shall be heard of or seen,
Unless, when beneath the pale moon,
His ghost shall glide over the green.[106]

The song itself represents the misfortunes in the love life of the aforementioned writer Joseph Addison (1672–1719), with whose works Ritson was very familiar.[107] It was by no means a new song when Ritson and his friend were drinking gin up at Appleton Wiske in what was probably the late 1760s or early 1770s. It was originally written by the dramatist and Poet Laureate Nicholas Rowe in 1712. The poem was never included in any of Rowe's collected works but is thought to have first come to public notice when it was published in the *London Magazine* in 1744.

When Ritson wrote that letter reminiscing about former times, he was living in London. At Ralph Bradley's urging, early in 1775, Ritson began exploring the feasibility of securing a position in London where his legal talents would be put to better use rather than in the quiet town of Stockton-on-Tees. The correspondence by means of which Ritson approached the law firms in London is now lost, but by mid-1775 he had secured a position in the conveyancing department in the firm of Masterman and Lloyd, based in London, on a salary of £150 per year— richer than some but poorer than many members of his profession. It is unknown how the son of a lowly farmer in Stockton-on-Tees secured a position in the MP William Masterman's firm, who was also the Clerk of the Council of the Duchy of Lancaster. However, Bronson in his previous biography uncovered an interesting fact: Ritson may have married into the family. *The Newcastle Chronicle* on 18 June 1774 revealed that

> Last week was married at Northallerton, by the Rev. Mr. Wood, Mr. Ritson, attorney (late clerk to Mr. Bradley, of Stockton) to Miss Masterman, of Northallerton; an accomplished young lady, with genteel fortune.[108]

This is beyond doubt 'our Joseph Ritson', as Bronson said. It dispels
the idea that was held by many in the Victorian era that Ritson never
married. Ritson never mentioned his wife in any of his letters. We might
assume that the lady in question was Catherine Masterman, perhaps a
distant relative of William Masterman, for the latter owned some land in
North Yorkshire.[109] There are many questions which remain of Ritson's
wife: why does no record of the marriage appear in official records? Did
she die soon after the marriage, maybe in childbirth? Was this a simple
mistake by the newspaper, for there were several Ritsons in the area in the
late eighteenth century? Why did Ritson never refer to her subsequently
if indeed he did marry her? Was Catherine Masterman the 'early
disappointment' in his love life that many of Ritson's friends mentioned
after he died? Such questions remain unanswered. Yet married to a relation
of William Masterman, Ritson must have been because when Masterman
died Ritson lamented that Masterman 'left me nothing but a ring, nor
did I look for anything'.[110] This suggests that, as a family member might,
Ritson expected something from Masterman's estate after the latter's
death. It was without a wife, however, that Ritson set off to London in late
1775. It is in the capital that we join Ritson in the next chapter.

Chapter 2

'Attention Requisite in Certain Branches of his Duty': Joseph Ritson the Gentleman

The journey that Ritson made to London in November 1775 was completed on foot. Travelling by coach was expensive and Ritson was yet to make his way in the world financially. When a person had no money to travel by coach, then just as Fielding's Parson Adams and Joseph Andrews do, they had to walk to their destination. For

Ritson it was probably a full seven days' walking, and maybe more depending on whether he stopped anywhere. It was also easy to get lost on England's country roads, as Ritson once found to his dismay.[111]

When he arrived in London for the first time, he would have had quite a culture shock. It was a busy metropolis. The pace of life would have been very different to what Ritson was used to in the 'small matter' of Stockton, which boasted a population of probably no more than 3,000 people in Ritson's day. London (in 1780) was home to over 750,000 people.[112] It was one of the largest cities in the world. Warehouses lined the banks of the River Thames, indicative of the unique trading opportunities that were available to ambitious tradesmen seeking to enlarge their fortunes through trade with Britain's colonies via the agency of the many joint-stock companies.[113]

London's political and legal societies were situated in the western part of the city while the eastern part of the metropolis was emerging of as a centre of industry and manufacturing. It was to the western part of the city that Ritson went on his first arrival in London when he took up lodgings with a man named Mr Robinson—not related to the Stockton-based Mr Robinson—near Gray's Inn, one of the Inns of Court. There are four Inns of Court: The Inner Temple, the Middle Temple, Lincolns Inn, and Gray's Inn, all of which were responsible for training barristers. Although it was located in what people may think was an increasingly fashionable West End of London at the time, and in spite of the fact that Gray's Inn itself looked rather genteel, the area around Ritson's new home was actually a bit dirty and smelly. Some of the streets around Gray's Inn were not paved, meaning that puddles of dirty, muddy water built up in inclement weather. It was not until the early nineteenth century that the area around Gray's Inn began to be paved.[114] A short distance away from Gray's Inn was Mount Pleasant, originally a tongue-in-cheek name given to an area which consisted of a rubbish tip, on top of a mound of soil, at the foundation of which was debris from the Great Fire of London in 1666.[115]

Ritson remained as a lodger with Mr Robinson near Gray's Inn for the five years he spent in Masterman and Lloyd's offices, based in chambers at Gray's Inn. Five years was the minimum term which, according to the Attorneys and Solicitors Act (1728), would-be attorneys and solicitors had to serve in an apprenticeship before they could enter

Gray's Inn during the late eighteenth century. (Wellcome Collection)

the profession in their own right. The pay of an apprentice, or 'clerk under article', may have been low but there were some advantages: Masterman allowed Ritson to make use of government franks to send his correspondence. It is from this period of employment that Ritson's letter-writing activity began in earnest. He was able to write letters to his family quite frequently, which was lucky, for his father back in Stockton was gravely ill. Writing to his father in March 1777 Ritson thanked him for letting him have an education and he lamented the fact that his present circumstances as a lowly legal apprentice meant that he could not offer his father any financial assistance when Mr Robinson, back in Stockton, refused to repay the debts owed to Ritson's father, the struggling grain farmer:

> Dear Father,
> I really waited (as Nanny tells me you thought I did) to hear how you were before I wrote. I every day hoped to have better news and am very unhappy in being so much disappointed. Heaven knows how much I have all along pleased myself with thinking I should be able in a few years to render you some assistance towards making you easy and happy in your old age for the education and indulgence you bestowed on

me in my youth … If we should be deprived of you now
(the very thought of which distresses me beyond description)
my sorrow will be sincere and such as my duty to so good a
parent, whose loss I shall long mourn, ought to prescribe.[116]

The family's financial outlook was bleak but Ritson at least had some
friends in London, notably his employer, Mr Masterman. Masterman
took a bit of a shine to Ritson and often lent him money when he was
feeling the pinch of poverty in London.[117] The cordiality between Ritson
and Masterman, and the latter's generosity, is of course easily explained
if we consider that Ritson and Masterman were probably related in
some way.

Ritson's father died shortly after he wrote that letter—his final
letter—to his father. Women tended to outlive their husbands and this
was the case with Jane, who survived her husband and, as many a rural
widower did, carried on the family business.[118] Ritson's sister Anne was
still living in Stockton, however, so in all likelihood she assisted her
mother in winding up her father's affairs while the property passed to
Ritson. The latter, having married at some point in the 1770s and given
birth to Joseph Frank, had also by 1777 become a widow. Ritson was
to become a father figure, from a distance, to Frank, through frequent
letters to him.

It would be a while until Ritson returned to Stockton. He decided to
strike out on his own in 1780 as a conveyancer and accordingly took
rooms at 8 Holborn Court, Gray's Inn, initially rented from Masterman,
which he occupied until the end of his life.[119]

An unqualified conveyancer such as Ritson would have completed
his legal work in his rooms at Holborn Court, but he would, much
like a salesman, have had to tout for clients in taverns, coffeehouses
(which before the establishment of the London Stock Exchange in
1801 functioned as places to buy and sell shares) where he would
have been able to meet with rich merchants eager to make investments
in properties.[120] He also supplemented his conveyancing with the
drawing up of official documents such as, in some cases, drafts of
parliamentary bills (a bill is the name given to a proposed law before
it becomes an Act of Parliament). It would have been difficult at first:
Ritson had very few contacts and the customer base was quite small.

At one point, his dire financial situation and gloomy business outlook caused him to think occasionally of returning to Stockton-on-Tees, although contacts back home informed him that the few conveyancing opportunities in his home town were already well taken care of by the existing firm of Mr Reed, who seemed to have a monopoly on the business.[121]

Whether Ritson would have been welcomed back to the small town of Stockton is unclear. The year before, he published a satirical work entitled *The Stockton Jubilee*, which, using phrases from Shakespeare's plays, was intended as a light-hearted lampoon about some of his former acquaintances from his home town. A flavour of some of these jokes is given below:

> L[u]k[e] Els[o]b, C-st-mh-se Off-c-r
> He stalks up and down like a peacock; a stride and a stand:
> ruminates like a hostess that hath no arithmetic but her brain
> to set down her reckoning; bites his lip with politic regard,
> as who should say, there were wit in this head, an 'twould
> but out.——Troilus & Cressida

> S[a]m[ue]l Sm[i]th, Esq.
> There can be no kernel in this light nut; the soul of this
> man is in his clothes: trust him not in matter of heavy
> consequence; I have kept of them tame, and know their
> natures.——All's Well.

> J[o] M[el]l[o]nb[y]
> I know thee for a knave, a rascal, an eater of broken meats; a
> base, proud, shallow, beggarly, three-suited, hundred pound,
> filthy worsted-stocking knave; a lilly-livered, action-taking
> knave; a whoreson, superserviceable finical rogue; a one
> trunk inheriting slave; one that would be a bawd, in way
> of good service, and art nothing but the composition of a
> knave, beggar, coward, pandar, and the son and heir of a
> mongrel bitch; one that I will beat into clamorous whining,
> if thou deny'st the least syllable of this addition.——
> King Lear.[122]

This seems like an odd thing to publish to a modern mind, but similar publications were a brief literary trend in the 1770s, as James Boswell explained:

> This season there was a whimsical fashion in the newspapers of applying Shakespeare's words to describe living persons well-known in the world; which was done under the title of *Modern Characters from Shakespeare*; many of which were admirably adapted. The fancy took so much that they were afterwards collected into pamphlet. Somebody said to [Doctor] Johnson, across the table, that he had not been in those characters. 'Yes (said he,) I have. I should have been sorry to be left out.' He then repeated what had been applied to him, 'I must borrow from Gargantua's mouth.'[123]

The pamphlet to which Boswell referred was published in 1778. No one was sacred. It satirized the whole royal family, the bishops in the House of Lords, Lord Bolingbroke, the Earl of Bute, and Hannah Moore to name but a few. If you 'mattered' in the world, so to speak, then you appeared in *Modern Characters*, which is why Johnson wanted to be included in it. It was a joke but Ritson's mistake seems to have been thinking that the residents of Stockton-on-Tees kept up with the latest literary trends. The citizens in his home town were less than impressed—shortly after the publication of *The Stockton Jubilee* Ritson remarked that he dared not now come back to Stockton lest he be killed on sight.[124] In fact, once Ritson was established in his business, he regularly made the trip back home to Stockton every summer and returned to London alive, not having been lynched—maybe the hostile reaction to *The Stockton Jubilee* had been exaggerated. The worst response was a short poem written by a Stockton resident lampooning Ritson and mocking his literary aspirations:

> With sacrilegious hand he tears,
> The wreath from Shakespeare's tomb;
> And, with presumptive folly, wears
> A meanly-pilfered plume.
>
> Thus, dressing each malignant thought,
> In language not his own,

This would-be wit, with envy fraught,
Disturbs a peaceful town.

His grov'ling mind directs his aim,
And drives him headlong forth;
To vilify superior fame,
And slander envied worth.

But judging minds he can't deceive;
They'll scorn the prating elf
Who fain would make the world believe,
That all are like himself.[125]

The residents of Stockton-on-Tees should have grown a sense of humour!

For a man of the law, Ritson occasionally sympathised with those who broke it, an attitude which shows in sharp relief in two letters to his mother in the summer of 1780, when he was an eyewitness to one of the most famous events in working-class history: the Gordon Riots. The riots were occasioned by the recent passage of the Catholic Relief Act (1778). Jacobitism was becoming a romantic fad and the government in London had thought it prudent to extend to Catholics certain rights. As we have seen, Catholics had been 'bending over backwards' to prove their loyalty to the Hanoverian regime. Lord Kenmare, to take one example, who was one of the leading Catholic landowners in Ireland—which although ruled by Britain had its own separate parliament and legal system—donated money and even allowed 1,900 of his tenants to enlist as auxiliary volunteers in the American War of Independence. The conciliatory approach seemed to be working, and by the late 1770s there seemed to be, in the words of Robert E. Burns, a good 'rapport' between the king and his Catholic subjects.[126] The Catholic Relief Act, also colloquially known as 'The Papists Act', required Catholics to swear loyalty to George III and renounce any loyalty to the Stuarts. If Catholics took the oath then, according to the terms of the Act, Catholics could, if they wanted, purchase freehold and leasehold land, which previously they had been barred from doing, and bequeath it to their descendents. The provisions also allowed Catholics to live in London, which had been banned for many years. It permitted them to found their own schools and allowed them to join the British army if they wished—a growing empire needed soldiers after all. The act passed through all stages of parliament without a dissenting voice.

One bigoted Scottish nobleman was against giving Catholics *any* civil liberties. This man was Lord George Gordon (1751–93), who has been called 'insane' by one historian.[127] He was a member of the Protestant Association—a kind of early modern extra-parliamentary pressure group—and became its president in 1779. He organised petitions to King George III on numerous occasions to get the government to repeal the Papists Act. The government humoured him for a time by listening to his concerns but he could never secure an audience with the king and his petitions were rejected. Annoyed with the rejection of his appeals Gordon rallied the members of his Protestant Association to London. On 2 June, Gordon and his mob marched on the House of Commons

For about a week in the summer of 1780, London descended into mob rule. Initially inspired by a bigoted objection to the passage of the Papists Act (1778), the rioters' aims expanded beyond their initial goals and began attacking symbols of authority. Joseph Ritson's sympathies were with the rioters. This image is a reproduction of John Seymour Lucas's *The Gordon Riots*, completed in 1879 and published in Joseph Clayton's *The Rise of Democracy* (1911).

to deliver a final petition. The anti-Catholic crowd grew in size and eventually numbered 60,000, all chanting 'No Popery' and other such slogans. When parliamentarians refused to debate the public's petition, the crowd got angry and began attacking parliamentary representatives outside the House. Events spiralled out of control quickly and the mob began rioting. Ritson wrote to his mother back in Stockton—who at this point was gravely ill—to tell her the news, and to reassure her that he had come to no harm:

> Dear Mother,
> I am very well and am much grieved to find that you should continue otherwise, but hope to God you will soon get better of your complaint ... the confusion which reigns here would have prevented me from writing sooner. A general spirit of discontent has long been increasing among the people: it has at last broken out among the lower class in London.[128]

Ritson placed great emphasis on the 'spirit of discontent' among the poorer classes rather than the anti-Catholic sentiments which had initially fuelled the riots. Ritson acknowledged later in his letter that he personally saw many people chanting 'Down with the Papists' and 'No Popery' slogans, and that some very rich Catholics had their homes burnt down, but poor Catholics were generally safe during the riots. Ritson saw the mob's primary concerns as being a general disillusionment with the establishment. To him, the following events were more representative of the riot's nature:

> Five of the mob having been committed to Newgate, and the keeper refusing to set them free, their comrades yesternight, burnt it to the ground, and set not only their own people, but all of the debtors and felons at liberty, three or four of whom were to be executed within these few days ... Sir John Fielding's house was also plundered of everything, and the furniture, &c. burnt in the street ... Lord Mansfield's house, in Bloomsbury Square, was burnt this morning ... Lord Mansfield's country seat, about four miles from town, is said to be now in flames ... destruction has been

vowed against the houses and persons of several noblemen, bishops, and gentry.[129]

Lord Mansfield (1705–93) and Sir John Fielding (1721–80) were not Catholic. They were both members of the Church of England and respectable judges. The non-Catholic institution, the Bank of England, was also looted. The mob's cause had evolved. In another letter written to his mother the following week, Ritson told her,

> The same evening on which I wrote my letter to you, but after I had finished and sealed my letter, the mob burnt the Fleet and King's Bench prisons, and set all the debtors at liberty, and likewise the toll gates on Black-friars bridge, and the greatest part of Holborn was in flames.[130]

The rioting lasted for several days—the constables of London did what they could to arrest some of the rioters, but eventually on 7 June the army had to be called in. It is unlikely that Ritson was ever in danger. Although Gray's Inn had been a target during previous riots, some of the attorneys stood guard ready to protect Gray's Inn, and Ritson never expressed any apprehension over danger to his person. As riots were common in eighteenth-century London, he might have placed a candle in the window of his rooms. Doing this, as many people did during the frequent times when 'King Mob' resumed his reign in London, would have signalled to the world that he supported the rioters in whatever cause they were protesting, and he could consequently be assured that his property was safe.

Ritson held the government solely responsible for the riots:

> No person any way innocent either has or (except by consequence) will suffer, and most of those whom they single out as examples of their vengeance, have long and deservedly been objects of public detestation, such as Lord Mansfield, Lord North, Lord Sandwich, Lord George Germaine, and others of the present scoundrel ministry.[131]

The mob's attacks on symbols of wealth and power led the neo-Marxist historian E.P. Thompson to designate the Gordon rioters as a 'revolutionary crowd'. These crowds begin with a vulgar mob gathered in support of some cause, much like the anti-Catholic protestors gathered in front of parliament on 2 June. In the next stage of a revolutionary crowd's evolution, localised rioting occurs in the aftermath of their demands being rejected. Governments tend not to concern themselves with the mob's demands at this stage, and statesmen are generally confident that they can ride out this second stage of mob evolution— Georgian governments had faced many riots. Indeed, most mobs usually end their activities in this second phase; as the movement fades, people realise that they will get no satisfaction from the powers that be, and go home. The final—and most dangerous phase—of any riotous crowd is when 'licensed spontaneity' occurs, which is what occurred with the Gordon Riots. People unrelated to the original cause join the mob and at this point and generally 'anything goes' when it comes to settling concerns with the rich and powerful. Although Ritson had not yet adopted the revolutionary ideology that he was to become an advocate for in the 1790s his approval of the Gordon rioters' targeting of the rich and powerful anticipates it.

It took three days for the militia to put an end to the riots and restore the rule of law. It had to be the army, because at this point in time Britain had no professional police force but relied on a corrupt system of thief takers and bailiffs to uphold law and order. There were some constables charged with keeping the peace, known as Bow Street Runners, who worked out of John Fielding's Bow Street Magistrates Office, although the punishment meted out to Fielding's house gives us an indication of what the crowd thought of this office. After the army had quelled the rioters, reports estimated that the cost of the damages inflicted by the mob totalled £200,000. Thirty-two private homes were destroyed as were as numerous businesses. The authorities quickly hunted down and arrested Lord Gordon, who was imprisoned without bail in the Tower of London on a charge of High Treason. He was ostracised in public life and his little bigoted anti-Catholic crusade which had been the cause of so much strife lost credibility in the eyes of the public. Gordon achieved nothing of note after 1780. Although he was eventually acquitted of High Treason in December he was excommunicated from his beloved protestant faith in 1785. In 1787 he was convicted of another crime and thrown into Newgate gaol where he remained until his death from typhoid fever in 1793.

Ritson's mother did not survive long after the letter recounting the events of the Gordon Riots. She died in the family home at Silver Street on 22 November 1780. What Jane Ritson died of is unknown— the duty of arranging the funeral devolved upon Ritson's sister, and in a letter on 25 November, Ritson wrote to her lamenting the death of 'our good mother' while recognising that 'it could be only unthinking cruelty to have wished her continuance in misery and disease'.[132] There are some sources, which amount to little more than malicious gossip, that attribute his mother's death to 'madness'. Ritson never mentioned such an illness in his letters so it seems safe to disregard it as mere hearsay.[133]

At some point before 1782, in addition to the family home in Silver Street, Stockton, Ritson inherited some property in Hartlepool and in Strickland from his uncle. The extent of the property he owned is unclear for in one letter Ritson refers to the Hartlepool property as consisting of 'two or three small old houses' and the 'little property' at Strickland.[134] Elsewhere Ritson described his properties as being an 'estate', which conjures up images of a larger property portfolio than 'two or three small old houses'.[135] It was probably some farmland with a few houses attached to it, and Ritson rented these out to tenants while the house in Stockton was tenanted by his sister and nephew. To his tenants in Hartlepool and Strickland, Ritson, who was eking out a living in the capital, was never anything more than an absentee landlord and it is doubtful that he ever met his tenants. He entrusted the management of his estates to Matthew Wadeson and John Russell Rowntree. These two stewards were somewhat remiss in the management of Ritson's affairs and Ritson had to constantly badger them to send him the rents. A note that he sent to Wadeson in 1783 is evidence of one such letter:

> My Hartlepool estate, I fancy, is sunk into the earth, or the houses are empty and the tenants insolvent. Render up an 'account of thy stewardship'—thou just steward![136]

The exact value of Ritson's property remains unknown but we do know that he could vote in general elections so it must have satisfied the forty shilling freehold property requirement for voting rights.[137] That Ritson could vote highlights one of the many oddities in the eighteenth-century electoral system. It is, with some justification, assumed that only a very small number of super-rich people could vote. Yet there were situations where, in Ritson's case, a man could be relatively poor, earn very little from his property, and still have the right to vote because he owned property *worth* over 40s.

In spite of Wadeson's poor management of his property portfolio, Ritson was an amiable man and would not let that get in the way of their friendship and in the same letter expressed the hope that he could return to Stockton soon to once again experience 'the pleasure of drinking a tankard of ale and eating a pan of toasted cheese with you and two or three fellows of our old fellowship'.[138]

Although he struck out on his own, Ritson remained good friends with his former employers. Advancement in the legal profession depended, in part, on the patronage of a well-respected superior, and Masterman helped Ritson secure the position of High Bailiff of the Liberty of the Savoy in May 1784. Although it was initially a temporary appointment, Ritson was granted the position for life in 1786. He expected that it would bring him in at least another £200 per year, but he did not always earn that much. He took his duties seriously and resolved to study law to perform his duties to the fullest. To this end, he enrolled at Gray's Inn as a student in the same month as he received his bailiff appointment.[139] There was no formal requirement for a person to be a fully qualified barrister to practice conveyancing, and his job as bailiff could have been undertaken without any formal legal training. Ritson started studying because he reasoned that the qualification would not only be useful for his job but would be useful in attracting business— prospective clients would want to do business with a man who had formal qualifications for his trade rather than one who had not sat a single exam.[140] He needed to make money. He was too generous at times: he had a good and charitable nature and often gave friends and their clients free legal advice where more savvy businessmen would have charged them. From time to time people took advantage of his good nature by asking him to take on *pro bono* cases. He often did so under duress, and privately confessed that he hated working for free and wished that people wouldn't ask him to do so. He was a student from a poor family after all.[141] His decision to begin studying for a formal qualification was a wise move. The century was marked by the ongoing professionalization of the legal and medical sectors. Although members

SAVOY PRISON.—1792.

Left and below:
Images of the
Savoy in the late
eighteenth century.

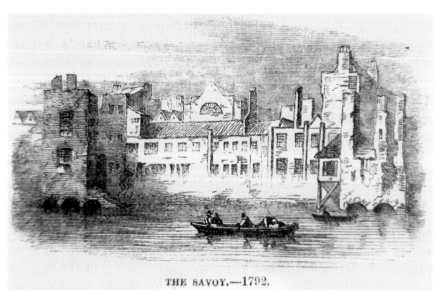

THE SAVOY.—1792.

of these professions would have probably completed an apprenticeship, many of them, not just Ritson sought formal qualifications in their trades because the public increasingly wanted to do business with qualified experts in their fields.

Increasingly many members of the legal profession sought to obtain a qualification and advertise to the world that they were skilled at what they did.[142] There was a decline in law apprenticeships, such as the one that Ritson had completed, and from the late 1780s many would-be barristers began to dive straight into formal study. Another manifestation of the increasing professionalization of the legal sector was the fact that the first annual *Law List*, containing the details of all qualified barristers and solicitors, was published in 1790.

In 1789 Ritson was called to the bar, but he would never practise in court. He now held a fairly respectable station in the world and was entitled to place 'esquire' after his name. He possessed a moderately successful private conveyancing practice and occupied the position of High Bailiff of the Liberty of the Savoy. A liberty was a special kind of parochial district which originated in the Middle Ages. It was a place where, at some point in the past, central and local government authority over a particular place had been ceded to a mesne lord. Under the feudal system, the mesne lord could sublet these lands to tenants, most likely his sons, who would then hold authority over the inhabitants. As such, liberties were separate and distinct from the usual system of local government into which areas were divided into hundreds and boroughs and run by a local corporation. The Liberty of the Savoy was an area of London where sovereignty over it had been granted by Henry III to Peter II, Count of Savoy, in 1246. The Liberty of the Savoy became part of the Duchy of Lancaster in 1284 when the district was bequeathed to Edmund, Earl of Lancaster. Essentially, then, the Savoy was a self-governing domain with its own laws and court system—the Court Leet. The remit of the Courts Leet involved its officials enquiring

> Regularly and periodically into the proper condition of watercourses, roads, paths, and ditches; to guard against all manner of encroachments upon the public rights, whether by unlawful enclosure or otherwise; to preserve landmarks, to keep watch and ward in the town, and overlook the common

lands, adjust the rights over them, and restraining in any
case their excessive exercise, as in the pasturage of cattle;
to guard against the adulteration of food, to inspect weights
and measures, to look in general to the morals of the people,
and to find a remedy for each social ill and inconvenience.
To take cognisance of grosser crimes of assault, arson,
burglary, larceny, manslaughter, murder, treason, and every
felony at common law.[143]

Very few Courts Leet remain in the United Kingdom; the statutes they
passed independently in their own districts laid the groundwork for
the modern system of by-laws. And in Ritson's day, royal writs were
technically unenforceable in the lands of the Duchy of Lancaster,
including the Savoy. This meant that in theory criminals could escape
to one of these districts and have no fear of arrest from one of the king's
officers. A bailiff in a liberty had significantly wider powers than those
of a bailiff in another part of the kingdom.[144]

Ritson did not record in his letters any of the duties that his
position of High Bailiff required of him. However, we know exactly
what Ritson's duties as High Bailiff were because he wrote down
what he did and these notes were then published posthumously by his
nephew as *The Office of Bailiff of a Liberty*. Ritson decided to research
what the duties of a High Bailiff were because, due to the somewhat
ad hoc judicial development of the liberties and franchises, his fellow
bailiffs in other liberties throughout the kingdom did not always know
what their duties entailed. Ritson's book, therefore, was the first one of
its kind to spell out *exactly* the powers that high bailiffs possessed, as
he said in his preface:

> The subject of the following digest is not, as may be hastily
> imagined, a matter of mere curiosity or antiquarian research.
> The officer of whom it treats exercises his function in many
> parts of the kingdom, in its fullest extent, at this day; though
> the attention requisite in certain branches of his duty may in
> some places, no doubt, have induced him to neglect them.
> The want of such a compilation as the present must have
> been more or less felt by every one who has acted in the
> execution of this office; and indeed it ought to seem much

more extraordinary (considering the multitude of similar publications on other subjects) that it should not have been attempted long ago, than that it appears at present. Little can, and less need be said in favour of a work which has no obligations either to genius or to judgement: some labour, however, has undoubtedly been exerted in the compilation, which, should it have the good fortune to prove so far serviceable to those whom it most concerns, as to render the discharge of an ancient and honorable office an object of less difficulty or hazard, the 'compiler' will not have reason to regret.[145]

Listed among the many responsibilities and duties of a High Bailiff was the swearing in of jurors; arranging for the repairs of local bridges and overseeing the smooth running of public amenities. Ritson was required to collect rents from tenants who occupied various buildings owned by the Duchy of Lancaster.[146] He was also responsible for the keeping of law and order in the liberty because high bailiffs had to direct the activities of the constables under him:

> If any man have suspicion of evil of roberdesmen, wastours and drawlatches, be it by night or day, they shall be incontinently arrested by the constables of the towns. And if they be arrested within franchises, they shall be delivered to the bailiffs of the franchises, and kept in prison till the coming of the justices assigned to deliver the gaols.[147]

'Roberdsmen' was a colloquial term for 'robber' which, so the legal commentator Edward Coke (1552–1634) had earlier assumed, was taken from the name of the band of men who followed that legendary medieval outlaw, Robin Hood.[148] The high bailiff of the Liberty of the Savoy was equivalent to a sheriff. Thus, in one of many ironies of history, Ritson—whose writings on Robin Hood ensured the legend's longevity—was in effect a latter-day sheriff charged with arresting Robin Hood's eighteenth-century counterparts.

Local government systems were complex and the numerous bodies which governed the various parts of London did not always see eye-to-eye.[149] Ritson had his fair share of disagreements with local officials in neighbouring parishes: because the Liberty was supposed to be self-governing and had to manage its own resources, Ritson took offence at any official from outside the liberty who used its facilities. As High Bailiff, Ritson was in charge of the 'common prison house' or 'roundhouse' on Strand Lane. However, constables in the adjoining Parish of St Clement Danes were also using the liberty's roundhouse to detain the felons they had caught in their own district. In August 1789, Ritson sent a polite letter to remind officials in the neighbouring parish that the common roundhouse was for the sole use of the bailiffs of the Liberty of the Savoy, and he signed off the letter with the customary phrase

> I am,
> Gentlemen,
> Your Obedt. and Humble Servt.[150]

Nevertheless, the problem persisted and neighbouring parishes were still depositing their criminals in the roundhouse. Ritson later sent a letter to the board of St Clement Danes parish vestry, which was probably read out in the weekly meeting, the following statement rebuking the head beadle, James Talboys, and threatening him with legal action if he did not relinquish control of the prison:

> Mr. James Talboys
> Take Notice that I Joseph Ritson of Grays Inn in the County of Middlesex Esquire Chief Bailiff of the Liberty of the Savoy in the said County and legally and rightfully Intitled to the Possession and Custody of the common Prison house of and for the said Liberty situate in Strand Lane within the said Liberty now in Your Occupation or in the Occupation of some Person whom you take upon Yourself to let or dispose of the same to or Authorize or Permit to inhabit and dwell therein and that unless You do forthwith deliver or cause to be delivered up the Possession and Custody of the said Prison house to me or my Order for the common good and service of the said Liberty and for the more convenient and effectual execution of my Office Application will be made in the ensuing Term to his Majestys Court of Duchy

Chamber in Order that you may be compelled so to do by and under the Process and Authority of that Court Dated this 5th. day of Novr.1789 J. Ritson.[151]

We notice here that the customary polite signature of 'Your Obedient Servant' is not included—Ritson must have been angry and in no mood for pleasantries. Although this may seem quite petty of Ritson to have insisted upon retaining the prison house only for the use of officers of the Liberty of the Savoy, it should be noted that what he refers to as a 'common prison house' and 'roundhouse' was a very small lock-up, probably of one room. This was separate to the larger prison in the Savoy which all officials from neighbouring parishes could use. A criminal would be taken by a constable to the roundhouse and deposited there for the evening until they could be arraigned in front of a magistrate the following morning.

While Ritson claimed that his *Office of Bailiff of a Liberty* was not a matter of antiquarian research, he did find the time to publish a history book relating to his profession. This was *A Digest of the Proceedings of the Court Leet of the Manor and Liberty of the Savoy* (1789). It was inscribed to 'The Gentlemen of the Jury of the Manor and Liberty of the Savoy' and contained the details of notorious criminal cases from the year 1682 onwards.[152] Contained within are details of cases such as brothel keepers who were fined for the crime of 'keeping a disorderly house', such as a man named James Keate, who was charged with 'keeping a lewd disorderly house, and entertaining lewd and disorderly persons att [sic] unseasonable times of the night, to the disturbance and annoyance of his neighbours'.[153] The details of those who ran illegal gambling dens are also recorded, such as one man who was fined £5 for

> Keeping a billiard table … for public use, being a great inconveniency to the neighbours, especially to the youth, by inducing them to play at the same, and by loosing [sic] their money there are put to difficulties to obtaine more, and that by unlawful means.[154]

There were some rather mundane misdemeanours recorded in the *Digest* as well, such as rogue landlords like Hans Wintrop Mortimer who in

1779 was fined £10 for an 'incroachment on his majesty's soil', having extended part of his house into the public highway.[155]

There was an existing market for works recounting historical crimes and misdemeanours. Publications such as the frequently reprinted *History of the Highwaymen* by Alexander Smith and the series of books published under the name of *The Newgate Calendar* were regularly issued from various publishers' presses. The monthly *The Proceedings of the Old Bailey* featured the latest trial news from the famous London courthouse.[156] There were likewise many standalone works, often pamphlets of about eight pages, as well as broadside ballads, which retold the deeds of contemporary and historical criminals (there are over 2,000 such pamphlets in the British Library's archives). These works were popular because the government, the press, and many of the people-at-large believed that England, and particularly London, was experiencing an epidemic of crime.[157] The author and Magistrate of Westminster, Henry Fielding, struck an alarmist tone in 1751, declaring that the roads leading to London 'will shortly be impassable without the utmost hazard, nor are we threatened with seeing less dangerous gangs of rogues among us, than those which the Italians call the banditti.'[158] However, there was much exaggeration in the press: in the mid-eighteenth century, robbery and property theft accounted for 44 per cent of all newspaper reports, yet only 7 per cent of crimes tried at the Old Bailey were thefts and robberies.[159]

This being said, Ritson's *Digest* differs from the more sensational true crime works simply by being incredibly detailed, whereas other criminal biographers rarely gave a fig for facts and often invented stories. Alexander Smith, for example, assumed that Shakespeare's John Falstaff, as he appeared in the Henrician plays, was a real person. Another reason why Ritson's work was more of a serious work than that of his contemporaries is the fact that he told cold hard facts and did not engage in any moral commentary on the actions of criminals. The purpose of most true crime literature was, at least superficially, to provide moral instruction to readers; the audience was supposed to heed the moral lessons to be gleaned from the lives of criminals to ensure that they too would not end on the gallows in the same way that the felons in their pages had.[160] Such works often took the moral high ground but they had few scruples with depicting sex and violence, and they were sometimes used by readers as erotic literature.[161]

Ritson followed up his *Digest* with *The Office of Constable* (1791). As we have seen, England did not have a professional police force and the keeping of law and order fell on the shoulders of thief takers, constables and watchmen, and a small, semi-professional team of Bow Street Runners founded by Henry Fielding and his brother, John. In the case of serious rioting, the militia might be called in, which had happened during the Gordon Riots. English people rejected a police force because it was seen as an instrument of government tyranny; the memory of the English Revolution and subsequent dictatorship of Oliver Cromwell, who used a standing army to police the people of England, loomed large in discussions of law enforcement; the fact that many absolutist rulers on the continent had police forces in their employ did little to convince hearts and minds for the need of a uniformed police force. So Englishmen, ever jealous of their political liberties, were contented with a haphazard system of law enforcement. Thief takers were people who would recover people's stolen goods from criminals for a fee.

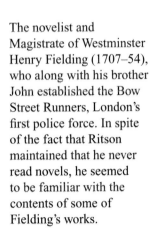

The novelist and Magistrate of Westminster Henry Fielding (1707–54), who along with his brother John established the Bow Street Runners, London's first police force. In spite of the fact that Ritson maintained that he never read novels, he seemed to be familiar with the contents of some of Fielding's works.

The notorious case of Jonathan Wild (1682–1725), who styled himself 'Thief Taker General of Britain' but was actually the head of a vast criminal organisation and was finally executed, meant that thief takers were widely viewed as corrupt. Nevertheless, they were useful, for the victim of a crime had to pay to prosecute an offender. It was less hassle for victims to simply pay someone to get their possessions back. Ritson refers to Jonathan Wild in two of his letters: the first instance is a jocular remark to his friend Rowntree, who back in Stockton had been hired to collect the rents from Ritson's estates. Ritson was expecting to be paid £15 but ultimately received only £5 once Rowntree had deducted his legal costs. Ritson exclaimed, 'Jonathan Wild was a fool to you, that's all.'[162] The second instance of Wild's name in Ritson's letters appears when Ritson got word that Rowntree was conning a count out of some money—no wonder Ritson queried the meagre £5 he received earlier from Rowntree! He urged Rowntree to be cautious:

> You cannot say that I have ever been backward in doing justice to your ingenious contrivances and unremitting assiduity in pursuit of money. I foresaw the success of your design upon the poor Count, too well concerted, indeed, to give him a chance of eluding it. But I am not yet sufficiently hardened to congratulate you upon an event which affords the immediate prospect of a jail for your client, and the not very distant one of a gallows—or at least a pillory—for yourself. Jonathan Wild was a great man, to be sure; but I would not have you forget that he was hanged at last.[163]

We do not know the details of this scheme that Rowntree cooked up to embezzle money from the count, but it reminded Ritson of the notorious thief taker. It should not be inferred from Ritson's remarks that he admired Jonathan Wild in any way by calling him a 'great man'. Ritson had probably read Fielding's *Jonathan Wild the Great* (1743). It was a satirical novel which mocked society's ideas of 'great men' and highlighted the difference between 'greatness' and 'goodness'. As Fielding said in the first chapter of *Jonathan Wild*: 'Greatness consists of bringing all manner of mischief on mankind, and Goodness in removing it'.[164] It is easy to see why Ritson might have been a fan of Fielding's works even though he would never admit to reading novels.[165]

The latter's fiction was usually written 'in the manner of Cervantes', and Cervantes's *Don Quixote* was one of Ritson's favourite books. Both Ritson and Fielding were also men of the law: Fielding was a magistrate and the founder of the Bow Street Runners.

Fielding's Bow Street Runners were a semi-professional police force founded in 1749, when government funding to the tune of £200 was secured to police Westminster. The team was small and consisted of the magistrates Henry Fielding and his brother John, 'the blind beak', along with a team of a few ex-constables and thief takers. Initially the runners could only do so much and the responsibility for law enforcement devolved onto the shoulders of constables and nightwatchmen. Constables were part-time and often unpaid. A person did not apply to become a constable but was chosen much as jurors are chosen in the UK today: he would simply receive a letter telling him that he had been selected to serve as a constable—this could be a major disruption to one's life and trade. The person chosen would then be summoned in front of a jury to take the Oath of a Constable. If the person refused, he would be fined for not attending to his civic duty. A person had to serve as a constable while also carrying on his own daily business. It is no wonder that people often tried to wriggle out of the obligation to serve. In his *Digest*, Ritson recorded several people in the Liberty of the Savoy who had either refused to take the office or absconded from their duties, such as Benjamin Walwyn, a glover, and Michael Connor, a peruke maker, who in 1761 were each fined £7 for refusing to take the constable's oath.[166]

The fact that untrained civilians had to serve as constables made Ritson think that such a manual as his *Office of Constable* was all the more urgent. In the preface he states that he wrote this work because he wished 'to benefit the community, by furnishing its most ancient, most constitutional, and most useful officer, with a compendious system or manual of his duty and powers'.[167] The historian and linguist in Ritson shines through at the beginning of the book: in the introduction he delves into the etymology of the word 'constable', and the appearance of constables in classical, medieval, and early modern literature. The word, so Ritson remarked, came from the office of *comes stabuli* in the Eastern Roman Empire.[168] Modern etymological dictionaries agree with Ritson: the word is indeed taken from an office in the Ancient Roman Empire which means 'count of the stable'.[169] Ritson went on to point out the many different kinds of constables that have existed in various parts of England since the Middle Ages, such as the Lord High Constable of

England, who was the leader of the king's armies; constables of the castles; constable of the exchequer and so forth. It is doubtful whether the brief history of the word 'constable' and the history of the office would have been hugely beneficial to the public servants at which the book was aimed, and the historical research was probably only included because Ritson enjoyed reading history. After the introduction, Ritson minutely chronicled all the duties of the High Constable and the Petty Constable, and their powers in maintaining law and order.[170] Alongside the usual powers of arresting law-breakers the constable had further powers: he may take into custody any 'ruffian' who verbally or physically assaults him, and he may use reasonable force against the said villain either in self-defence or to restrain him until assistance arrives. A constable could detain any 'madman' who posed a threat to public order. He might, if needed, command his neighbours to assist him in arresting someone, and he may even deputize another citizen temporarily, and fine anyone who refused. The constable could dispense summary punishments for minor offences such as drunk and disorderly conduct by placing offenders in the stocks without needing to haul them in front of a magistrate.[171] In appendices at the end of the book, Ritson reprinted 'The Constable's Oath' as well as the Riot Act. And no book written by Ritson would be complete without a ballad, so he reprinted James Gyffon's 'Song of a Constable' (1626), which contains an early use of the phrase 'the truth and nothing but the truth' in the English language:

> I a constable haue tooke myne oath;
> By which shall plaine appeere
> The troth and nothing but the troath,
> Whoseuer my song will heere.[172]

It would be a mistake to assume that Ritson's writings on the law were bestsellers. Yet two of them did receive a favourable review from a reader of the *St James's Chronicle*:

> *To the* Printer of the St. J. Chronicle.
> Sir,
> In your Chronicle of Thursday last I observed a curious paragraph, mentioning that a quondam *Remarker* on Shakespeare had lately employed his pen in some Law

productions ... I was at first indeed puzzled to comprehend whom, and to what, the paragraph related—but a friend to whom I appealed put into my hand two little *tracts*, on subjects not much or well treated, *Court-Leets* and *Constables*; which bear on the face of them the marks of great knowledge in the antiquity of our laws, and are not without some of those *home strokes* at the deficiency in the practice as well as theory of our law, which, tho' perhaps delivered with a little too much of the writer's usual asperity, are too well founded in justice and reason. That the writer of these tracts is a remarker on Shakespeare, seems pretty plain—*Aut Erasmus aut Diabolus*—And the Publick are indebted to him for employing his talents on subjects of instruction as well as amusement.[173]

A late-eighteenth-century engraving of a polite and fashionable gentleman taking morning tea with a lady in her boudoir. Any self-respecting man making his way in the world endeavoured to fashion himself into a polite gentleman; having read some of the many conduct books that were being published, he would have been expected to make himself agreeable in the company of others and be able to hold his own while discussing the latest philosophical or literary works. (British Library)

There was sufficient demand for *The Office of Constable*, the *Digest*, and *The Jurisdiction of the Court Leet*, to be combined into a larger book entitled *Law Tracts* (1794).[174] Ritson's interest in the legal profession has been downplayed by scholars who focus to a larger degree on his literary work. Sometimes they claim that Ritson was uninterested in his profession but the evidence does not bear this out. The catalogue of his unpublished manuscripts lists a further seven projected books and pamphlets on the law: 'Precedents in Conveyancing', 'Treatise on Conveyancing', 'Precedents by Mr Bradley', 'Wills Drawn up by the Late Ralph Bradley', 'The Privileges of the Duchy of Lancaster', 'Antient and Modern Deeds, Charters, Grants, and Surveys', and 'The Institution, Authority, Acts, and Proceedings of the Burgesses of the Savoy'.[175] On occasion Ritson moaned about his job, but a man who hated his job would not have penned several book-length manuscripts relating to his profession.

Being a gentleman was about more than a mere job title and placing 'esquire' after one's name. A man's conduct should immediately mark him out as a gentleman among his peers, and throughout his letters Ritson had a firm idea of how gentlemen should act. He communicated these precepts to his nephew whom he tried to fashion into a *polite* gentleman. In 1784 he wrote,

> My good boy (for so I trust you are)
> I shall always be glad to hear of your improvement in dancing or anything else. But I hope while you are polishing the rusticity of your body, you will not neglect that of your mind, which it is infinitely more requisite you should attend to…. You must learn and study to behave with politeness and propriety—all that is, to render yourself agreeable to all your acquaintance. I know of no branch of learning of half so much value.[176]

Today 'politeness' has a fairly narrow definition, meaning that one should act respectfully and considerately of other people. It meant this in the Georgian period of course, and in another letter Ritson counselled his nephew to be

> Civil, good-natured, and obliging to your school-fellows … have no bad connections, nor be guilty of any wicked, base,

or dirty actions or expressions. Especially lying, swearing,
abusive, or nasty language, which many boys will practise,
and most of them come afterwards to the gallows.[177]

However, politeness had a much wider meaning as a code of conduct
and a marker of taste. It had its roots in the seventeenth-century
culture of courtly civility practiced by the aristocracy. Yet with the
shift in power and influence away from the royal court towards the
moneyed middle classes in the early part of the eighteenth century, a
new means of public conduct had to be formulated. This new code was
politeness.[178] Politeness promoted the emulation of aristocratic culture,
but the important point was that one did not have to be a nobleman to
be considered polite; anyone, no matter from which class one came,
would be welcome in the new polite society that was emerging, as long
as they endeavoured to be agreeable to those whom they met. This
included not only cultivating the art of good conversation and good
manners, but also keeping one's self well-groomed and neat, which is
another facet of the advice Ritson doled out to his nephew who urged
him to perfect 'delicacy (that is, a pretty obliging manner) in your
language and conversation; neatness in your clothes, and cleanness
in your hands and face, which never lose the skin by too much
washing'.[179] As Paul Langford tells us: politeness was sought after by
the bourgeoisie, which included wealthy tradesmen and professionals,
because it conveyed 'gentility to a much wider élite whose only
qualification was money'.[180]

Joseph Addison and Richard Steele—with whose work Ritson was
well-acquainted—were the first to theorize ideas of politeness in *The
Tatler* and *The Spectator*. They were originally published in penny
numbers between 1709 and 1715 and then appeared in four- and
eight-volume reprints right into the 1950s, after which they went out
of fashion among the reading public. Book-length manuals on how
to be polite soon followed. It was an urban, cosmopolitan ideology
because politeness was practiced mainly by the middle classes, who
lived in or near towns. For this reason, Steele's first essay in *The Tatler*
stated that his essays would be written from the locations of various
London coffee houses.[181] This meant that people from rural areas were
often considered, as Addison stated in *The Spectator*, a bit backward
or 'behindhand'.[182] This is why Ritson counselled his nephew to finish

'polishing' the 'rusticity' of provincial Stockton-on-Tees out of his character because the aim of any aspirant member of polite society should be to 'improve' themselves and fit in with other members of polite society. A polite gentleman had to be able to hold his own in a conversation on all manner of subjects including art, literature, and philosophy. The sons of the aristocracy would have had a formal education in these subjects, and they perhaps finished their education by undertaking a 'Grand Tour' of the continent and viewing the Greek and Roman antiquities. For the bourgeoisie, where they lacked formal education in this area, their improvement might take the form of reading philosophical books, and Ritson was well-versed in the works of Voltaire and Rabelais.[183] Alternatively, this might involve learning a new language—learning French would, according to Ritson, help his nephew improve himself and become a polite gentleman, and our antiquary taught himself several languages.[184] From a young age, Ritson impressed upon his nephew Frank the importance of learning to read, and in these letters he usually gave advice to his young relative as to what he should improve upon.[185] Ritson continued advising his nephew even when the latter was an adult and a professional in his own right.[186] Painting was another activity that might signify that a man was polite: in many of the letters that Ritson sent to his nephew, we find that he endeavoured to encourage his nephew's cultural pursuits by sending him children's books, history books, and novels, as well as painting materials.[187] As a man of business but also a doting uncle, however, Ritson realised that sometimes children needed an extra financial incentive to complete these 'improving' activities: it was not unusual for Ritson to dispense his advice on politeness and improvement to his nephew and finish by enclosing a guinea (£1 1s) in the expectation that young Frank would complete his uncle's tasks as required.[188]

Only by aspiring to be polite could a member of the upper middle and lower middle classes claim gentility; in an ideal world, if everyone practised politeness, social harmony would be the result. The emergence of an aristocratic code of behaviour that could be practiced even by the humble tradesman led the legal commentator William Blackstone (1723–80) to call the British people of his own time 'a polite and commercial people'.[189]

The salary that Ritson earned earned from his legal business and role as High Bailiff meant that he had the time and money to devote to his real passion: historical research. His position as a man of the law coloured his attitude towards the study, preservation, and publication of historical texts. A literary forger, in his view, was just as morally bankrupt as a forger of money and, by extension, shoddy scholarship should always be condemned. Yet this commonsense approach to the study of primary sources made him widely despised among his fellow antiquaries who were not above tinkering with ancient English texts, as we shall see in our next chapter.

Chapter 3

'Judgments are Formed, Critics Arise': Joseph Ritson the Scholar

In 1694, Joseph Addison, in his poem 'Account of the Greatest English Poets', had a somewhat sneering attitude towards England's medieval literary heritage. Of the works of Geoffrey Chaucer, Addison complained that 'Age has Rusted what the Poet writ,/Worn out his Language, and obscur'd his Wit'.[190] Addison was equally dismissive of Edmund Spenser who 'warm'd with Poetick rage':

> In Antick Tales amus'd a Barb'rous Age;
> An Age that yet uncultivate and Rude,
> Where-e'er the Poet's Fancy led, pursu'd

> Through pathless Fields, and unfrequented Floods,
> To Dens of Dragons and Enchanted Woods.
> But now the Mystick Tale, that pleas'd of Yore,
> Can Charm an understanding Age no more;
> The long-spun Allegories fulsom grow,
> While the dull Moral lies too plain below.
> We view well-pleas'd at distance all the sights
> Of Arms and Palfreys, Battles, Fields, and Fights,
> And Damsels in Distress, and Courteous Knights.
> But when we look too near, the Shades decay,
> And all the pleasing Lan-skip fades away.[191]

In the reign of Queen Anne, George I, and George II, the culture of Ancient Greece and Rome was venerated by English polite society as the pinnacle of human intellectual achievement. It was in a neoclassical architectural style that the middle and upper classes built their houses; neoclassical buildings sprang up in cities such as Calcutta, with the British rulers there evoking the glories of antiquity; sculptors such as John Baker the Younger depicted the heroes of the British Empire, such as the Marquess Cornwallis, in the habit of a Roman centurion; and the military heroes of Ancient Greece were often considered as the epitome of selfless heroism.

This reverence for antiquity, its rationalism and its rules, was reflected in the writings of men such as John Dryden, Joseph Addison, Richard Steele, Alexander Pope, Jonathan Swift, and Henry Fielding—they called themselves 'Augustan' because of their artistic and intellectual connection with the age the Roman Emperor Augustus. As Addison wrote in his 'Account of the Greatest English Poets', Spenser and Chaucer were okay to read out of curiosity but in his opinion the greatest English poet was Dryden. As Kenneth Clark put it: for many English artists, dramatists, and poets, 'the middle ages was a foggy sea with but one landmark—the Norman Conquest—round which the Gothic cathedrals drifted like rudderless ships.'[192] It was not unusual, as Rosemary Mitchell states, for episodes from English history in art and literature to be given a baroque or neoclassical overlay.[193] On occasion, medieval British heroes such as King Arthur and Robin Hood were sometimes given such a baroque or neoclassical facelift.[194]

Yet after 1764, the art, architecture, and literature of the medieval period was increasingly held in high esteem. In that year, Horace Walpole published *The Castle of Otranto*, a gloriously silly gothic horror set in a remote castle in Italy, which features chases in the vaults of a castle, mysterious prophecies, armies of knights, and ghosts. Soon further gothic novels issued from the printing presses to widespread approbation. Authors readily claimed inspiration from Walpole. In the preface to her novel *The Old English Baron* (1777–80), for example, Clara Reeve admitted that her tale was 'the literary offspring' of Walpole's novel.[195] While Walpole's tale was rather fanciful—the novel begins with a giant stone helmet falling from the heavens and crushing a young boy to death—the public's enthusiasm for all things medieval acquired a scholarly foundation.[196] Richard Hurd wrote *Letters on Chivalry and Romance* in 1762. While polite society had hitherto venerated the architecture of Ancient Greece and Rome, James Essex wrote a treatise on Lincoln Cathedral in 1776 and argued that 'the previously despised style' of the medieval period was in fact well adapted to an age of politeness and gentility.[197] The publication of Thomas Percy's *Reliques of Ancient English Poetry* in 1765 showcased the 'select remains' of the early 'martial and unlettered' English nation.[198] Scholars such as Hugh Downman began researching the history of the Vikings in England.[199] The lines between scholarship and fiction were blurred by some writers on occasion. James MacPherson's epic poem *Ossian* (1760) drew on Irish and Scottish folklore and claimed to have been taken from 'ancient' sources. Many readers believed that it was indeed the remains of a 'lost' Celtic poem until the nineteenth century, although more savvy readers like Samuel Johnson saw right through MacPherson's scam. Others turned their attention to the works of Chaucer, Shakespeare, and Spenser (Dryden had, of course, 'translated' Chaucer into modern English and 'smoothed' the language and the rhymes enough to make him acceptable to ears attuned to neoclassical verse).[200] Far from sneering at pre-modern English poets like Addison had done, writers and readers alike now drew inspiration from the medieval or 'gothic' period of English history.[201]

Ritson's own research into English medieval history was part of this cultural trend towards the Gothic. As early as April 1775, we find Ritson asking one of his associates whether he might peruse 'several papers relative to the History and Antiquities of Stockton'.[202] But nothing engaged his interest more than the study of 'ancient' English poetry, songs, and ballads. We have seen how Ritson sought to inculcate in his nephew a love of English history and old ballads by sending him books and directing him towards the learning of new songs. Young Frank was only too eager to please his loving uncle and receive his praise by telling him when he had mastered ballads such as 'The Battle of Chevy Chase' by heart.[203] As Ritson's nephew grew up, the pair of them continued to converse on various literary subjects. It was not only with his nephew that he discussed historical and literary matters but with his many associates. When times were hard for him financially, it was living in London, with its easy access to the British Museum and the capital's

An example of the 'Neoclassical medieval': this frontispiece to the 1731 edition of John Dryden's *King Arthur* depicts the legendary British king as a Roman centurion.

proximity to Oxford and Cambridge's libraries that made him stay. He would visit the reading rooms of these libraries not only to conduct his own research but also to transcribe documents for his likeminded literary friends from all around the country. His friends would often return the favour either by visiting one of their own local archives or reading the manuscripts of his books before they went to press.[204]

During Ritson's early years in London, while he was building up his business, he was fairly unknown in the literary world. But he soon made a name for himself by writing, in 1782, a little volume titled *Observations on the Three First Volumes of the History of English Poetry by T.W. in a Letter to the Author*. This was a scathing response to Thomas Warton's *History of English Poetry* (1774–78). Warton's book was an overview of

An engraving from a scene in Horace Walpole's *The Castle of Otranto* (1764). The first gothic novel, it was set in the medieval period and featured an array of sinister supernatural occurrences, evil barons, damsels-in-distress, and chases through the dark vaults of the castle. (British Library)

the development of English poetry over several centuries and contained excerpts of a number of early modern poems. With this book Warton had established himself as the foremost expert on the history of English poetry—or, rather, he was considered thus until Ritson came along. Ritson was polite in the preface to his *Observations*:

> Sir,
> You will have no reason to be either alarmed or offended at a mode of address which every reader has the right to adopt … The "History of English Poetry" stands high in public estimation; the subject is equally curious, interesting, and abstruse: much, very much, of its success is, undoubtedly, to be ascribed to the opinion generally entertained of your veracity and care as a historian … I have read and examined your great and important work with some degree of attention and accuracy; and I now present you with the result of my enquiries.[205]

Ritson's main gripe with Warton's *History of English Poetry* was the fact that Warton never included the history of Anglo-Saxon English poetry in his book because he thought it would, quite literally, be too much work for him. In any case, reasoned Warton, the Saxons were too 'rude' and 'uncivilised' to appeal to a reading public with polite tastes.[206] To study the history of English poetry, Warton concluded, one could simply begin with Chaucer in the fourteenth century. Ritson took umbrage to the characterisation of Old English poetry:

> But "that the Saxon poetry has no connection with the nature and purpose of 'your' present undertaking," is an assertion, one may safely venture to say, as new as it is ill-grounded, and full of mischief ... You, Sir, have sometimes been a biographer; and did you ever find it necessary to commence the story of your hero at the 15th or 16th year of his age, and to assert that the time of his birth and infancy had no connection with the story of his life ... the truth is, that the origin and fundamental principles, as well of our language as of our poetry, are to be sought for among the remains of the Saxon literature; and he who shall tell us that the English and Saxon languages have no sort of connection with each other, is either deceived himself, or finds it in his interest to deceive others,—by sheltering his own ignorance and inactivity under a formidable and laboured shew of difficulty and uselessness, equally visionary, delusive, and pernicious.[207]

What Ritson said was common sense: it was disingenuous of Warton to pretend to write a history of English poetry without mentioning the earliest examples. But this was not the end of the matter: a reader turning the pages of Ritson's little book would have discovered that this was not a few simple corrections of the errors that inevitably seep into any large literary work but a complete dissection of it. Over 51 pages, Ritson pointed out every single page of Warton's history which contained, in his view, a factual error or misinterpretation.

Some commentators could not object to the substance of Ritson's attack but objected to the tone. One publication stated that it would have been better 'if [he] had done it in more civil language'.[208] The antiquary Edmond Malone told the Earl of Charlemont in November 1782 that

> There is a young man, one Wrightson [Ritson] … who has published a most furious attack on Warton's History of English Poetry. There is a good deal of good matter in the pamphlet, and he has caught Mr Warton tripping pretty often; but the whole is spoiled by the petulance and indecency of the manner.[209]

Later revised editions of Warton's *History of English Poetry* addressed some of Ritson's criticisms directly and incorporated his suggestions into the work.[210] Ritson was mightily pleased with himself for having exposed Warton's errors and Ritson cheekily sent Warton a signed copy of his *Observations* 'with compliments'.[211] Ritson then wrote to his long-time friend Robert Harrison asking 'what say you to my scurrilous libel against Tom Warton?'[212] We do not know what Harrison's response to this question was, but in the same letter Ritson vowed to 'turn the world upside down' with his next publication and he soon turned his attention to the two most eminent Shakespearean scholars of the age. These men were Samuel Johnson and George Steevens who had published critical editions of Shakespeare's plays.

Some context is needed. Shakespeare's folios containing the earliest complete copies of his plays had all been published in the early seventeenth century but his material was

The title page of Shakespeare's First Folio. (British Library)

never sacrosanct. Later poets and playwrights often hacked his storylines up, added new characters, new scenes, and even songs into the mix. These later playwrights then repackaged them as their own works. In 1667 William Davenant and John Dryden wrote *The Tempest; or, the Enchanted Isle* in which they added two new characters: Miranda was given a sister and Ferdinand now had a rival suitor for Miranda's love. Dryden and Davenant's play, not Shakespeare's original, remained the standard version of *The Tempest* until the 1750s. *King Lear* was reworked by Nahum Tate in 1681. Tate reasoned that many of the scenes in Shakespeare's original were unsuitable for the stage. In Tate's new refined version, Edgar and Cordelia were now lovers; the fool from Shakespeare's original was 'too low' a character to be included in a tragedy so he was cut from the story; and King Lear does not die of grief as he does in Shakespeare's version but is restored to his throne meaning that Cordelia and Edgar can marry and live happily ever after.[213]

It was not until the actor-manager David Garrick (1717–79) made Shakespeare's name fashionable again through his own performances on the London stage c. 1740 onwards that a newfound respect for the bard emerged at the level of high culture. Garrick still reworked the plays but he kept Shakespeare's name prominent in their marketing, whereas Dryden and Tate often left Shakespeare uncredited. Garrick even held a Shakespeare Jubilee in 1769 to celebrate the opening of Stratford's Town Hall where, although the weather was bad, he performed some of his Shakespearian roles and unveiled a statue of the playwright which he donated to the town. Afterwards tourists hacked small pieces of Shakespeare's Chair from the Hathaway family home in Shottery, Stratford-upon-Avon.[214] (It is also Garrick who must be thanked for preserving a fifteenth-century copy of the 'Playe of Robyn Hode', which Ritson later consulted for his book on Robin Hood in 1795).[215]

Audiences' emerging love for Shakespeare was part of the aforementioned cultural shift from the veneration of Ancient Greek and Roman culture towards that of the medieval and early modern period. The public's new-found love of their literary heritage was also acquiring an element of nationalism: the British nation was great and its historical heritage had to be extolled. The many wars against the French during the century gave a further stimulus to the rise of this emerging *British* national identity and the celebration of national history. The deeds of major players in British history—generals, statesmen, kings,

THE

TEMPEST,

OR THE

Enchanted Island.

A

COMEDY.

As it is now Acted

At Their Majesties Theatre

IN

DORSET-GARDEN.

LONDON,
Printed by *J. M.* for *H. Herringman;* and fold by *R. Bentley,*
at the Poft-Houfe in *Ruffel-ftreet,* Covent*Garden.*
1690.

Late-seventeenth- and early eighteenth-century playwrights and dramatists admired Shakespeare but they thought that some of the bard's plots were ridiculous, some of the comedy and characters too 'low', so they often rewrote his plays, added new characters and subplots, and passed them off as their own. This is the title page to John Dryden's *The Tempest* (1674).

queens, writers, poets—were increasingly viewed as a source of national pride.[216] Thus theatre-goers, instead of hankering after foreign French and Italian operas, were counselled to look to their own country's dramatists for cultural enrichment, as the prologue to one play urged:

Too long, *Britannia*, hast thou blindly err'd,
And Foreign Mimes to *English* wit preferr'd!
Eunuchs to Sloth your senses have betray'd,
And *British* spirits (as they sung) decay'd.
But see, behold! A better time returns,

74

Each Bosom now, with nobler Rapture burns!
Immortal Shakespear's [sic] matchless Wit revives,
And now the Bard in speaking Marble lives.[217]

Shakespeare's plays, especially his histories, offered all classes
something by depicting both high-born noblemen and low-born
commoners taking part in major historical events. In this sense the
bard was perfect for what was, in some respects, a socially diverse
polite audience. In tandem with the popular interest in Shakespeare,
scholars began publishing new editions of Shakespeare's works, which
is where George Steevens came in. In 1766 Steevens published *Twenty
of the Plays of Shakespeare* in four volumes, earning the praise of such
literary luminaries as Samuel Johnson. Johnson convinced Steevens to
collaborate with him and produce a new edition of Shakespeare's works
which would rectify some of the flaws in Steevens's original (Steevens
had not consulted the earliest copies in his *Twenty Plays*). The result of
Johnson and Steevens's labours was *The Works of Shakespeare with the
Corrections and Illustrations of Various Commentators*, published in ten
volumes in 1773 based on readings of the earliest folios available.

Johnson and Steeven's edition of Shakespeare's works was critically
acclaimed, but it was, in Ritson's eyes, hardly the most accurate. Ritson
set to work again and in 1783 produced another little book in the style
of his earlier *Observations* that pointed out multiple flaws in Johnson
and Steevens's work. Ritson's book was titled *Remarks, Critical and
Illustrative, on the Text and Notes of the Last Edition of Shakespeare*.
Johnson claimed to have consulted the earliest Shakespeare folios to
produce the 'best' version of his plays available, but on this point Ritson
accused him of lying to the public:

> The remarks in the following sheets, will prove that he never
> collated any one of the folios,—no not for a single play,—or
> at least that of his collations he has made little or no use.
> That he picked out a reading here and there from the old
> editions, is true: all [Johnson's] predecessors did the same:
> but this is not collation. So much for dr. Johnson.[218]

Johnson *had* actually consulted the earliest copies of Shakespeare's
work and Ritson was wrong to accuse him otherwise.[219] Nevertheless,

what followed in the *Remarks*, as in the *Observations*, was a page-by-page breakdown of every single fault in Johnson and Steevens's edition. To take just one example, reprinted below is one of Ritson's remarks on Johnson and Steevens's version of *King John*:

> p. 64.

> *Pand.* For that, which thou hast sworn to do amiss,
> Is't not amiss when it is truly done?
> And being not done, where doing tends to ill,
> The truth is then most done not doing it.

> For this nonsense the reader is indebted to dr. Johnsons emendation; the old copies have it thus:

> *Is not amiss when it is truly done.*[220]

Ritson was not perfect himself of course, and he felt compelled to publish a supplement to the *Remarks* five years later, in 1788, entitled *The Quip Modest; A Few Words by Way of Supplement to the Remarks*. In this book he acknowledged some of his own errors but pointed out—over forty pages no less—all the further errors which he had spotted in Johnson and Steevens's work after the publication of his *Remarks*.[221] So thorough were Ritson's criticisms of Johnson and Steevens's work, however, that the editors incorporated Ritson's suggestions in their 1793 edition of Shakespeare's plays.[222]

Johnson and Steevens's *Shakespeare* was supplemented by Edmond Malone in 1780 with a book entitled *Supplement to Johnson and Steevens's Edition of Shakespeare's Plays*, and Malone produced his own edition of the works of Shakespeare in 1790. Very oddly, Malone's supplement contained reprints of plays that he assumed were partly written by Shakespeare such as *A Yorkshire Tragedy*, *Pericles Prince of Tyre*, and *Thomas Lord Cromwell*. To include these in an edition of Shakespeare made no sense, thought Ritson, and he published his criticisms in *Cursory Criticisms on the Edition of Shakespeare Published by Edmond Malone* (1790). Just as his previous Shakespeare books did, this was a line-by-line take down of both Malone's *Supplement* and the rest of his multivolume edition of Shakespeare. Ritson's exasperation with all of the Shakespeare editors was evident from the outset:

Above and right: Dr Samuel Johnson and George Steevens who produced a critical edition of Shakespeare's plays in the late eighteenth century. Joseph Ritson found many faults with their work which he published in *Remarks, Critical and Illustrative, on the Text and Notes of the Last Edition of Shakespeare*. (British Library and Wellcome Library)

I thought proper, in the following pages, to make a few observations on some of Mr Malones [sic] notes. Now Mr. Malone will take this exceedingly ill; for Mr. Malone has a very high opinion of himself, and a very mean one of everybody else. But I confess I do not seek to please Mr. Malone: I wish to rescue the language and sense of an admirable author from the barbarism and corruption they have acquired in passing through the hands of an incompetent and unworthy editor. In a word, I mean to convict and not to convince him.[223]

To be sure, his mode of writing was direct and Ritson could have softened his tone a little, but he did not castigate the whole of Malone's Shakespearean scholarship. His only gripes with Malone's work were set down in the *Cursory Criticisms*. As we shall see, Ritson was an admirer of Malone in other respects.

Ritson had truly made a name for himself in the literary world with his responses to Warton, Johnson, and Steevens. He later contemplated publishing his own edition of Shakespeare's plays which, in his own view, would be free of the errors that Johnson and Steevens made, but this never materialised because Ritson, taking a look at the literary marketplace, assumed that it was 'glutted' with editions of Shakespeare.[224] After the publication of the *Remarks*, Ritson laid Shakespeare aside for a while and published his own collection of medieval and early modern English songs and ballads: *A Select Collection of English Songs* in 1783. Each of the songs that were reproduced were well-edited faithful reproductions and were prefaced with a commentary on each text. The unassuming title obscures its impact somewhat. In these volumes, Ritson criticised the conclusions of Britain's most eminent ballad scholar and editor of the *Reliques of Ancient English Poetry*: Thomas Percy, Bishop of Dromore (1729–1811). Ritson first came to Percy's notice back in 1782 after the publication of the former's criticism of Warton. One of Percy's friends warned him to be wary of the 'young lawyer' from Gray's Inn who was something of a 'Drawcansir' (a fictional character from George Villiers's *The Rehearsal* who kills many people and spares neither friend nor foe).[225]

Percy's *Reliques* was a collection of a few medieval and mostly early modern popular songs, poems, and ballads

> In the Editor's possession, which contains near 200 poems, songs, and metrical romances ... of all times and dates, from the ages prior to Chaucer, to the conclusion of Charles I. The manuscript was shown to several learned friends, who thought the contents too curious to be consigned to oblivion, and importuned the possessor to select some of them and give them to the press ... Accordingly such specimens of ancient poetry have been selected as either shew the gradation of our language, exhibit the progress of popular opinions, display the peculiar manners and customs of former ages, or throw light on our earlier classical poets.[226]

According to what has become a semi-legendary event in the history of folk songs and English popular poetry, Percy was visiting a friend one day in the 1750s and saw a maid about to throw a book on the fire to keep the house warm.[227] Percy enquired what the book was and found that it was a manuscript containing long lost poetry, among which was the famous 'Robin Hood and Guy of Gisborne'. Percy rescued the manuscripts from the flames. He then reprinted some of the poems in the *Reliques* along with many newer 'popular' songs and ballads. Percy's work was a hit with readers: successive editions appeared in 1766, 1767, and 1775. He became a household name because of his *Reliques*.[228]

Percy may have made the old songs and ballads of bygone eras accessible but he often edited or 'refined' the texts to make them more appealing to readers. 'His object', as one contemporary observer recognised, 'was to please both the judicious antiquary and the reader of taste; and he hath endeavoured to gratify both without offending either.'[229] This is all well and good—both editors and publishers would

Bishop Thomas
Percy, editor
of *Reliques of
Ancient English
Poetry* (1765).

have wanted to make sure a book appealed to readers—but Percy was not honest about his edits, often adding whole stanzas into some songs, and some of his emendations simply did not make sense. To take one example, there was Percy's version of 'Robin Hood and Guy of Gisborne' printed in the first volume of the *Reliques*. In the first edition of Percy's work, Robin shoots the sheriff through the 'backe-syde'.[230] The original text from the seventeenth century sees Robin shooting the sheriff through the heart. It was an odd emendation to make in view of the fact that Percy retained the violent episode earlier in the ballad which sees Robin decapitate Guy and mutilate his face with a knife. This practice of tinkering with the text went against Ritson's principles: modern editors of ancient texts did not have a right to alter them. In Ritson's view, those in the present should care for and look after the poems which had been handed down to them, in the same way that a decent retirement should await 'a superannuated domestic, whose passed [sic] services entitle him his old age to a comfortable provision and retreat'.[231]

When Ritson published his *Select Collection of English Songs*— with illustrations by the celebrated artist and engraver William Blake (1757–1827)—he had a few bones to pick with Percy's scholarship. He attacked the idea that most of Percy's 'reliques' were from a bygone age because, with the exception of a few poems in the first volume, most of the songs were too modern in style and composition:

> The learned and ingenious bishop Percy has, indeed, published a work, in which a considerable number of songs and ballads, that have never otherwise appeared, are ascribed to a very remote antiquity; an antiquity altogether incompatible with the stile and language of the compositions theirselves [sic], most of which, one may be allowed to say, bear the strongest intrinsic marks of a *very* modern date.[232]

Ritson was not wrong: the poems and ballads in the first volume of Percy's *Reliques* could properly be described as late medieval in origin but those contained in the second and third volume were quite modern, evinced by the inclusion of the 'Ballad of George Barnwell' in the third volume of Percy's books.[233] This particular ballad was based upon George Lillo's play *The London Merchant* (1731). It was not a 'relique' and it was disingenuous, in Ritson's view, for Percy to claim it as such.

Percy also assumed that there was, in the Middle Ages, a much-venerated professional body of minstrels who had entertained kings and their courts with heroic ballads and poems. Ritson thought this was utter tosh:

> Of the English minstrels ... all the knowledge we have of them is, that by a law of queen Elizabeth, they were pronounced "rogues, vagabonds, and sturdy beggars;" a sufficient proof that they were not very respectable in her time.[234]

Afterwards came Ritson's most savage criticism: he cast doubts on the authenticity of Percy's claim that his manuscript even contained medieval ballads by saying that 'the genuineness of the pieces in the "Reliques" cannot be properly investigated without an inspection of the original manuscript from which they are said to be extracted.'[235] There has been a lot of uninformed writing on this point with some scholars having alleged that Ritson cast doubt on the existence of the manuscript itself. This is not the case, as Ritson never doubted its existence, merely Percy's claims about it.[236] Some poems in Percy's folio manuscript did in fact date from the Middle Ages, but he was very cagey about showing it to people and wanted people to take him at his word. Percy should have had some common sense. If his claims as to the antiquity of the ballads was being doubted then he should have allowed the young upstart to look at it, but he never did. In fact he was rather petty about the whole thing, exclaiming, 'he shall be disappointed: the manuscript shall never be exposed to his sight in my lifetime.'[237] Nevertheless, after Ritson's remarks, Percy's authority on all things relating to ballads and poems was irrevocably eroded. Even after Ritson made amends in subsequent publications, Percy remained bitter towards Ritson, although when Percy revised future editions of the *Reliques* he did incorporate some of Ritson's suggestions.

Ritson's vegetarian diet was well-known among the London literati and he was viewed as an eccentric because of it. His criticisms of eminent scholars led the *St. James's Chronicle* to satirize Ritson by contrasting his humane treatment of animals with his savage treatment of other humans whom he 'ate up' for dinner:

> By wise Pythagoras taught young R-ts-n's meals
> With bloody viands never are defil'd;
> For Quadruped, for Bird, for Fish he feels:
> His board ne'er smokes with roast meat, nor with boil'd.
> In this one instance, pious, mild, and tame,
> He's surely in another a great sinner;
> For man, cries R-ts-n, Man's my game!
> On him I make a most delicious dinner.
> To venison and to partridge I've no Gout;
> To W-rt-n Tom such dainties I resign;
> Give me plump St-v-ns and large J-hns-n too,
> And take your turkey and your savory chine.[238]

Ritson took no note of this little satire, at least as far as we can ascertain, and it is to be noted that nowhere does the satire say that Ritson's 'attacks' were in any way unjustified.

In the midst of his literary research, Ritson never neglected his family in Stockton-on-Tees. By January 1784 his sister was gravely ill. Ritson promised her that should the worst happen, he would adopt Frank as his own son: 'You may be assured,' declared Ritson, 'that my attachment to [Frank] will only cease with my life.'[239] We have seen how Ritson often sent Frank books, and sometimes painting materials, so that his nephew might 'improve' himself. Frank had been sent to Norton Grammar School, on the High Street in that town which is close to Stockton, so Ritson was adding to the young man's homework in order to mould a boy who would become a gentleman.[240] Although the now 15-year-old Frank, in June 1784, wanted nothing more than to come and join his uncle in London and get an apprenticeship in a law firm, Ritson *commanded* him to stay in school. An education would be too important to his future prospects to waste it by finishing too early.[241] For the time being, Frank remained in Stockton with Matthew Wadeson acting as his guardian during his mother's illness.[242]

In 1784 and 1785 Ritson used his interest in historical songs and poems to produce two little children's books: *Gammer Gurton's Garland, or, The Nursery Parnassus* and *The Spartan Manual, or Tablet of Morality*. The first consisted of a number of nursery rhymes 'for the amusement and instruction of all little children'. The rhymes in the collection included ones which are still well-known 200 years later, such as 'London Bridge is Broken Down', 'Sing a Song of Sixpence', 'The Cat and the Fiddle', and 'Mistress Mary Quite Contrary'. The book was much sought after, and because of subsequent reprints was read by children and to children into the Victorian age.[243] *The Spartan Manual* contained no ballads but was a collection of wise sayings and precepts from the Ancient Greeks—Ritson had recently taught himself Greek—which would educate children and improve their minds and morals.[244] Teaching young men to follow 'Spartan' or Ancient Greek morals would have been recognised by contemporaries as an attempt to inculcate a sense of manly and heroic virtue.[245] Virtuous youths who had been educated properly would grow up into virtuous citizens. Childhood was a good time to teach these precepts. Since John Locke's *Some Thoughts Concerning Education* (1693) was published, an idea grew that the mind of a child was like a 'blank slate' upon which it was possible to imprint good principles and, eventually, produce a virtuous adult citizen.[246] The secular approach to teaching was in marked contrast to the primarily religious subjects in which pupils had been educated before Locke.[247] A largely secular education in moral principles was all-important because a child was innocent and only became 'corrupted' through experience and exposure to wrong habits. As a result, a flourishing market for children's literature emerged during the eighteenth century.[248] These children's books were simple, as was Ritson's:

CONTENT.

He is richest who is contented with least; for content is the riches of nature. *Socrates.*

It is better sleeping in peace on the earth, than lying unquiet in a soft bed. *Phocion.*

He is well disposed who grieves not for what he hath not, and rejoices for what he hath. *Democritus.*[249]

While it was usually the middle classes who availed themselves of the latest educational books, Ritson's children's books were cheap and both retailed at the very modest price of 2d. His nephew, of course, received a copy *gratis*.[250]

By late 1785, Ritson had sold the house in Silver Street, Stockton, and his sister had moved into smaller lodgings. He still owned property in Hartlepool but there was no need for a big house in the centre of the town because Ritson had secured Frank an apprenticeship to a law firm.[251] Frank was to take a boat from Stockton to London, live on ship's biscuit for however long the journey took, and he should, so Ritson commanded, welcome this opportunity because it would be a character building exercise.[252] As Ritson wrote in *The Spartan Manual*: 'pleasing things are delightful, and hardships glorious'.[253] Frank remained silent as to whether he was grateful for this opportunity to improve his character.

Frank lived with his uncle in London for several years, perhaps between late 1785 and 1793, for Ritson's letters to his nephew cease in 1785 and begin again in the latter year. This was to be a Spartan existence with his uncle, for in a letter sent to Frank—which arrived after Frank had already set out to London—Ritson advised him to acquire the following skills:

> Frying and dressing potatoes, making puff-paste, pickling, preserving and mending stockings, or any other similar kind of knowledge which you may never have an opportunity of coming at, and can have no idea of the vast utility of. In short, to make a pudding, and set a button on your shirt, will be of more use than all your reading and writing. You will think, perhaps, that such a lesson would be more fit for one who was coming into a cook's shop, than a conveyancers chambers—but when you have been here a year or two you will probably be of a different opinion.[254]

According to Ritson's gossipy servant, Mrs Kirby, Ritson turfed Frank out of the house at one point when he caught him eating meat. If this did happen—and B.H. Bronson believed this was just malicious gossip from someone known to tell tall tales—the fall out between the two cannot have lasted long.

ANCIENT SONGS,

FROM THE TIME OF

KING HENRY THE THIRD,

TO THE

REVOLUTION.

——CALAMIS AGRESTIBUS INSONAT ILLE,
BARBARICOQUE MIDAN——
CARMINE DELINIT.—— OVID.

LONDON:

Printed for J. JOHNSON, in St. Pauls Church Yard,
M DCC XC.

Title page to Joseph Ritson's *Ancient Songs* (1791).

Ritson was never a man to work on only one project at a time. While he was collating his children's books, and arranging for Frank's apprenticeship once he was in London, it will be recalled that he also starting to study law and began his employment as High Bailiff of the Liberty of the Savoy. Always interested in local history, he produced two little books of songs from the north of England: *The Bishoprick Garland; or, Durham Minstrel* (1784) and *The Yorkshire Garland* (1788). Ritson's friend Mr Harrison had reviewed the manuscript of these two works before they went to press.[255] A few years later, in 1793, Ritson went on to publish *The Newcastle Nightingale*, a collection of local ballads and poems arranged along similar lines as the Durham and Yorkshire songbooks. All three little books contained the texts of a few songs that were, even in Ritson's time, probably of interest only to those from the north of England, such as 'Newcastle Beer', a patriotic song about beating the French, and 'The Joyful Maid and Sorrowful Wife'. Not many copies were printed but they did sell well in those regions on their first release.[256]

While Ritson criticised Percy's conclusions in *A Select Collection of English Songs* it should be remembered that notwithstanding Ritson's criticisms of Percy, he had always admired the *Reliques* as 'a publication of uncommon elegance and poetical merit':

> I have always been, and still am, a warm admirer of Bishop Percys [sic] *Reliques*, and though I have been persuaded that he has not on every occasion been so scrupulously attentive to his originals as the work required, I shall be very glad to find the idea unfounded, and readily confess that what you have been so obliging as to tell me about the folio Ms. has in a great measure removed my prejudice on that head.[257]

Ritson looked to Percy as an authority on etymology when his own knowledge was lacking in certain areas.[258] Ritson soon made amends in the preface to his next major work, *Ancient Songs and Ballads from the Reign of King Henry the Second to the Revolution in Two Volumes* (1790). The tone was more respectful of Percy's contribution to scholarship, describing him as that 'learned, ingenious, and elegant writer', although he did criticize Percy's scholarship on certain points in several footnotes.[259] Ritson still disagreed with Percy's conclusions about the minstrels and also outlined why he at first accused Percy of lying about the existence of the manuscript he rescued from the fire.[260] Ritson was respectfully disagreeing with Percy.

In truth, the public dispute between Ritson and Percy has been a little bit overblown by scholars who maintain that Ritson's attacks in print were *always* venomous and unforgiving. Such an impression seems to have been given by an anonymous reviewer in the *Critical Review*—a magazine that had always been hostile to Ritson—who accused him of attacking Percy with 'the most shameful and disgusting virulence'.[261] The magazine never actually said where these 'shameful and disgusting' criticisms could be found. The result, however, is that Ritson has been caricatured as an irascible man. William Godwin (1756–1836) recognised the misrepresentation and remarked to Ritson,

> I have often heard you accused as an irritable man, but never having had the smallest ground to reproach you in that respect in an intercourse of considerable length, I have always defended you from the accusation with earnestness and zeal.[262]

The more unreasonable actor in this feud was Percy, who took Ritson's criticisms on his work *very* personally, fell out with friends who took Ritson's side on scholarly matters, and remained bitter even after Ritson died. When Percy visited the antiquary John Pinkerton in London in 1792, Percy must have had a grumble about Ritson's criticisms of his minstrel thesis. Pinkerton promised Percy that he would look into the matter and write an article in the *Critical Review* exposing Ritson's mistakes. Percy went back to his home in Ireland no doubt contented that the man he viewed as an enemy would be publicly humiliated. Yet when Pinkerton researched the matter closely he reached the same conclusions as Ritson—there was never a professional class of minstrels in the medieval period. Pinkerton then wrote in the *Critical Review* that Ritson was in fact correct and that his friend Percy had made a mistake. Percy and Pinkerton's friendship came to an abrupt end.[263]

The truth is that whenever Ritson endeavoured to critique other scholars' arguments, he often acknowledged, privately and publicly, that even if he disagreed with them, they still deserved respect. We should note that while Ritson had published responses to Malone, he approved of Malone's other work on Shakespeare, particularly his *Plays and Poems of William Shakespeare* which was published in ten volumes in 1790. When one of his associates mocked Malone, Ritson responded by saying, 'You will do Mr. Malone a great injustice if you suppose him to be in all respects what I have endeavoured to represent him in some'.[264] It was the same with Percy, whose scholarship on one or two specific points was criticised and not the body of his work as a whole.

A small book followed in 1791 entitled *Pieces of Ancient Popular Poetry*. This book was, much like his previous volumes, a work for learned scholars. In the preface, we again find Ritson referring to Percy's work as 'ingenious and elegant'.[265] In the introduction to his transcript of the ballad of 'Adam Bell, Clim of the Clough, and William of Coudeslie', for example, Ritson cites Percy as an authority, as Ritson does in the preamble to the copy of 'The King and the Barker'. One gets the sense that Ritson was laying on the compliments as thick as possible to lessen any offence caused by their disagreement; there are brief notes which suggest that Percy may have been wrong on one matter, but that was it. Indeed we note that there are absolutely no offensive references to Percy in the body of Ritson's letters. Scholars often disagree with scholars and the way they do so is through their publications, offering counter-arguments to previous works of scholarship. In this way, Ritson was simply following the path resorted to by modern academics.

It might be asked: would it not have been more gentlemanly and *polite* for Ritson to suggest amendments to Johnson, Steevens, Malone, and Percy through private correspondence? In his *Life of Thomas Warton* (1810), after all, Alexander Chalmers stated that, in his criticisms of the *History of English Poetry*, Ritson should have been more 'decorous'.[266] To think thus would be to fail to take account of the fact that the enjoyment of high culture in the eighteenth century was largely something that people 'purchased'.[267] As people were now buying cultural products like Percy's book, then they, as consumers, had a *right* to publicly express their approval or disapproval of what they had purchased and read. To be able to express a reasoned critical opinion on anything related to high culture was a marker of 'taste' and politeness. It was to facilitate the development and improvement of public taste and knowledge that a flourishing periodical press emerged which specialised in literary and art criticism. Anonymous reviewers provided commentaries on the latest cultural products by printing book reviews and critiques of paintings—and those anonymous reviewers could be much more scathing than Ritson. A culture of free and open debate into all political, social, and cultural matters was assumed to be beneficial to the British nation because it would 'improve' the country's culture, just as individual people could 'improve' themselves. As the Earl of Shaftesbury said:

> Without a public voice, knowingly guided and directed, there is nothing which can exalt the genius of the workman, or make him emulous of fame, and of the approbation of his country and of posterity … When the free spirit of a nation turns itself this way, judgments are formed, critics arise; the public eye and ear improves; a right taste prevails and in a manner forces its way.[268]

Just as the *Critical Review* censured Ritson, so too did Ritson censure Percy where he saw the latter's errors. The criticisms which flowed from Ritson's pen should be viewed as a contemporary literary mode. By providing commentaries on the flaws in Malone's, Johnson's, Steevens's and Percy's works, Ritson was, by the standards of the time, performing a public service. His manner of writing may have been direct but he was hardly the first and he certainly would not be the last person to voice their disapproval of a work of art and literature in the press. In fact most of the accusations towards Ritson, with charges that he was venomous and cruel, were aired in private correspondence between the men whose scholarship Ritson had criticised. These remarks were then made public after Ritson's death, and our antiquary's reputation has been unfairly maligned as a result.

Thus far Ritson had published books on Shakespeare, songs, and ballads. He soon turned his attention to poetry. One of the most

popular kinds of works was the poetical anthology or 'miscellany'—
it was 'the age of anthologies' according to Carly Watson—which
were collections of short poems and extracts of larger ones.[269]
An early pioneer of this format was John Dryden, who, with the
publisher Jacob Tonson at the end of seventeenth century, published
six volumes of *Miscellanies* containing the latest popular poetical
works. Other publishers soon realised that the format could earn
them good money and countless others appeared. Poetry was widely
read by the middle classes and by poorer families. People would read
poetry, perhaps before church as Dorothy Wordsworth records doing
in 1802, or they might, as a family, engage in the polite, improving,
and entertaining activity of reading to each other on an evening.[270]
It was with the general reader in mind that Ritson produced one
of his most comprehensive and, with engravings that he personally
chose, his most beautiful publication to date, entitled *The English
Anthology*, published in three volumes in 1793. In the preface Ritson
did not address his fellow antiquaries, as he did with the Shakespeare
pamphlets and *Select Collection of English Songs*, and neither did
he begin by criticising the scholarly arguments of another literary

An engraving from Joseph Ritson's *English Anthology* (1793) depicting famous
English poets from history receiving inspiration from the Muse.

critic. Instead he dedicated the book to 'a generous and discerning public, whose approbation is the sole reward of his disinterested endeavours'.[271] Neither was there any critical commentary on the texts of the individual poems which he included, which contrasts with his editorial practices in previous song collections. *The English Anthology* was a book to be enjoyed.

The English Anthology reads like a 'who's who' of English literary history. Contained in the collection are sonnets from Shakespeare; extracts from Chaucer's *Canterbury Tales*; selected passages from Edmund Spenser's *Faerie Queene*, passages from William Langland's *Piers Plowman* (c. 1377); excerpts from Thomas Warton's poetry; as well as extracts from the works of a whole host of minor poets from the late medieval period to the eighteenth century. Ritson did not simply favour men either, for, in keeping with current trends which saw some women rise to the heights of poetical fame, the works of a number of female poets, to whom he devoted a lengthy section in the second volume, were included in his collection. Among the woman poets were leading lights such as Aphra Behn, Anna Laetitia Barbauld, Lady Mary Wortley Montague, Elizabeth Rowe, and Letitia Pilkington. Ritson cited them by name at a period when most women, if they had their poetry published in a literary magazine, were often published anonymously or pseudonymously. Thus we have in Ritson a man who, at a period when women poets were sometimes viewed as second-rate, respected their works and had no qualms about including their poetry alongside that of Chaucer, Spenser and Shakespeare.

There was much else that Ritson wanted to learn. He enjoyed learning about the Ireland's medieval history and culture and in 1789 thought of publishing a collection of Irish songs but, as he expressed to one of his Irish acquaintances, Joseph Cooper Walker, his lack of knowledge on old Irish languages impeded him in this ambition.[272] Ritson had however been researching the historical poems and songs of Scottish authors since the 1770s and even privately published 420 copies of a fragment of a collection known as *The Caledonian Muse* in 1785, but the rest of the manuscript, so Ritson thought, had been destroyed by a fire in the printer's office. In reality only the introduction to *The Caledonian Muse* had been destroyed and the manuscript, probably without Ritson's knowledge, passed from the printer to the bookseller

Robert Triphook in 1809.[273] Having had to collect all the materials on Scottish poems and songs after the destruction of the manuscript, it was not until 1794 that *Scotish Song* appeared, although he began compiling the manuscript for it in the summer of 1790.[274] Most of the material in Ritson's *Scotish Songs* anthology came from transcriptions of Scots ballads he had completed by visiting archives as well as reprints of songs from earlier ballad collections such as D'Urfey's *Pills to Purge Melancholy* (1698–1720). Again Ritson appealed to Percy's ego and complimented him by calling him 'an ingenious writer'.[275] In *Scotish Song* Ritson proved to be a man ahead of his time in the interpretation of historical matters: many antiquaries assumed that all popular songs and poetry originated in an oral tradition and had come down in their 'pure' state to people in the eighteenth century. Ritson was hesitant to accept this theory:

> Obsolete phrases will be perpetually changing for those better understood, and what memory loses the invention must supply. So that a performance of genius and merit, as the purest stream becomes polluted by the foulness of its channel, may in time be degraded to the vilest jargon. Tradition, in short, is a species of alchemy which converts lead into gold.[276]

He much preferred to trust printed sources and argued that even if a story or song once existed in an oral tradition, what survived in his own day was in all likelihood very different to that which existed in times gone by. Ritson's view is now the one taken by most folklorists.

Ritson never made huge amounts of money from his books. His letters reveal that it was a mere £500 in royalties which he obtained from the sale of his books over the course of his life. This may sound like a lot of money but, given that Ritson's first book appeared in 1782 and the fact that he died in 1803, this amounted to less than £24 per year—hardly enough to allow him to live a life of luxury. His research should be seen more as a labour of love. Yet Ritson's legal and scholarly activities highlight only one aspect of his life of continued variety. In the next chapter we shall see how Ritson became a revolutionary.

Chapter 4

'He was Active, Brave, Prudent': Joseph Ritson the Revolutionary

Jonathan Swift said: 'If a man would register all his opinions on love, politicks, religion, learning and the like; beginning from his youth, and so go on to old age, what a bundle of inconsistencies and contradictions would appear at last?'[277] No statement could have been more apt in Ritson's case. As a young adult he was a romantic Jacobite. By the end of the century he was a revolutionary and a democrat. But it was a slow journey.

During the 1780s Ritson made sporadic comments on politics. After the American War, British public opinion was on the side of the king. Lord North's government fell in 1782 when it became clear that the colonies would be separated from Britain. A new coalition government was formed, composed of both Whigs and Tories, with the Earl of Shelburne as Prime Minister. Ritson approved of the new ministry, and remarked that the new ministry was composed of 'all men of approved abilities and integrity—the ablest heads and the soundest hearts'.[278] The Jacobite had become Whig.

There were two main political parties in Britain: the Tories and the Whigs. The old Tory party, with its Jacobite sympathies, had disintegrated by c. 1760 after which there existed what might be termed various subsections of the Whigs. The term 'Tory' continued to be used, however, to describe those who were the 'King's Friends'. These Tories believed in the need for a strong monarchy, a strong Church of England, and wanted to maintain the pre-eminent social position and rights of the landowners at the expense of the moneyed middle classes (although the leader of these 'Tories', William Pitt, would have identified himself as an 'independent Whig', so these labels can sometimes be misleading). The Whigs stressed the need for a very limited role for the monarchy, were tolerant of dissenters, and were the party most friendly to business and trade. They were essentially the party of the middle classes and Ritson enthusiastically endorsed their leader, Charles James Fox.[279] Ritson's political sympathies were clearly changing. This being said, we should not make the mistake of thinking that the Whigs were a modern political party by any stretch. The electorate was very small and people could only vote if they owned freehold property worth over 40 shillings. There was also little in the way of party organisation, and the party system, such as it was, was merely a system of loose alliances between MPs who found that they had common interests.

In 1787 Ritson lamented that there would be 'immediate ruin' if Charles Fox did not get into power. That year was a fairly smooth one in politics so it is not clear what particular event made Ritson make such an exclamation—it may just have been a general grumble about the government.

In any case, an election was three years away. General elections usually lasted slightly over a month because each constituency polled on a different day and it took a while for the results from all over the country to travel to London to be counted. There were two seats up for grabs in Ritson's home constituency of Durham County.[280] In the general election of 1790, which took place between 16 June and 28 July, Rowntree asked Ritson to make the journey from London back to Stockton-on-Tees to cast a vote for the local Whig candidate, Captain Ralph Milbanke (1776–1850). Ritson thought that this was rather cheeky:

> Dear Rowntree,
> I this morning received your favour of the 20th … how can it have happened that you should *expect me down*? … I most certainly had no intention … it would have been highly inconvenient, if not altogether improper, to have set out immediately on receipt of your letter. I am nevertheless perfectly desirous, if a single vote can be of consequence, to give mine to Mr Milbanke, and for that purpose am ready to sacrifice my convenience to my inclination, and come down, as a freeholder, in the same way that a gentleman does: though I shall certainly make it a point to return the moment I have polled. No one, I should think, could expect me to make such a journey at my own expence: nor, if I do come down, shall any thing I here say be construed to prevent me from splitting my vote if I see occasion for it in favour of Sir John Eden.[280]

As a property owner, Ritson was inclined to 'do his civic duty' and return to Stockton to cast a vote. But Ritson expected payment for his services as a voter and this was the usual practice: candidates would canvass voters before an election to see if they could count on their support; if a voter had to travel a long way to cast his vote for a candidate, the voter expected to be paid expenses. This is why Ritson's letter to Rowntree is rather standoffish. Ritson was a property-owning *gentleman* and it was barefaced cheek for anyone—even his friend—to ask him to make a journey and spend his *own* money to cast a vote. Ritson disapproved of the 'bribery and perjury' which flourished at election times,[282] but he wanted his expenses paid were he to vote in person.[283]

In any case, Ritson would use his vote as he saw fit and would not be railroaded into voting solely for Rowntree's friend Milbanke but would also vote for the other Whig candidate, John Eden (1743–1812). This requires some explanation: in general elections, each constituency normally sent two representatives to the House of Commons. When a person gained voting rights as a result of having met the property qualification, he gained the right to cast *two* votes.[284] Under this system,

A reproduction of an image by William Hogarth depicting an eighteenth-century general election. Rowdy and noisy events, people cast their votes in public, while before and after polling prospective MPs would wine and dine their voters.

if a voter wanted to support only one party, he could opt for a 'straight-party vote' and cast his votes for the two candidates who had been nominated by a single party. If a voter could not decide which party to vote for, he might even cast one vote for a Tory candidate and one vote for a Whig candidate. Ritson would, if he did come down, obviously opt for a straight party vote by casting his vote for the two Whigs, Milbanke and Eden.

It is doubtful that Ritson ever made the journey up to Stockton to cast his vote and it did not make much difference to Captain Milbanke's electoral fortunes. He won his seat with a comfortable majority. John Eden was not so lucky because he lost his seat to the Tory landowner Sir Rowland Burton, who held his seat until 1806. This was a good thing for constituents because Eden could rarely be bothered to make the trip down to London, sit in parliament and actually represent his electors anyway—doing so would curtail the time he was able to spend in hunting on his country estate. Even in the 'rotten' parliament of the eighteenth century it is unsurprising that voters opted for someone else.

Although Ritson was reluctant to make the long journey simply to cast a vote, he always took an interest in Stockton's local politics. Even after his removal to London, his letters contain, here and there, remarks on Stockton's local issues. At one point, in 1788, his friends persuaded him to stand for Durham at the next election, and he seems to have greeted the suggestion with some enthusiasm. However, he did not win enough votes.[285] His friends prevailed upon him to stand again in local elections in 1791; this time he seems to have put himself forward more to please them rather than for his own benefit. He was not sad when he lost.[286]

Soon Rowntree and Ritson fell out over money matters. In business, the two men referred clients to each other and Rowntree was the steward of Ritson's properties, responsible for collecting rents. Ritson considered him a good friend. But Ritson had, for some unknown reason, temporarily run into money problems early in 1791 and asked Rowntree if he could borrow £100. Rowntree prevaricated and never sent Ritson a reply to his first request. After a little while, Ritson wrote to Rowntree and declared that he would never bother him with money matters, or anything else for that matter, again. Ritson then turned to Matthew Wadeson and excoriated Rowntree for being a false friend:

> What is the value of either friendship or the man? Rowntree, to be sure, is a very clever as well as a very useful fellow, and was not, perhaps, to blame that I placed more confidence in his sincerity than it was able to bear. One should have some sort of mental thermometer to ascertain the boiling and freezing points of a mans [sic] friendship. At least (to change my metaphor) it would be very important to know "the sticking place" of the machine, lest by screwing too high you break it into pieces … My friend Rowntrees zeal might be up to the loan of fifty, or perhaps sixty, or even seventy pounds, but the mention of a hundred extinguished his fires and converted his hot water into cold ice. I am therefore content to let him freeze.[287]

Rowntree could have just declined Ritson's request by claiming he was short of funds or something. Unfortunately the pair would never correspond with the same warmth which they had in times past. The friendship was largely over.

Ritson's anti-Hanoverian and 'damn the king' views would soon develop into republicanism. He became a revolutionary. A revolutionary is somebody who seeks a fundamental change in their society's constitution. The ideology that they hold sets them at odds with mainstream society, its citizens, and its government. There are two types of revolutionary. The first type is a person who participates in a revolution. These are the kind of people who build barricades and actively fight against an oppressive state; they are the kinds of people who we find in 1789 storming the Bastille. The second kind—and they are by no means mutually exclusive—is someone who holds a revolutionary ideology. They may not take up arms themselves, but through their writings and

Radical thinker Thomas Paine, a leading intellectual during both the American and French Revolutions and author of *Common Sense* (1776) and *The Rights of Man* (1791). Ritson had an engraving of Paine on the door of his apartment (Wellcome Library)

political activism they advocate for a revolutionary change in society. Thomas Paine was such a man. In *Common Sense* (1776), which was addressed to the inhabitants of the Thirteen Colonies in America during the Revolution, Paine argued that monarchical systems of government had no place in the modern world:

> But there is another and greater distinction for which no truly natural or religious reason can be assigned, and that is the distinction of men into KINGS and SUBJECTS. Male and female are the distinctions of nature, good and bad the distinctions of Heaven; but how a race of men came into

the world so exalted above the rest, and distinguished like
some new species, is worth inquiring into, and whether they
are the means of happiness or of misery to mankind.[288]

Although Ritson disagreed with the American revolutionaries during the
1770s, in the 1790s he became a Paineite. But it took an event across the
English Channel to light the fuse of Ritson's radicalism, an event which
Charles James Fox called 'the greatest event ... in the history of the
world': the French Revolution.[289]

On 5 May 1789, the French king, Louis XVI, convened the Estates
General. It was a citizens' assembly, with representatives from the clergy,
the nobility, and the third estate, convened with the purpose of finding
a solution to the nation's parlous financial state. The French had lent a
great deal of military and financial assistance to the American colonists
in their war of independence, with little thought of the monetary burden
such an endeavour would place on the nation. The French government was
reaping what it had sowed: the country was heavily in debt. However, the
clergy and nobility attempted to block any reforms which might damage
their privileges by insisting on voting collectively by estates (which would
ensure the clergy and nobility's pre-eminence) rather than voting by
head (which would increase the power of the third estate). Justifiably
annoyed, the representatives of the third estate refused to take part in
the proceedings any longer and instead, on 20 May, gathered in a nearby
tennis court where they all took an oath and vowed 'not to separate, and
to reassemble wherever circumstances require, until the constitution of
the kingdom is established and consolidated upon firm foundations'.[290]
This was a pivotal moment in the history of the revolution: the third
estate was signalling to the king, the clergy, and the nobility that their
power came not from a divinely ordained place in the feudal structure but
from the people at large. The representatives who assembled at the tennis
court that day would soon become known as the National Assembly.
Although the king attempted to shut it down by denying them the use
of the tennis court, the third estate's representatives simply reconvened
to a local church. In light of this, Louis thought it prudent to grant the
National Assembly a royal charter. The Assembly now had legitimacy not
only from the nation (hence it was a 'national' assembly—an assembly
of representatives from the nation) but also from the king. Soon some
members of the clergy and the nobility joined the National Assembly,

PARIS GARDÉ PAR LE PEUPLE
la nuit du 12 au 13 Juillet 1-89.

The Parisian mob on the day before the storming of the Bastille. (Wellcome Library)

after which it was reconstituted as the National Constituent Assembly, and Louis was forced to formally request that voting was carried out by head. The Estates General was dead in the water.

The people were growing suspicious of the king however, for he had at his command an army of mercenaries in Paris which he refused to dismiss. His refusal to dismiss the troops spurred a mob of Parisians, on 14 July 1789, to storm a castle in the centre of Paris named the Bastille. It was used as a prison primarily for political prisoners and for a long time was reviled as a symbol of despotic royal power. All seven of the prisoners were released when the mob entered and the rioters achieved their other aim: to secure the arsenal of ammunition stored in the castle. After the crowd of approximately 1,000 people had 'liberated' the bastille, its governor and four of his officers were killed by the mob.

The French nobility were getting scared. Some decided to leave the country, many went to Britain. The revolution signalled an end to the feudal privileges the nobles had enjoyed since time immemorial.

On 4 August the National Constituent Assembly abolished feudalism, and three weeks later the assembly adopted the Declaration of the Rights of Man and Citizen, which had been drafted by the progressive clergyman Abbé Sieyès (1748–1846) and the Marquis de Lafayette (1757–1834) who had fought in the American War. In drafting the document they had consulted with the future president of the United States, Thomas Jefferson (1743–1826). It contained seventeen articles, inspired by the American Declaration of Independence, Enlightenment ideals of civic virtue, and the social contract. A selection of the declaration's provisions are laid out below:

1. Men are born and remain free and equal in rights. Social distinctions may be founded only upon the general good.
2. The aim of all political association is the preservation of the natural and imprescriptible rights of man. These rights are liberty, property, security, and resistance to oppression.
3. The principle of all sovereignty resides essentially in the nation. No body nor individual may exercise any authority which does not proceed directly from the nation.
4. Liberty consists in the freedom to do everything which injures no one else; hence the exercise of the natural rights of each man has no limits except those which assure to the other members of the society the enjoyment of the same rights. These limits can only be determined by law.

...

7. No person shall be accused, arrested, or imprisoned except in the cases and according to the forms prescribed by law. Any one soliciting, transmitting, executing, or causing to be executed, any arbitrary order, shall be punished. But any citizen summoned or arrested in virtue of the law shall submit without delay, as resistance constitutes an offense.

...

10. No one shall be disquieted on account of his opinions, including his religious views, provided their manifestation does not disturb the public order established by law.
11. The free communication of ideas and opinions is one of the most precious of the rights of man. Every citizen may, accordingly, speak, write, and print with freedom, but shall be responsible for such abuses of this freedom as shall be defined by law.

The revolution seemed unstoppable. Although the Declaration of the Rights of Man stressed the rights of men only, women also got involved in the action. Parisian women led a march from Paris to Versailles, 'kidnapped' Louis from his palace, and brought him back to Paris in October 1789. In 1790 the National Constituent Assembly continued its assault on the *ancién regime* by proclaiming the abolition of nobility. They also passed a decree requiring the clergy to swear allegiance, not the to the king, who was considered as God's representative on earth, but to the nation. The year 1791 saw further developments. Pope Pius VI condemned the Civil Constitution of the Clergy in May, while Louis and his queen, Marie Antoinette, attempted to flee Paris and go to Austria to seek refuge with Marie Antoinette's family. They might have escaped but were captured at Varennes and thereafter the royal pair rapidly lost any public sympathy they had.

It was into this fray that Ritson and his friend William Shield arrived in Paris in August 1791 where they stayed until November.[291] This was a holiday and not business trip. He had always wanted to visit Europe. As early as January 1788 he said that he was 'considering of a trip to Paris or Madrid, being ashamed to have lived so long in the world and seen so little of it'.[292] It was of course the custom for the sons of the wealthy to go on a Grand Tour of the continent at this time, and Ritson probably wanted to undertake such a visit because it was what gentlemen did.

Before Ritson set out to Paris, he appears, like many in Britain, to have been watching the events of the revolution with interest, as he told a friend in June 1791:

My desire to reside for a few weeks at or near Paris has been increasing ever since the Revolution, and is in reality very strong; which you will easily conceive when I give it as a decided opinion that no people ancient or modern was ever so deserving of admiration.[293]

Ritson's favourable disposition towards events across the channel may have had something to do with the fact that his political hero, Charles James Fox, once turned up wearing a French Revolutionary cockade to the Commons.

In the early years of the revolution, many British newspapers initially expressed approval of the revolution. *The English Chronicle; or Universal Evening Post* declared that 'the hand of JUSTICE has been brought upon France' in her 'great and glorious REVOLUTION'.[294] *The London Chronicle* reported that 'in every province of this great kingdom [France] the flame of liberty has burst forth'.[295] Romantic poets such as William Wordsworth (1770–1850) added their voice to the debate: 'Bliss it was in that dawn to be alive,' Wordsworth would later exclaim.[296] It seemed as though mankind was entering a new age of reason, unshackled from the dead weight of tradition and feudalism.

When Ritson arrived in Paris he was captivated with the energy and excitement of the revolution, as he wrote to Mr Harrison in November:

Well, and so I got to Paris at last; and was highly gratifyed with the whole of my excursion. I admire the French more than ever. They deserved to be free and they really are so. You have read their new constitution: can anything be more admirable? We, who pretend to be free, you know, have no constitution at all … The French read a great deal, and even the common people (such, i mean, as cannot be expected from their poverty to have had a favourable education, for there is now no other distinction of rank,) are better acquainted with their ancient history than the English nobility are with ours. They talk familiarly of *Charlechauve*,[297] and at St Denis i observed that all the company, mostly peasants or mechanics, recognized with pleasure the portrait of *La Pucelle*. Then, as to modern politics, and the principles of the constitution, one would think that half the people in Paris had no other employment than to study and talk about them. I have seen a fishwoman reading the journal of the

National Assembly to her neighbours with all the avidity of Shakespeare's blacksmith. You may now consider their government completely settled, and a counter-revolution as utterly impossible: they are more than a match for all the slaves in Europe.[298]

Ritson was right: both rich and poor avidly read the latest political news. What Ritson was witnessing in Paris during that summer was the newly-born French public sphere of political debate in action. Before the French Revolution, political power had been held by a small elite of nobles and the king. By 1791 popular sovereignty was exercised through the representatives of the Third Estate. While statesmen debated in the National Assembly, their representatives and supporters had an excellent tool with which to shape public opinion: a newly-freed newspaper press. Before 1789, newspapers had to obtain a licence from the French king and the licenced newspapers were heavily censored.[299]

From the beginning of the Estates-General in May 1789, however, journalists defied official regulations and from then until 1799 over 1,000 new newspapers and periodicals appeared, along with countless other pamphlets catering to every political persuasion.

Ritson was of course correct to say that the British nation did not boast a constitution as wonderful as the Declaration of the Rights of Man and Citizen. To this day the British nation does not have a written constitution. Back in Britain, it took Edmund Burke in his *Reflections on the Revolution in France* (1790) to define what the English constitution was. For Burke, the English

Edmund Burke, author of *Reflections on the Revolution in France* (1790).

constitution was not based upon abstract principles of 'the rights of man'. Instead it was the inheritance bequeathed to us by our forefathers who had tried and tested various modes of governance and laws, through balancing equally the power of the crown, the lords, and the commons. The result of this delicate balance was that the British people, in his opinion, enjoyed a degree of liberty and security which surpassed that of any other nation. Therefore the British did not need a revolution as the French had, who had essentially rejected the political heritage of their ancestors. As Burke wrote, the very idea of completely overthrowing the system 'of government which is our only security for law and liberty … is enough to fill us with disgust and horror.'[300] Although in Britain, Burke's book was popular with many conservative-minded people who feared that French Revolutionary ideology might spread to Britain, many were unimpressed by Burke's text and a 'pamphlet war' ensued. Among those who opposed Burke was the visionary thinker Mary Wollstonecraft who wrote *A Vindication of the Rights of Men* (1790) and later *A Vindication of the Rights of Woman* (1791). Perhaps the most high-profile riposte came from the pen of Thomas Paine, who published *The Rights of Man*, in two parts in 1791 and 1792 in which he set forth his opposition to hereditary government again:

> All hereditary government is in its nature tyranny. An heritable crown, or an heritable throne, or by what other fanciful name such things may be called, have no other significant explanation than that mankind are heritable property. To inherit a government, is to inherit the people, as if they were flocks and herds … We have heard the Rights of Man called a levelling system; but the only system to which the word levelling is truly applicable, is the hereditary monarchical system. It is a system of mental levelling. It indiscriminately admits every species of character to the same authority. Vice and virtue, ignorance and wisdom, in short, every quality good or bad, is put on the same level. Kings succeed each other, not as rationals, but as animals. It signifies not what their mental or moral characters are. Can we then be surprised at the abject state of the human mind in monarchical countries, when the government itself is formed on such an abject levelling system?[301]

It would be hard to overestimate the popularity—or notoriety—of Paine's *Rights of Man* in England when it was first published. Read aloud in taverns and coffeehouses, it reportedly sold over 50,000 copies in its first year.[302]

No doubt Ritson availed himself of a copy when he returned to England in November. He became well-versed in the principles of Paine's political philosophy. It was clear to everyone that the old Jacobite who wished for a restoration of the Stuart monarchy was gone. The Joseph Ritson who returned from France was now decidedly anti-monarchy, pro-democracy, and pro-equality. Perhaps the best illustration of Ritson's newly adopted republican ideals is to be found in an impromptu poem, written by his friend Thomas Clio Rickman, which he included in a letter to his nephew in November 1793:

> With heartfelt joy to you I send,
> This precious relic of my friend,
> With *this*, our *Paine*, those pages wrote,
> Which all the good with rapture quote;
> And which, ere long, from Pole to Pole,
> Shall *purge* and *renovate* the whole;
> Shall monarchy, and man's *greatest* curse,
> And all its satellites disperse,
> And make the human race exclaim,
> We owe our happiness to Paine![303]

So enamoured was Ritson with the writings of Thomas Paine that he placed a print of his likeness on the door to his apartment to publicly signal to the world that he sympathised with the revolutionaries across the Channel.[304] In emulation of the French, he began addressing all his acquaintances as 'Citizen' in his letters. He also, on occasion, used the French Revolutionary Calendar. The French Revolutionary government used this calendar between 1793 and 1805, having redesigned the existing calendar to remove all royal and religious references. So we see Ritson sign off a letter to his nephew in 1793 with the date 18 Germinal, II, which meant 18 March in Year Two of the French Republic.[305] (It is a rather confusing calendar, and Ritson only signed a few of his letters with a revolutionary date, and the French nation soon returned to the Gregorian Calendar).

However, Ritson still had some lingering sentimental attachment to his old Jacobite beliefs. The Jacobite Royalist anthem, 'When the King Enjoys his Own Again', was incorporated into *Ancient Songs* and Ritson declared,

> It is with particular pleasure that the editor is enabled to restore to the public the original words of the most famous and popular air ever heard of in this country. Invented to support the declining interest of the Royal Martyr, it served afterwards, with more success, to keep up the spirits of the Cavaliers, and promote the Restoration of his Son; an event it was employed to celebrate all over the kingdom. At the [Glorious] Revolution it of course became an adherent of the exiled family, whose cause it never deserted … It is believed to be a fact, that nothing fed the enthusiasm of the Jacobites, down almost to the present reign, in every corner of Great Britain, more than 'The King Shall Enjoy His Own Again'.[306]

Ritson's description of Charles I as 'the Royal Martyr', as late as 1793, indicates that he retained some admiration of and affection for the executed Stuart king even into later life. Indeed, Ritson's seemingly easy switch from Jacobitism to republicanism might also be interpreted as having been inspired by an intense dislike of the Hanoverian dynasty— perhaps realising that Jacobitism was dead, and harbouring a long-running disdain of George III, it made sense for him to throw in his lot with the republicans.

Tragedy struck the family again in April 1793 when Ritson's sister, Anne, passed away.[307] In the nineteenth century one Mrs Wright, who knew the family well, stated that Anne 'was a woman of melancholy and nervous temperament' and gave 'madness' as a reason for her afflictions, although Ritson himself never alluded to such an illness.[308] Anne had moved from the house in Silver Street to smaller lodgings elsewhere in Stockton. In the last few months of her life she was well cared for by Mr Rowntree's wife and Mr Wadeson, who arranged her funeral, although neither Ritson nor Frank (still living in London but no longer with Ritson) attended, as is indicated when Ritson wrote to his nephew to comfort him on his mother's death:

Dear Nephew,

If there had been any hopes that the longer duration of your mother's life would have been accompanied with an increase of health and happiness, I should be very much concerned for her untimely loss; but as we could not reasonably flatter ourselves that this would be the case, it ought to afford us great consolation that her afflictions are at an end. I think you give a very sufficient reason for not attending her funeral, which appears, by a letter I have had from our friend Wadeson, to have been conducted with great propriety and as nearly as possible in accordance with her own request.[309]

What little property Ritson's sister had was sold off with Ritson keeping a few trinkets and the rest of her annuity, which at the final reckoning amounted to £23 7s 6d and was bequeathed to Frank.[310]

Even when he was offering his condolences, Ritson still found space in his letter to offer Frank advice on the virtues of hard work—all the more important because, with the exception of his uncle, Frank was

The political philosopher and novelist William Godwin, of whose work Ritson was fond. (British Library)

WILLIAM GODWIN.

109

now alone in the world and had to make his own way. Ritson was in no position to help him out financially either, for he had made some unwise investments on the stock exchange, 'having turned stock-jobber and disabled myself by buying into funds'.[311] This was to be the first of many naïve investments which towards the close of his life would ruin him financially. It was no use for Frank, now a fellow radical, to simply disengage from his studies and wait for a revolution to happen in England, as Ritson warned:

> But suppose a revolution do happen, how is it to provide for you? People will have to work for bread I presume, pretty much as they do at present; for a long series of years at least; and he who has nothing will be in equal danger of starving. In fact the idea of an approaching change should influence you the rather to fix your self in a business or situation which would enable you to take advantage of it when it did come.[312]

Ritson may have been a revolutionary but he was not a utopian; a post-revolutionary Britain would not mean an end to toil. There have always been revolutionary thinkers guilty of utopianism. The poets Samuel Taylor Coleridge and Robert Southey were both radicals and in 1794 concocted a hare-brained scheme of moving to the United States and building a Pantisocracy or 'government of equals' on the banks of the Susquehanna River. Karl Marx and Friederich Engels's brand of communism was developed in 1848 in response to the more abstract 'feel good' utopian socialism peddled by Henri Saint-Simon, Charles Fourier, and Robert Owen.[313] Even Lenin, writing shortly after the Russian Revolution in October 1917, had to remind Russian workers that their country was not a utopia and that the Soviets were building 'a republic of labour [and that] he who will not work, will have to go without food'.[314] In Ritson's view, a person should look forward to the 'approaching change' but they had to ensure that their material circumstances enabled them to weather the storm. Thus there was nothing for Frank to do but continue to apply himself to studying for the bar and serving his employers. Frank could do little to further the cause of a revolution by quitting his studies and discussing politics all day in coffeehouses wearing tatty clothes.[315] Ritson found his own legal profession a bit tedious at times, and he regarded most attorneys as 'ignorant and capricious ... insincere, unprincipled, and in every respect, worthless', but it was still a good profession to be in if and when a revolution occurred.[316]

Ritson forged amicable associations with fellow London-based radicals such as the novelist and political philosopher William Godwin, and the latter visited Ritson's home twice in November 1793.[317] Godwin was Mary Wollstonecraft's husband and these two were parents to the great Mary Shelley, author of *Frankenstein; or, The Modern Prometheus* (1818). When Ritson became acquainted with him, Godwin had recently published *Enquiry concerning Political Justice and its Influence on General Virtue and Happiness* (1793). According to Richard Gough Thomas, this book—a heavy tome of over 800 pages in two volumes—earned Godwin a kind of celebrity status among contemporary British radicals as one of their foremost intellectuals. While the book was expensive, retailing at £1 1s, British radical clubs and debating societies often clubbed together to buy a copy which would then be read out at their meetings. While the British government had issued a Royal Proclamation against 'seditious writings' in 1792, it was probably the cost of Godwin's book and its serious philosophical nature which meant that Godwin avoided getting into trouble with the authorities—after all, what harm could come from a book which very few could afford?[318] In contrast, Paine's writings were cheap and more accessible to 'the lower orders'; the government, fast becoming paranoid about anything which vaguely smacked of political reform, sought to contain the spread of his writings and Paine eventually had to flee the country. Luckily for him he did so just a few months before he would have been indicted for seditious libel. He was tried and convicted *in absentia*.

Godwin was also a novelist, and having read his *Enquiry*, Ritson was initially enthusiastic upon learning that Godwin had a novel in the works.[319] *Things as They Are; or, The Adventures of Caleb Williams* (1794) incorporated many of the radical sentiments found in Godwin's philosophical works. Yet as he confessed to his nephew, Ritson was less than impressed when he read *Caleb Williams*:

> Did you ask (for I don't exactly know what I have done with your letter) whether Godwins book [*Political Justice*] was about to appear in 8vo? I can only tell you that he is preparing for such an edition, but I do not think it is likely to be published these twelve months. I suppose he will give

me timely notice, as I myself have the *4to* edition — though it cost me, by the by, no more than 18s. — You have read his novel [*Caleb Williams*], I presume; he has got it sufficiently puffed in the Critical Review, but, between ourselves, it is a very indifferent, or rather despicable performance, — at all events unworthy of the author of Political justice: I have no patience with it.[320]

Ritson never told his friend Godwin that he disliked the novel, which was probably for the best, otherwise Godwin may have thought fit to revise his friendly assessment of Ritson's character.[321]

Another radical who made Ritson's acquaintance was John Thelwall of the London Corresponding Society (LCS). The modest name of this organisation obscures its aims: its members were dedicated to campaigning for political reform. The measures they called for included universal male suffrage and annual elections (the rationale behind the last was that, if an MP was potentially in office for only one year, it would be difficult for him to succumb to bribery and corruption). Its members included 'respectable' tradesmen who paid a fairly cheap subscription to attend its meetings. Ritson was never a member of the society himself however, because he was under the impression that the rank-and-file LCS members did not like lawyers.[322] There was also a bit of snobbery towards the members of the LCS: Ritson was obviously intelligent; he was a professional and fairly affluent; had risen through society's professional ranks and he perhaps took umbrage at the 'poor mechanics' in the organisation; his dedication to egalitarian ideals did not always translate into the real world. Thus in May 1795 Ritson advised his nephew against trying to join the society:

The London Corresponding Society is chiefly composed of poor mechanics who find it a sufficiently hard matter to support themselves and their families, setting aside several of their members who are languishing in penury, sickness, and confinement, and whose wives and children are literally perishing for want. I would therefore recommend it to you to make no more applications of this sort ... To confess the truth, the more I see of these modern patriots and philosophers the less I like them.[323]

Ritson's dislike of the LCS aside, he became an evangelist for the cause of democracy: he may not have been religious but in Paine's teachings he had found a message to spread. In spite of his counselling his nephew to lay aside his politics, he continually sent Frank books and pamphlets such as 'Thelwalls Vindication, Paines (new) Rights of man'.[324]

Yet Ritson had to be careful. At several points during the 1790s he felt he was under surveillance by the authorities.[325] While he occasionally addressed his associates as 'Citizen', by 1794 he wrote to Mr Laing and said:

> I dare not call you Citizen, lest … your scoundrel judges should send me for fourteen years to Botany Bay; only I am in good hopes, before that event takes place, they will all be sent to the devil.[326]

Although Ritson had exchanged transcripts of songs and ballads with friends since his late teenage years, he decided against sending his friend Mr Harrison a copy of the French Revolutionary anthem 'Ça Ira' because 'it is become high treason either to sing or whistle it, and of course, I presume, misprision of treason, at least, to possess, communicate, or speak of it.'[327] Whether or not Ritson's communications were being monitored by the government is hard to determine, but he had good reason to be paranoid. As Anglo-French tensions spilled over into outright war in 1793 the British government further restricted the activities of English radical clubs up and down the country. A series of

JOHN HORNE TOOKE.
(From an old Print.)

John Horne Tooke, one of several radicals arrested on spurious charges of treason during Pitt's Terror. (British Library)

113

repressive measures which curbed freedom of assembly and censoring 'seditious libel'—supported by none other than that 'saint', the anti-slavery campaigner William Wilberforce (1759–1833)—were enacted by the government. The British government's campaign against English radicals seemed, in government's eyes, increasingly necessary because the French Jacobin-dominated Committee of Public Safety in Paris had begun executing the enemies of the French Revolution, beginning with the beheading of Louis XVI by guillotine in 1792. They did not want similar scenes breaking out in Britain. The French Reign of Terror lasted until 1794, after the deaths of 40,000 people, with the fall of the Terror's architect Robespierre, who was also despatched via the guillotine. Ritson actually despised Robespierre and lambasted fellow radicals who sought to 'wash the blood' from Robespierre's hands, although Ritson remained a radical.[328] Because of the Terror the British government, led by William Pitt the Younger, was not above spying on its citizens. At one point during 'Pitt's Terror' members of the LCS felt themselves 'surrounded by spies' who would intercept their correspondence and infiltrate their meetings.[329] The authorities took still more direct action against suspected 'traitors': local magistrates in provincial towns often directed gangs of loyalists to attack local political clubs.[330]

During the 1790s there were over 200 prosecutions for sedition in Britain.[331] Between 1792 and 1794 over thirty radicals found themselves in gaol charged with sedition. The most notorious cases were the arrests and trials of LCS members Thomas Hardy (1752–1832), John Horne Tooke (1736–1812), and John Thelwall (1764–1834). These trials were a sensation—tickets were sold to the public at vastly inflated prices because the men had become famous, or infamous. To get free admission to the trial, for the first and last time in his career, Ritson wore his wig and cloak and sat with his fellow barristers to watch the proceedings. He admired Horne Tooke even before his 'radicalisation', for in 1790 the latter stood for the parliamentary seat of Westminster, but Horne Tooke lost, collecting only forty-three votes, Ritson remarking that he did so because of his refusal to bribe anybody.[332]

Ritson offered Thelwall free legal advice before the trial. He had learnt that a magistrate, John Reeves—the founder of the reactionary Association for Preserving Liberty and Property against Republicans and Levellers—intended to break the law and arrest Thelwall without a warrant and deliver him into the hands of the 'press gang', or impress

One of the reasons the British government began suppressing home-grown radicals' activities was because of the Reign of Terror in France, when the Jacobin-dominated Committee of Public Safety decided that 'terror' would be needed to safeguard the revolution.

service. This would have seen Thelwall compelled to serve in the royal navy. Ritson advised Thelwall that he was within his rights to resist arrest and flexed his professional muscles as High Bailiff to Thelwall's advantage, as Thelwall recorded in his memoirs:

> Mr Ritson sent me word that Mr. [Reeves] (the magistrate) had determined to take me into custody … and to deliver me into the hands of a pressgang, whom he had engaged to be in waiting for the occasion; and advised me, if the attempt were made, to resist. This advice, however, I deemed imprudent, and consulted Mr. Gurney upon the occasion, who confirmed my opinion. I went, determined to try the issue upon legal grounds; and being, as well as others, in possession of the facts, to see if such a judicial conspiracy could, even in such times, be acted upon with impunity. Mr. Ritson, seeing me there, and finding me determined on

> my course, called up the beadle and other inferior officers of
> the court, and, in my hearing, instructed them, one by one, if
> Mr. [Reeves] should order me to be taken into custody, not
> to obey him. They all promised to follow Ritson's direction,
> and did, in fact, as I was afterwards informed, refuse to obey
> the magistrate when he gave them the order.[333]

Thanks to Ritson, Thelwall obtained a temporary reprieve from the harassment of corrupt law enforcement officials who were unafraid to break the law to imprison radicals.[334] We should not underestimate Ritson's bravery in holding steadfastly to his revolutionary beliefs, especially given his position as High Bailiff of the Liberty of the Savoy. His own bailiwick was in fact 'the white hot core' of conservative and reactionary sentiment in London.[335] By the end of the Napoleonic Wars in 1815, the British government had become so repressive with its networks of spies and informants, and its curbs on freedom of speech and assembly, that the historian Robert Reed declares that Britain became 'closer in spirit to that of the early years of the Third Reich than at any other time in modern history'.[336] Eventually Thelwall's trial, like that of Horne Tooke and Thomas Hardy, completely collapsed. Luckily for them the jurors realised that the charges were so obviously malicious that they were fully acquitted.

However, if the magistrates wanted to arrest someone they would soon have another weapon in their arsenal: the suspension of *habeas corpus* in 1794. The government had egg on its face not only because of the trials of Horne Tooke, Thelwall, and Hardy but also as a result of the acquittal of LCS members Paul Thomas Lemaitre, John Smith, Robert Thomas Crossfield, and George Higgins, who were alleged to have been involved in what was called the Popgun Plot—a conspiracy to assassinate George III by shooting him with a poison dart. The case collapsed when the chief witness against them had apparently died the previous year. With the suspension of *habeus corpus*, troublesome radicals could now be locked up indefinitely without a trial and save the embarrassment of having proceedings dismissed by a judge. Ritson suspected that local officials in provincial areas were pulling even dirtier tricks to get rid of those who advocated even mild political reform. In 1795, Ritson asked his nephew—who now had his own legal practice in York—about a case in which a known Bradford-based radical had been imprisoned on a charge of burglary:

> Do you know any thing about the trial of William Britton of
> Bradford, clothworker, and his man who were convicted at
> your last summer assizes of burglary, and afterward hanged?
> The charge of felony, as the brother (who was likewise
> indicted) had been telling at Eatons, was not only totally false
> and groundless, but was actually (or apparently) a diabolical
> contrivance … to take away these poor innocent people out of
> the way as suspected democrats. There had been some sort of
> riot or disturbance, in which, I do not know how, one or other
> of them was thought active … But I only learned the story at
> second-hand, and have already forgotten or confounded many
> of the particulars: the men, however, were hanged. I wish you
> would recollect, or enquire into, the nature and complexion
> of the evidence (which was that of the mistress, man and
> maid of the house, in the neighbourhood of Bradford, where
> the burglary was committed) and other circumstances of
> the prosecution; as it seems a curious method to suspect a
> man of Jacobinism, and hang him for felony. The brothers
> [sic] narrative, at any rate, appeared to have been simple and
> affecting, and to have had all the semblance of truth.[337]

One might suspect that Pitt's attacks on the rights and liberties of the British people would cause the population to protest against his government. But the British government's approach to radicals at home seemed to be winning the hearts and minds of the general public, many of whom were disgusted at the violent turn the French Revolution had taken. Even some of those famous British radical artists, writers, and intellectuals, such as Southey, Wordsworth, and Coleridge, who had initially been enthusiastic supporters of the revolution, began to turn their backs on their youthful idealism because of the Terror. France's invasion of Switzerland in January 1798 certainly did nothing to endear the revolutionary government to these British radicals who were wavering in their support for revolutionary principles. However, Ritson was a man with the courage of his convictions and would not forsake his revolutionary beliefs, and regretted that Britain's working classes seemed unwilling to fight for a more egalitarian world:

> With respect to a revolution, though I think it at no great
> distance, it seems to defy all calculation for the present.

> If the increase of taxes, the decline of manufactures, the
> high price of provisions, and the like, have no effect upon the
> *sans culottes* here, one can expect little from the reasoning
> of philosophers and politicians here.[338]

Yet nothing would dampen Ritson's belief that a great revolutionary
upheaval in Britain was imminent. He wrote to Matthew Wadeson in
1794 of 'the great change which I hope and believe is about to take
place'.[339] Wadeson did not share Ritson's politics and was probably
anxious as to whether Ritson advocated a policy of Terror in England
and whether radicals sought to redistribute wealth. So Ritson sought to
reassure his friend:

> No reformer, Painite, or whatever you please to call us,
> proposes to put himself in a worse condition than he is at
> present: and everyone has something of his own, such as it
> is—I myself have a little. You may therefore be assured that
> the most violent revolutionist is as little anxious as yourself
> for any change that would put in jeopardy the well earned
> fruits of honest industry. If, indeed, you were a sinecure
> placeman or pimping pensioner of ten or twenty thousand a
> year you might I confess have some little reason to fear.[340]

(A 'pensioner' was someone who was in receipt of an annual government
stipend, which was usually granted for having advanced the interests of
the government or the nation in some way). Ritson ended his letter by
advising Wadeson to read Thomas Paine's book and, if he has no interest
in furthering the cause of an English revolution, then Ritson advised
Wadeson 'to remain a temperate spectator'.[341]

However, Ritson was not intolerant of those with differing political
opinions, and the same letter to Wadeson proves that he could find
some humour in the contrast between his own Paineite beliefs and
conservatism:

> Well, you heard that I had got into France at last, knowing
> how long and anxiously I had waited to see it. My sentiments
> are and ever have been so entirely correspondent to the
> ruling measures that I had only to rejoice at seeing a theory

I had so long admired reduced to practice. I know that you and I do not exactly agree in our political principles. Your creed, if I mistake not, is that a few men, whether born with boots and spurs or at least who have got them on, have a right to bridle, saddle and harness the rest, and ride or drive them with as much gentleness or violence as they occasion; and that it is much more for the latter to jog on peaceably and quietly than by kicking or flinging to provoke a larger portion of hard blows and hunger. This is I believe a pretty fair representation. I must however do you the justice to allow that you are an aristocrat of the most moderate description, since I believe you only wish to ride with a single spur and a little switch. They order these matters very differently in the country I was speaking of, which, owing to the dissemination of those sacred and fundamental principles of liberty and equality, enjoys a degree of happiness and prosperity to which it has hitherto been a stranger: but which is very typical of that to which it will shortly arrive.[342]

Theodora McNutt lists Mr Wadeson as a grocer, although Ritson in that letter calls him an aristocrat.[343] Wadeson does appear to have been a local official of some note, although I can find no records of him being an aristocrat of even the most minor rank. Perhaps Ritson was implying that he an aristocrat 'in spirit'; it may even have simply been a private joke between the pair.

When all is said, Ritson was a minor figure in the world of eighteenth-century radical politics. He never wrote great political treatises, as did his friend William Godwin or his idol Thomas Paine. Ritson became interested in the history of men who had fought against the establishment, especially those from the north of England. It was for this reason that, from his friend Mr Harrison, Ritson borrowed the manuscript of the autobiography of Captain John Hodgson, a man from Halifax, Yorkshire, who, during the English Revolution of the 1640s, took up arms on the side of the Parliamentarians and fought alongside Thomas Fairfax at the Battle of Leeds and Capture of Wakefield during 1643. Ritson had transcribed it in full by 1794 but never published it. Perhaps he was busy putting the finishing touches to his next publication.

𝕽𝕺𝕭𝕴𝕹 𝕳𝕺𝕺𝕯:

A

COLLECTION

OF ALL THE ANCIENT

POEMS, SONGS, AND BALLADS,

NOW EXTANT,

RELATIVE TO THAT CELEBRATED

ENGLISH OUTLAW:

TO WHICH ARE PREFIXED

HISTORICAL ANECDOTES OF HIS LIFE.

IN TWO VOLUMES.

VOLUME THE FIRST.

In this our fpacious ifle I think there is not one,
But he ' of ROBIN HOOD hath heard ' and Little John;
And to the end of time the tales fhall ne'er be done
Of Scarlock, George a Green, and Much the miller's fon,
Of Tuck, the merry friar, which many a fermon made
In praife of ROBIN HOOD, his out-laws, and their trade.

DRAYTON.

LONDON:

PRINTED FOR T. EGERTON, WHITEHALL, AND
J. JOHNSON, ST. PAULS-CHURCH-YARD.

MDCCXCV.

Title page to Joseph Ritson's *Robin Hood: A Collection of All the Ancient Poems, Songs, and Ballads, Now Extant, Relative to that Celebrated English Outlaw* (1795).

Ritson's next publication would be one which, thanks to his new-found radical politics, would bequeath to posterity a legacy that, arguably, would eclipse the famous political philosophers of his day. He took the legend of the medieval outlaw Robin Hood, who had hitherto been imagined as a comic figure and lowly thief, and fundamentally reshaped it into that of a revolutionary freedom fighter. Having toned down the radicalism in his letters during the time of Pitt's terror, Ritson needed an outlet through which to express his revolutionary zeal. And so we come to our examination of Ritson's magnum opus: *Robin Hood: A Collection of All the Ancient Poems, Songs, and Ballads, Now Extant, Relative to that Celebrated English Outlaw* published in two volumes in 1795. He had collected a lot of material and was planning a full volume on Robin Hood as early as 1791, for in the preface to *Pieces of Ancient Popular Poetry*, which includes the ballad of a now 'forgotten' medieval outlaw named Adam Bell, Ritson 'apologised' to his reader by saying,

> It might naturally enough excite the surprise of the intelligent reader, that in a professed republication of popular poetry, nothing should occur upon a subject indisputably the most popular of all—the history of our renowned English archer ROBIN HOOD. Some apology is undoubtedly necessary on this head, as the omission is by no means owing to ignorance or neglect. In fact, the poems, ballads, and historical or miscellaneous matter, in existence, relative to this celebrated outlaw, are sufficient to furnish the contents of even a couple of volumes considerably bulkyer [sic] than the present; and fully deserve to appear in a separate publication, 'unmix'd with baser matter'.[344]

Ritson's *Robin Hood* retailed at 12 shillings, which was more expensive than previous anthologies of Robin Hood songs that were published under the title *Robin Hood's Garland*, which retailed at 4d. However, it was worth the cost because Ritson included four of the earliest sources which, until his book, had been languishing in archives away from public view. These were 'A Gest of Robyn Hode' (1495), which Ritson probably transcribed as early as 1782 when he visited Cambridge University Library,[345] 'Robin Hood and the Potter' (1468), 'A True Tale of Robin Hood' (1632), and 'Robin Hood and Guy of Gisborne'. This

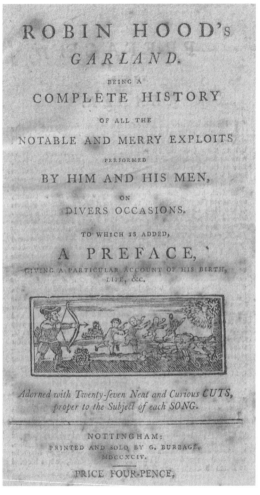

ROBIN HOOD's
GARLAND.

BEING A
COMPLETE HISTORY

OF ALL THE
NOTABLE AND MERRY EXPLOITS

PERFORMED
BY HIM AND HIS MEN,

ON
DIVERS OCCASIONS.

TO WHICH IS ADDED,
A PREFACE,
GIVING A PARTICULAR ACCOUNT OF HIS BIRTH,
LIFE, &c.

Adorned with Twenty-feven Neat and Curious CUTS, proper to the Subject of each SONG.

NOTTINGHAM:
PRINTED AND SOLD BY G. BURBAGE.
MDCCXCIV.

PRICE FOUR-PENCE,

Before the publication of Ritson's *Robin Hood*, stories of the outlaw had circulated in cheaply made 'garlands', which only included songs of seventeenth- and eighteenth-century origin, or he was simply a common criminal in true crime books such as Charles Johnson's *History of the Highwaymen* (1734).

last one was first printed in Percy's *Reliques*.[346] As well as printing these early sources, Ritson scoured archives around the country and found virtually every scrap of information relating to his hero and from these was able to write a biography of Robin Hood.

Before Ritson, in most retellings of the Robin Hood legend the outlaw been a common thief who did not even steal from the rich and give to the poor, as in the three earliest Robin Hood tales. He had also been a rather inept outlaw in seventeenth-century ballads, which usually see Robin Hood get beaten up by a stranger in the forest. He was also something of a brute in the works of Charles Johnson and Alexander Smith. Being well-acquainted with Robin Hood's 'former biographers', Ritson's footnotes reveal the fact that his own publication was partly an attempt to improve upon what he saw as Johnson's sub-standard scholarship.[347] Ritson's account reads as though it were a criminal biography: Robin Hood was born c.1160 and the reader is told that he became an outlaw as a result of having led a wild and profligate youth:

> In his youth, he is reported to have been of a wild and extravagant disposition; insomuch that, his inheritance being consumed or forfeited by his excesses, and his person outlawed for debt, either from necessity or choice, he sought an asylum in the woods and forests.[348]

Charles Johnson had come to a similar conclusion in 1734 by stating that Robin Hood was 'of a roving disposition' in his youth and, because of an inability to follow a trade, became an outlaw.[349] Finally Ritson gave an account of the outlaw's death in 1247 based on the ballad tale of 'Robin Hood's Death' found in Ritson's second volume. It was through the treachery of a woman that Robin met his end. When Robin was an old man he was said to have fallen ill and applied to the Prioress of Kirklees to be bled, but the prioress, in concert with Roger of Doncaster, bleeds him to death.[350]

Following the account of Robin Hood's death, Ritson gave the reader a brief account of Robin's moral character:

> He was active, brave, prudent, patient, possessed of uncommon bodly strength, and considerable skill; just, generous, benevolent, faithful, and beloved or revered by his followers for his excellent and amiable qualities. Fordun, a priest, extols his piety, and piety, by a priest, is regarded as the perfection of virtue; Major (as we have seen) pronounces him the most humane and the Prince of all Robbers.[351]

While earlier criminal biographers appropriated Robin Hood's story to warn readers of the consequences of following a life of sin, Ritson had a political point to make: Robin Hood's life was one of struggle against tyranny. Ritson's Robin Hood is both an outlaw and freedom fighter who 'set Kings, judges, and magistrates at defiance'.[352] Robin Hood appeared as a truly heroic figure:

> A man who, in a barbarous age and under a complicated tyranny, displayed a spirit of freedom and independence, which has endeared him to the common people, whose cause he maintained, (for all opposition to tyranny is the cause of the people,) and, in spite of the malicious endeavours of pitiful monks, by whom history was consecrated to the

crimes and follies of sainted idiots and titled ruffians, to suppress all record of his patriotic exertions and patriotic acts, will render his name immortal.[353]

Although Ritson's Robin Hood appeared at the beginning of the Romantic era, when writers and artists began looking back to the medieval past, the idea of Robin Hood as a patriotic 'independent' man actually draws upon neo-classical ideals of civic virtue combined with love of political liberty. At its more extreme end, neoclassical 'independence' was certainly inclined to republicanism.[354] This was perfectly in line with Ritson's Paineite radicalism. A kingless republic was the most perfect state of society, but in a republic people had both rights and obligations; a man had to work for the good of the community, and doing so was the ultimate patriotic act. Robin Hood was a patriot who sided with the *people* of the nation. His civic virtue was evinced in his clear social mission:

> In these forests, and with this company, he for many years reigned like an independent sovereign; at perpetual war, indeed, with the King of England, and all his subjects, with an exception, however, of the poor and needy, and such as were "desolate and oppressed," or stood in need of his protection.[355]

Yes, Robin and his men were robbers but

> That our hero and his companions, while they lived in the woods, had recourse to robbery for their better support, is neither to be concealed nor denied. Testimonies to this purpose, indeed, would be equally endless and unnecessary. Furdun, in the fourteenth century, calls him, "*ille famosissimus siccarious*," that most celebrated robber, and Major calls him "*famatissimi latrones*." But it is to be remembered ... that, in these exertions of power, he took away the goods of rich men only; never killing any person, unless he was attacked or resisted; that he would not suffer a woman to be maltreated; nor ever took anything from the poor, but charitably fed them with the wealth he drew from the abbots.[356]

'He was active, brave, prudent': an illustration from Ritson's Robin Hood depicting the outlaw rescuing three men from being hanged.

Ritson presented the political situation in twelfth century England—for which we read also late eighteenth century England—as one of a clash between good and evil, tyranny and liberty.[357] To those who might question Robin's methods in establishing an 'independent sovereignty' in opposition to the King, Ritson simply replies, 'what better title King Richard could pretend to the territory and people of England, than Robin Hood had to the dominion of Barnsdale and Sherwood, is a question humbly submitted to the consideration of the political philosopher'.[358] This is a subtle nod to the writings of Thomas Paine, who questioned the legitimacy of a monarchy which was imposed on England through the actions of a medieval Norman warlord. As Paine said in *Common Sense* about William the Conqueror: 'A French bastard landing with an armed Banditti and establishing himself king of England against the consent of the natives, is in plain terms a very paltry rascally original. It certainly hath no divinity in it'.[359] Paine drew upon the idea of the 'Norman Yoke'. Before the Conquest it was thought by radicals such as Paine that the Anglo-Saxons, with their trials-by-jury and the idea of the king as 'first among equals' who was subject to their laws, enjoyed an unparalleled degree of political liberty. William the Conqueror's victory at Hastings in 1066 changed all of this and led to the centuries-long dominance of a small aristocratic oligarchy. They maintained their hegemony in the eighteenth century by ensuring, through bribes, pensions, and sinecures, their dominance of government, civil, and religious institutions. This modern system of corruption had a name: 'Old Corruption'. The term was used by both the middle and working classes to describe a political system that facilitated institutionalised corruption in government, exacerbated by the fact that before 1832 few people had the vote and so could not vote to change this state of affairs. Ritson also took aim, not only at medieval Catholicism but against the clergy in his own day:

> Our hero, indeed, seems to have held bishops, abbots, priests, and monks, in a word, all the clergy, regular or secular, in decided aversion [...] and, in this part of his conduct, perhaps, the pride, avarice, uncharitableness, and hypocrisy of these clerical drones, or pious locusts, (*too many of whom are still permitted to pray upon the labour of the industrious, and are supported, in pampered luxury, at the expence of those whom their useless and pernicious craft tends to remain in superstitious ignorance and irrational servility,*) will afford him ample justification.[360]

'Clerical drones and pious locusts' is not simply a manifestation of traditional English Protestant anti-Catholicism but an indictment of all clergymen. His anti-religious sentiments would have been relatively uncontroversial and his appropriation of the medieval figure of Robin Hood legend meant that he could avoid any censure from the government. After all, who in high places could have objected to a work which did not explicitly criticise the current government? This was a book about Robin Hood, an English hero whom everybody loved!

In some of the earliest texts from the fifteenth century, Robin Hood is said to be a humble yeoman, but Ritson alleges that Robin Hood was actually a lord. The depiction of Robin Hood as an aristocrat emerged in the work of a sixteenth-century playwright named Anthony Munday. One of the modern world's foremost Robin Hood scholars, Stephen Knight, argues that whenever the famous outlaw is cast as the Earl of Huntingdon, then it is a 'gentrified' portrayal. Ritson did indeed point out that Robin held the earldom of Huntingdon, but he qualifies it.[361] He says that

Right and below:
Engravings of Robin Hood
from the early modern
printed books which Ritson
consulted for his book on
the outlaw's legend.

Robin Hood was 'frequently stiled [sic], and commonly reputed to have been Earl of Huntingdon; a title to which, *in the latter part of his life, at least, he actually appears to have had some pretension*'.[362] This was not Ritson being a poor historian and overlooking inconvenient facts that did not fit his narrative. He was a highly skilled scholar and aware that the earlier texts depict Robin as a yeoman. The 'latter part of his life' statement in all probability stems from Ritson's familiarity with the 'Gest of Robyn Hode', at the end of which Robin joins the king's household.[363] Ritson was saying that Robin Hood *might* have become a nobleman. In his footnotes Ritson elaborated further upon the matter and acknowledged that there are debates on the issue.[364] He did believe that Robin Hood possessed 'nobility'—that is, *nobility of character*. As a possible answer to Thomas Percy—who maintained that Robin's earldom was entirely fictitious—he cites Munday's second play where, after Robin has turned to outlawry, he desires not to be known by any titles but as 'Robin Hood, plain Robin Hoode,/That honest yeoman stout and good'.[365] Evidence from Munday's plays allowed Ritson to explain why an engraving of Robin Hood's grave stone in Kirklees, West Yorkshire, called him a lord as several ballads did, and why early medieval texts depicted him as a yeoman. Thus, by Ritson's reasoning, it was Robin Hood's commitment to egalitarianism that accounted for seemingly contradictory tales about his nobility.

Some modern Robin Hood scholars have expressed surprise at the fact that Ritson depicted Robin Hood as a lord. But being a lord did not preclude one from leading a revolt or being on the side of the people. We recall that it was the bigoted Lord George Gordon who incited the Gordon Riots in 1780. A more progressive British aristocrat was Charles Lennox, 3rd Duke of Richmond, a member of the House of Lords, who brought forward a Bill to parliament in 1780 calling for manhood suffrage, equally-sized electoral districts, and annual elections. He even presented a draft of a projected written English constitution along with his bill in the Lords. Unfortunately, the bill was thrown out of the Lords, for it was presented on the same day that the Gordon Riots began. In his youth, Richmond was an avid reader of the works of many political reformers. His testimony in Horne Tooke's trial, where he stated that he had promoted the same views on parliamentary reform back in 1780 so Horne Tooke's views could not possibly be seditious, was one of the factors which led to the latter's acquittal. As a Francophile, Ritson may have had in mind either General Lafayette (1757–1854), who contributed to the writing of the Declaration of the Rights of Man and Citizen, or perhaps Louis Phillippe (1747—93), a member of the French Royal family who lent his support to the revolutionaries and even changed his name to Phillippe Égalité.

An eighteenth-century reader, having perused Ritson's biography of Robin Hood, would then have come to the collection of the ballads themselves. The first volume contained four of the earliest Robin Hood

Above, below and overleaf: A selection of the many engravings which John Bewick produced for Ritson's *Robin Hood.*

poems which Ritson had found, all painstakingly transcribed to be as 'accurate' as possible to the original printed books and manuscripts. The biography of Robin Hood was also placed in the first volume. Twenty-eight songs of seventeenth- and eighteenth-century origin were included in the second volume. This was a book for readers; very few melodies to the modern songs were included in spite of the fact that they had survived into Ritson's time.

Ritson's book was decorated by the famous Newcastle-based John Bewick (1760–95), brother of the more famous Thomas Bewick (1753–1828). The Bewick firm specialised in creating picturesque engravings of rural life for a variety of publications including books, newspapers, periodicals, and business cards. There is nothing in Ritson's letters to suggest that he was good friends with the leading men of the firm but he liked what they produced because he had previously commissioned the Bewick firm to produce illustrations for his *Pieces of Ancient Popular Poetry*. The Bewicks' images were one of the main selling points for *Robin Hood*, as is indicated in an advertisement in *The Morning Chronicle*:

> This day is published, price 12s … elegantly printed on fine paper with vignettes, by the Bewicks, "Robin Hood: A Collection of All the Ancient Poems, Songs, and Ballads, Now Extant, Relative to that Celebrated English Outlaw, to which are prefixed historical anecdotes of his life."[366]

Yet there was a tension between the radical ideal of Robin Hood conveyed in Ritson's text and the predominantly rustic rural images which Bewick made for the book which were anachronistic. Robin and his men appeared more like Georgian country gentlemen than medieval outlaws. The illustration which accompanied 'A Gest of Robyn Hode' depicts attests to the above statement. Robin and Little John are sitting peacefully under a tree while a deer can be seen in the background. The clothing that each man is wearing looks more Georgian than medieval. Robin is wearing a hat with a large feather attached to it.[367] In fact very few of Bewick's images for Ritson were decidedly medieval, with the exception of the view inside the Bishop of York's chambers to illustrate the second section of the 'Gest'. Yet in some ways, although the images were not historicist interpretations of medieval life, they were perfect for Robin Hood because they depicted an idealised vision of life in England, a time free from political tyranny, before the onset of industrialisation in Britain and enclosures of the common land. As one critic puts it, most of the images produced by the Bewick firm were 'snapshots of human life lived collectively in idealised harmony, they also reflect an overt dependence on a common good … which assert the right to gather water or game from common sources'.[368] Overall, when Bewick's images are considered, the image of Robin Hood that the reader received from Ritson's text was at once radical, utopian, and pastoral.

In spite of Ritson's portrayal of his revolutionary Robin Hood's actions as patriotic, Ritson's old foes at *The Critical Review* smirked at the book:

> [Robin Hood's] character is here estimated too highly. He certainly possessed a spirit of freedom and independence; but, however we may be inclined to excuse the manner in which that spirit was displayed, it was not without a smile that we saw it denominated patriotism.[369]

In spite of the reviewer's snarky comments, Ritson's book became highly influential in the overall development of the Robin Hood legend. It truly was Ritson's biography of Robin Hood that gave the world the image of the outlaw/freedom fighter that has persisted in so many retellings right through to the twenty-first century.

Chapter 5

'Farewell for the Present': Joseph Ritson's Later Life and Death

After *Robin Hood*, Ritson published very little. By the 1790s he was not a well man. Since the beginning of the decade he had complained that the 'little hope that the nervous complaint I have mentioned myself subject to, and which I suppose has been stealing upon me for years, will give way to medicine.'[370] Ritson sensed that his illness was affecting his ability to carry out small tasks and at times rendered his ability to write to friends difficult. 'I could indeed offer several apologies for my seeming neglect,' he told his friend Mr Harrison in June 1790, 'but shall content myself to trouble you with one, which is, that I am become so nervous, as they call it, that I have very seldom either resolution or capacity to write the shortest note on the most trivial occasion'.[371]

A 'nervous complaint' could mean a variety of ailments ranging from migraines or headaches to melancholy.[372] There were plenty of cynics in Ritson's day who thought that such 'nervous complaints' were merely hypochondria—men who suffered from nervous disorders were subjected to derogatory stereotypes and accused of being 'unmanly'.[373] Nervous problems were seen as something that women were subject to; Elizabeth Bennet's mother in Jane Austen's *Pride and Prejudice* (1813) is one famous fictional sufferer whose husband has 'no compassion for my poor nerves'.[374] Ritson was hardly a Mrs Bennet, but his complaint did caused him serious troubles. 'My complaint,' he stated in 1798, 'is neither a fever nor a consumption: but it renders my existence miserable, and I have no hope of getting the better of it … I am daily forgetting the most common words in the language.'[375] Some of Ritson's associates put his suffering down to his vegetarian diet. Judging by what would eventually happen to Ritson, his malady was more than just 'in his head'; severe headaches left him debilitated for days at a time or sent him raving in his apartment for hours.

It would be seven years after *Robin Hood* that Ritson mustered up the energy for another round of research and publishing. He had always been a stickler for editorial accuracy, even if in some of his more popular publications he had, for the benefit of the general reader, allowed a few emendations to the texts of ballads and poems to make them readable. However, produced, in 1802, a 'pure' edition, in three volumes, of Old and Middle English songs, poems, and ballads: *Ancient Engleish Metrical Romanceës*. Ritson had grown quite confident in his abilities and was aware that he was now numbered among the public as one of the foremost historians of the age, because for the first time ever, he attached his name to the title page, where previously his works had been published anonymously—perhaps this was a response to the Society of Antiquaries' refusal to admit him as a member. Ritson's 'literary patriotism' shined through in the introduction, for this collection of epic tales was meant to show the very best literary endeavours of the English people from past ages.[376] He may by this point have been a republican, but he was also a proud Englishman and took pride in his nation's heritage. He wrote that the work had been labour of love that had been in production over many years. Of course, no Ritson book would have been complete without a pre-emptive snipe at his would-be critics:

> Brought to an end with much industry and more attention,
> in a continue'd state of ill-health, and low spirits, the editour
> abandons it to general censure, with cold indifference,
> expecting little favour, and less profit; but certain, at any rate,
> to be insulted by the malignant and calumnious personalitys
> of a base and prostitute gang of lurking assassins, who stab
> in the dark, and whose poison daggers he has allready
> experience'd.[377]

'Prostitute gang of lurking assassins' must surely rank among Ritson's most inventive snipes, aimed no doubt at the hacks at the *Critical Review* who 'stab in the dark', that is, anonymously, as many reviews in magazines were then written. The first volume of the *Metrical Romanceës* contained, as was usual for Ritson's books, critical essays on the subject at hand—which repeated earlier criticisms of Warton and Percy—

before presenting readers with transcriptions of the primary sources. The *Metrical Romanceës* was certainly an important anthology for it included literary gems such as the Arthurian romance 'Ywain and Gawain', which until Ritson's book had only existed in manuscript form. He again accused Percy of having been dishonest with readers in having edited the texts of certain poems and Ritson stated that there was 'scarcely one single poem, song, or ballad' that Percy had not taken it upon himself to 'improve'.[378] The *Metrical Romanceës*, therefore, would allow readers to see some of the poems printed in Percy's books in their 'true' unaltered state.

In the end, Ritson need not have worried about the 'prostitute

Robert Southey

The poet Robert Southey, a fan of Ritson's *Metrical Romanceës*. Ritson particularly admired Southey's first collection of poetry.

gang of lurking assassins'; his foes at the *Critical Review* refused to review this latest work. But *Metrical Romanceës* was critically acclaimed in other quarters of the press. The future Poet Laureate, Robert Southey (1774–1843), praised Ritson's new book in the *Annual Review*.[379] Ritson had admired Southey since he came to public notice with the publication of his first anthology of poetry in 1799.[380] No doubt he would have been thoroughly pleased with the approbation of this up-and-coming author—Southey and Ritson's paths had probably crossed at some point in the 1790s; the former had attempted to enter the legal profession briefly during that decade and was also a radical. Southey, in fact, had written a Robin Hood novel in 1791 entitled 'Harold; or, The Castle of Morford', and one wonders whether the pair of them ever conversed on the subject.[381]

While *Metrical Romanceës* was lauded for its accuracy, Ritson gave his critics ammunition for criticism in one respect. For years, he had been devising his own 'pure' version of the English language—readers will notice the somewhat odd spelling of the words 'English' and 'romances' in his book's title. In the preface he included in this book, Ritson let loose his own curious orthography. A flavour of this is found in the 'advertisement' at the beginning of the first volume:

> The publication so much desire'd, and so eloquently recommended by this learned and ingenious writeër, has at length been undertakeën; and to what he has say'd in its favour nothing remains to be aded but some little information as to the mode in which it makes its appearance.[382]

The rationale for some of these changes was odd. It is unclear, for instance, why 'desire'd' was thought to differ in any way from the regular 'desired'. According to Bronson, Ritson's unpublished notes suggested that 'where a word is found in French as in Saxon, always derive it from the latter'.[383] This still does not quite explain 'desire'd' but presumably it made sense to Ritson. Ritson had among his unpublished manuscripts the beginnings of what he intended would be 'A New Dictionary for the Orthography, Pronunciation, and Etymology of the English Language', in which the definitions of several words revealed his own republican and anti-clerical biases:

DEMOCRAT. An advocate for liberty, equality, and fraternity.

[…]

MONKEY. An animal resembleing man. The name was, in all probability, given, originally, by the Spaniards, either to some species of this animal which reminded them of a monk, or to the whole tribe on account of their mischievous and odious qualitys.

[…]

SCEPTRE. A kings bauble.[384]

It was perhaps for the best that Ritson never published this dictionary.

Ritson published another book in 1802: *Bibliographia Poetica*. George Steevens, whose work Ritson had offered several criticisms upon in the 1770s, had evidently forgiven him at some point because the book, as Ritson says,

> Was originally suggested in the course of a conversation with the late George Steevens, of whose familiar acquaintance the editour is proud to boast; and whose rich and wel-selected library, supply'd the title of many a rare and curious volume.[385]

Steevens was not the only old 'foe' that Ritson cited as an inspiration, for he also stated that the work could not have been completed without the pioneering work of 'Warton's ingenious, though too frequently inaccurate, *History of English Poetry.*' The *Bibliographia Poetica* was a series of short biographical entries on poets from the twelfth to sixteenth centuries with a brief list of what they had written. Notable among them is one Ritson writes about a minor fifteenth-century parson named Gilbert Pylkynton:

> Parson, as some have thought, of the parish of Tottenham, in Middlesex, is supposed, by his successor, Wilhelm Bedwell, to be the author of an excellent song, intitled "The turnament of Tottenham, or the wooing, wenning, and wedding of Tibbe, the reeves daughter there."[387]

The next part of the 'Pylkynton' entry is most curious, for contained within the manuscript was 'a story of Robin Hood, and little Iohn'.[388] The Robin Hood tale to which Ritson refers was composed c. 1465 but now goes by the name of 'Robin Hood and the Monk'. It was never included in Ritson's *Robin Hood* in 1795 so his discovery of this little note must have been after that year. Yet it is evident that Ritson was the first Robin Hood scholar at least to have knowledge of the manuscript's existence. It would not be until Robert Jamieson published this 'Story of Robin Hood' in his *Popular Ballads and Songs* (1806) as 'Robyn Hode and the Munke' that it would be brought to public notice.[389]

We noted previously that Ritson was not intolerant of people with different political opinions. He maintained a warm friendship with a young Scottish Tory, a lawyer named Walter Scott. Scott was born in a third floor flat in 1771 in College Wynd, Edinburgh, 'a cramped, dimly lit alleyway with poor sanitation and little fresh air'.[390] In this squalid environment, six of Scott's siblings died and Scott, at two years of age, contracted polio, or 'infantile paralysis'. This resulted in him being

Vincent Brooks Day & Son.

The poet and novelist Walter Scott, who maintained a good friendship with Ritson in his later years, and who was inspired, after reading Ritson's *Robin Hood*, to write the most successful Robin Hood novel ever published: *Ivanhoe* (1819) (British Library)

disabled his whole life, with one of his legs being shorter and weaker than the other—a common occurrence in polio survivors (The Writers' Museum in Edinburgh has one of Scott's childhood rocking horses on display, with one footrest higher than the other to accommodate the young lad's disability).[391] After he had recovered from his illness, Scott was sent to rural Sandyknowe to live with his grandparents. It was under their guardianship that he imbibed a love of old ballads and heroic medieval tales. He went to school and became an advocate—the equivalent of a barrister in the Scottish court system—retaining his love of poetry into later life. In his early twenties, Scott began collecting, with a view to publishing, a collection of old Scottish songs, much as Ritson had done in *Scotish Songs*. Scott's antiquarian project brought him in touch with Ritson. He invited Ritson to stay with him for a couple of days in the summer of 1801. The two, in spite of their profound difference in politics, forged a friendship that would last to the end of Ritson's life. Scott recalled Ritson's visit well:

> I had a great kindness for poor Mr. Ritson; and always experienced from him the readiest, kindest, & most liberal assistance in the objects of our joint pursuit, in which he was so well qualified to direct the researches of an inferior antiquary. One thing I observed in his temper, an attention to which rendered communication with him much more easy than if it was neglected: it was, that Mr. Ritson was very literal and precise in his own statements, and, expecting you to be equally so, was much disgusted with any loose or inaccurate averment. I remember rather a ludicrous instance of this. He made me a visit of two days at my cottage near Laswade, where I then spent the summer. In the course of conversing on such subjects, we talked of the Roman Wall; and I was surprized to find that he had adopted, on the authority of some person at Hexham, a strong persuasion that its remains were nowhere apparent, at least not above a foot or two in height. I hastily assured him that this was so far from being true, that I had myself seen a portion of it standing almost entire, high enough to break a man's neck. Of this Ritson took a formal memorandum, and having visited the place (Glenwhelt, near Gilsland), he wrote back

to me, or rather I think to John Leyden, "that he had seen the wall; that he really thought that a fall from it would break one's neck: at least it was so high as to render the experiment dangerous." I immediately saw what a risk I had been in, for you may believe I had no idea of being taken quite so literally. I was very indignant at the insult offered to his memory, in one of the periodical publications, after his decease, imputing the unfortunate malady with which he was afflicted to providential vengeance and retribution, for which the editor, in exact retributive justice, deserved to be damned for a brutal scoundrel.[392]

The friendship was even more unusual in view of the fact that Ritson had always disliked Scots—one of Ritson's pseudonyms in *The Gentleman's Magazine* was 'Anti-Scot'. But Ritson really warmed to young Walter who by all accounts was one of the friendliest men one could ever meet.[393] After this visit, Scott and Ritson maintained a very friendly

LASSWADE COTTAGE

Walter Scott's cottage at Lasswade which Ritson visited in 1802. (From a photograph in Charles S. Olcott's *The Country of Walter Scott* (1913))

correspondence. Ritson was always on hand to provide Scott with an answer to any query he had and Ritson always addressed Scott in his letters as 'My Dear Sir', or 'My Dear and Honoured Sir'.[394] It was a friendship which, as Scott's comments reveal, was dear to him as well. Scott went on to achieve celebrity status as the author of a number of novels and poems in the early nineteenth century, and in the Victorian era was regarded as one of the best British novelists. It was Ritson's work on Robin Hood which would inspire Scott to write, in 1819, what is perhaps the best Robin Hood novel ever published: *Ivanhoe*.

Having lived all his life as a vegetarian, Ritson set down his thoughts on the subject in a lengthy pamphlet entitled *An Essay on Abstinence from Animal Food as a Moral Duty* (1802), published by the radical printer Richard Phillips, who earlier had printed Thomas Paine's *Rights of Man* and had even spent time in Newgate during Pitt's Terror.[395] *Animal Food* was written with a simple moral message: to convince people to stop eating meat. Bringing his historical knowledge to bear upon the subject, he quotes a long list of writers, ancient and modern, whose writings held that animals' lives were of equal worth to that of humans. He therefore had very little respect for butchers, saying in one part that

> The butcher knocks down the stately ox with no more compassion than the blacksmith hammers a horse-shoe, and plunges his knife into the throat of an innocent lamb, with as little reluctance as the tailor sticks his needle into the collar of a coat.[396]

It was lucky, then, that local officials in Ritson's home town of Stockton-on-Tees had removed the butcher's trade from the town centre before he was born. Another observation he made was that men should not eat animals because humans themselves were animals. Published over half a century before Charles Darwin published *On the Origin of Species* (1859), one of Ritson's observations on the nature of the animal kingdom is striking:

> Naturalists distinguish most, if not all, animals, by classes or *genera*: as the lion, tiger, leopard, and so forth, are say'd to be of the cat-kind, from a general resemblance, in form

or figure, though not in size or strength, to that individual. Man, in like manner, may, with equal propriety, be arrange'd under the monkey-kind; there being the same degree of analogy between the man and the monkey, as between the lion and the cat; and there being, allso, in each of these classes, intermediate animals of different sizees, ranks, or degrees, by which the several species, which compose it, are approximateed or connected, like the links of a chain: thus between the cat and the lion, are the serval, the syagush, the lynx, the tiger-cat, the ounce, the panther, the leopard, and the tiger; and just so, between the monkey and the man, are the maimon, the wandrow, the mandril, the gibbon or long arm'd ape, the pongo, and the ourang-outang; each gradually increasing in size and strength. Man, therefor, in a state of nature, was, if not the real ourang-outang of the forests and mountains of Asia or Africa at the present day, at least, an animal of the same family, and very nearly resembling it.[397]

When Darwin wrote his ground-breaking book he was 'standing upon the shoulders' of those scientists, or 'naturalists' as they called themselves, who had come before him. Benoît de Maillet (1656–1738), for example, posited that life in the universe developed without divine guidance.[398] In 1751, Pierre Louis Maupertuis claimed that over many generations, species could adapt to their environment and in some cases entirely new species would be formed.[399] Ritson's purpose in identifying mankind as part of the ape group was not, of course, to posit a theory of evolution but to highlight the barbaric nature of meat eating. Animals were mankind's near cousins, and in Ritson's reasoning meat eating was 'very little, if at all, inferior to that which … is practised by cannibals'.[400]

At least Ritson's diet would have been an inexpensive one, and he did live an austere life in his rooms at Gray's Inn. As a property owner and a voter, he was never destitute, and his salary from his official appointments, although sometimes it did not pay as well as he hoped, saw him through those times when business was slow. To try to make money in times past, he had previously dabbled in buying and selling shares on the stock exchange. Owning shares in commercial ventures and buying and selling them on the stock market was another marker of gentility. If a man was able to trade in stocks, he was effectively signalling to the world that he was a person of sound financial standing. In fact it was in the late eighteenth century when the *haute bourgeoisie*, or upper middle class, emerged. Members of this class usually had a professional qualification, they often owned land, and they had enough surplus capital to be able to trade on the stock market. There was another type of person too: the man who had *pretensions* to upper-class gentility and who might indeed make investments on the stock market but who, in reality, could not really afford to do so—Ritson would fall into this latter category.[401] The revolution in France presented the would-be entrepreneur with some sound investment opportunities if you knew where to look. As a result of the Eden Treaty, signed in 1786, Britain already enjoyed favourable trading terms with France, and the latter, in the throes of revolution, saw an unprecedented redistribution of wealth from the narrow aristocratic oligarchy to the French bourgeoisie and even the peasants—who all would have needed legal services and, in some cases, access to foreign capital to make further investments.[402] This is why, although knowing that his friend Mr Wadeson disapproved of the revolution, Ritson urged him to 'make your fortune by opening a little snug trade between Stockton and France!'[403]

AN

ESSAY

ON

ABSTINENCE

FROM

ANIMAL FOOD,

AS A

MORAL DUTY.

BY JOSEPH RITSON.

Unde fames homini vetitorum tanta ciborum,
Audetis vesci, genus ô mortale? quod oro,
Ne facite; et monitis animos advertite nostris.

OVIDIUS.

LONDON:

PRINTED FOR RICHARD PHILLIPS, NO. 71, ST. PAULS
CHURCH-YARD.

1802

Wilks and Taylor, Printers, Chancery-Lane.

Title page to Joseph Ritson's *Essay on Abstinence from Animal Food as a Moral Duty* (1802).

Any gains British shareholders made through investments in France would have evaporated with the onset of war between the two nations in February 1793. The assets of British banking houses based

The interior of the Royal Exchange in the late eighteenth century. Any self-respecting gentleman invested in the stock market. Ritson, unfortunately, made unwise investments and lost almost £1,000 in 1802. Illustration from Walter Thornbury and Edward Walford's *Old and New London* (1878).

in Paris, like Boyd and Benfield for example, were seized by the French government when the war began.[404] But after the war started there was more money to be made back in Britain: one simply had to invest in the war effort. Government spending on the entire war until 1815 was £1,657.9 million. In 1796, the Prime Minister, William Pitt, went directly to the public to raise a 'loyalty loan' of £18 million through the sale of government securities in the National Debt.[405] Ritson must have made investments specifically related to the war effort, perhaps through a purchase of a government security or maybe an investment in war materiel production. But when the Peace of Amiens came on 25 March 1802—which turned out to be nothing more than temporary truce—the stock market crashed. According to a letter written to his cousin Mary, Ritson revealed that he was completely ruined:

Times are unfortunately very different at present; being over head and ears in debt. Having a great opinion of an acquaintance who did business on the stock exchange, I was induced in hope and flattery, to speculate with all the money I had or was able to get. In my way from Durham towards London I came by Stockton, to see my nephew and remaining friends, where in a letter for me, I understood (in consequence of the sudden peace, by which so many in my situation suffered much greater losses) that I was utterly ruined, though partly by the mismanagement of him in whom I had placed confidence; the whole of my loss was considerably above a thousand pounds. I have been forced to sell my uncles [sic] land in Strickland, which I had always intended for my dear cousins Jane and Mary and shall as long as I live lament that I did not make it secure.[406]

Ritson was forced to sell part of his library to pay his creditors. This must have been heartbreaking for the book lover that he was. When his nephew was appointed executor of his uncle's estate he found there was barely anything left. So that he might leave something to his family in the event of his death, he attempted to get his life insured for £1,000, but when he attended the company's offices for an interview, they had somehow learned that he had pre-existing medical conditions and refused to insure him.[407]

On a trip back to Stockton early in 1802, illness struck again: he suffered two fits within twenty-four hours. By his own admission afterwards he was

Entirely deprived of memory, intellect, and speech; but got relief by the application to my temples of leeches and blisters. This was thought a narrow escape, and the next attack, I suppose, will carry me off.[408]

Ritson then suffered an 'attack of a paralytical stroke' in February 1803. This disappointed him severely because he had planned on setting out to Paris again that month, taking advantage of the Peace of Amiens, but instead he was partially paralysed. He was advised by his physician to visit Bath to bathe in the supposedly healing thermal waters.

Napoleon Bonaparte, First Consul of the French Republic and later Emperor of the French. Ritson and his nephew seem to have been great admirers of the young military general in 1803. (Wellcome Library)

The waters did not give Ritson any benefit however. He described them as 'altogether unprofitable and worthless'.[409]

The Peace of Amiens expired on 18 May 1803. Across the channel in France, a young army general had seized the reins of government—Napoleon Bonaparte. Both now confirmed radicals, Ritson and his nephew must have admired this general greatly. Frank even kept a bust of him in his apartment. Ritson counselled him, however, to keep the bust of Napoleon hidden away until Napoleon 'makes his appearance'.[410] Clearly Ritson was hoping for Napoleon to bring liberty, equality, and fraternity to Great Britain. Given Ritson's attitude towards kings it was perhaps for the best that he did not live to see Napoleon crown himself Emperor of the French in December 1804.

Ritson's reference to Napoleon occurred in his penultimate letter, which was addressed to his nephew. The final letter that he wrote on 16 August 1803, addressed to the same, reveals that he three other publications in the works: *The Life of King Arthur*, *Memoirs of the Celts*, and 'The Life of Jesus'. The manuscript of 'The Life of Jesus' is now lost but Ritson claimed that he had found, and would publish, all the evidence he had highlighting that Jesus was an imposter.[411] His final few letters to his nephew were written with the purpose of arranging a long-overdue meeting, and to enjoy a coffee and a morning paper together in London. He signed off his last with the following affectionate lines, apologising for having been neglectful and saying, 'farewell for the present … my letters are generally procrastinated till they would come too late and I should have nothing to say'.[412]

Whether Frank ever met his uncle for a coffee is unclear, for on 9 September 1803 shouting and swearing was heard emanating from Ritson's apartment in Gray's Inn. After this, Ritson's servant, the gossipy Mrs Elizabeth Kirby, was seen running down the stairs. She was accosted on the way down by Mr Robert Smith who inquired what the matter was:

> She answered that she believed *her master was out of his mind*, for his conduct in every respect proved him so, and that she was greatly afraid that in his delirium he would do himself or her an injury.[413]

Ritson's mental health was rapidly deteriorating. He was avoiding food and being aggressive to those who crossed his paths: he had verbally

BATHING AT BATH, OR STEWING ALIVE
By Robert Cruikshank

People in the eighteenth century thought that their ailments would be healed by bathing in the thermal waters in Bath. Ritson tried it and found the experience utterly worthless.

abused his maid the day before when she brought him his dinner. Smith went up to Ritson's apartment but he had barricaded himself inside. Later in the evening he calmed down and went to bed. He was quiet for most of the following day.

However, as Smith was returning to his chambers in the evening, 'there was,' he said, 'a great light in his room which had alarmed the people in the steward's office.'[414] The steward was nowhere to be found so Smith got the spare key to Ritson's apartment from the laundress and forced his way in through Ritson's barricade. Ritson was throwing many of his unpublished manuscripts onto the fire, and some papers strewn about the floor had caught fire. Ritson was shouting and swearing and, as he caught sight of Smith, who was now joined by Mr Quinn the steward, lunged at them with a knife and chased Smith, Quinn, and Kirby back through the landing before returning to his apartment.

Smith returned to Ritson's apartment and, presumably having put the fire on the floor out, managed to calm Ritson down. Ritson then asked if Smith might have a drink with him, which the latter declined. Ritson then began to ramble on about his passion for books and that he wanted to write a history of his life. Smith made sure to stay with Ritson till he had

148

got into bed, and took the knife back into his own apartment. Later that evening, however, Ritson's troubles started again and Smith—a fairly brawny man by all accounts—had to pacify our slightly-built antiquary.

A doctor was called for, who pronounced Ritson 'incurable'. A man in the doctor's employ stayed with him for the next five days in his chambers. Smith, who did not know Ritson that well, must have been a very kind and warm-hearted individual, and visited Ritson every day. Ritson was always glad to see Smith and used to exclaim, 'here comes my friend who will set me at liberty,' after which he would verbally abuse his 'keeper'—the doctor's man—saying that 'the devil would torment him for his cruelty in keeping him so confined.'[415] After the five days of confinement in his rooms at Holborn Court, Ritson was taken to a private 'madhouse' run by Sir Jonathan Miles, where he died on 23 September 1803. Ritson was buried with very little ceremony in Bunhill Fields, London. In his will, Ritson had stated,

> With respect to my funeral, (if I happen to die, that is, in the County of Middlesex, of the City of London), my most earnest request to my executor is, that my body may be interred in the burying ground of Burnhill [sic] Fields, with the least possible ceremony, attendance, or expense.[416]

An atheist to the end, Ritson stipulated that his funeral should be carried out 'without the presence of a clergyman'.[417] He wanted to be completely forgotten: 'Steal from the world, and ne'er a stone,/tel where I lye,' Ritson wrote to his associate Thomas Hill. The executors followed his wishes to the letter, and to this day there is no gravestone which marks his burial place. According to some accounts, Ritson did once sit for a portrait, but the only image we have of him is a caricature drawn by James Sayers in 1803. It depicts a slim man standing at a desk with a quill in hand, writing notes on parchment. In the image, Ritson dips his pen into an inkwell that is inscribed with the word 'GALL'. In his pocket rests a copy of *The Atheist's Pocket Companion*. Ritson's Spartan mode of life is illustrated by the sandals he wears—he is standing on a torn copy of one of Thomas Percy's ballads. Under the table, a picture of Thomas Warton has been impaled with a knife. Books adorn the shelves of the apartment and the room is filled with an abundance of vegetables—a cow can be seen poking his head in through the window helping himself to a basket

The caricature of Joseph Ritson drawn by James Sayers in 1803.

of lettuce on the table. Meanwhile, Ritson's pet cat is chained up so as to stop it from eating mice—this was not quite fair, for Ritson accepted that animals ate other animals, and that it was in cats' natures to kill mice.[418] During the Victorian era, some more sympathetic images of Ritson were published, based on Sayers' engraving, simply showing him with quill in hand standing at a desk, omitting the vegetables and animals.

Although Ritson desired to be forgotten, not everyone was ready to forget him, nor the injuries they thought he had done them. One reviewer of Ritson's *Animal Food* in the *British Critic* gloated over his mental health troubles saying,

> We had written thus far, when we were informed that he was no more! How fearful are the ways of heaven! The fool who, in the pride of his no knowledge, arraigned the wisdom of Providence; the worm that, in the conceit of his no-strength, aspired to pull the Almighty from his throne, sunk, in the twinkling of an eye, beneath the level of the lowest and most contemptible of the beasts that perish! It is said that he was found naked, at midnight, in the court of his inn, with a large clasp-knife in one hand, and a copper kettle in the other, on which he was exercising his impotent fury. The humanity of the neighbours conveyed him to a mad-house, where, in the course of a few hours, he expired in a paroxysm of frenzy. It is just, as well as charitable, to hope that his opinions were influenced by the imperceptible growth of that malady which destroyed him: for the rest he is now before a righteous tribunal, where we also must appear; and where, the least sinful of the human race must look, no otherwise than himself, for forgiveness to the mercy of a long-suffering Judge and Father.[419]

This is the only contemporary account that says Ritson was found naked—eyewitnesses to Ritson's final days do not record this, so we must assume that the *British Critic*, which had long been one of Percy's cheerleaders, was simply inventing stories (the editor, Mr Richard Nares, was good friends with Percy).[420]

News of Ritson's death travelled fast around London literary circles. George Chalmers, another historian with whom Ritson had had some dealings, wrote to Thomas Percy at his seat in Ireland to tell him the news. Percy had always eagerly lapped up any news his friends would tell him of Ritson's peccadilloes, and Percy and Steevens would gossip about him, as a letter from Steevens in 1788 reveals:

> I have been so long absent from the literary world, that the intelligence I offer you is scarce worth your reading. One circumstance, however, I must not omit. Your antagonist

Mr. Ritson, about a month ago, got drunk, and assaulted an inoffensive barber, who brought an action against him, and has obliged him to pay severely for his frolic; a proper warning to critics militant.[421]

Obviously not one to hold a grudge, Steevens, as we have seen, had evidently forgiven Ritson by 1802 and inspired Ritson to complete the *Bibliographia Poetica*. But when he learned the news of Ritson's death, the Christian bishop Percy lost sight of his Christian principles somewhat, for by all accounts he was positively gleeful over the death of the man who had pointed out two of his errors in the 1780s and 1790s.[422] His public enemy was dead and of course, surmised the bishop, he was always right to be suspicious of Ritson because he had gone mad.[423] In further proof of how petty Percy was, he had his own copy of Ritson's *Animal Food* specially bound with Sayers's satirical print, no doubt to have a small chuckle to himself when he opened it.[424]

However, Percy may have been the 'big player' in the literary world while he was alive, but it is Ritson whose legacy lives on in the form of virtually every Robin Hood novel, movie, and television show ever produced to this day—a legacy which Percy could never match.

Chapter 6

'In Praise of Robin Hood, his Outlaws and their Trade': Joseph Ritson's Legacy

While he was alive, Ritson garnered a 'starring role' in a novel written by his good friend Thomas Holcroft. In Holcroft's *Alwyn; or, The Gentleman Comedian* (1780), a character named Mr Handford appears. A humanitarian, Handford converts his house into a hospital for old, lame, and sick animals:

> I must be exercising my pity upon some distressed devil or another—I have taken a fresh freak—I know you'll laugh, but I don't care—I have turned my house into an hospital.— For what, say you?— The lame or the lazy?—I'll tell you, Sir—I have at this instant—nine dog-horses, seven of

them blind, forty young puppies, almost as many kittens, a tolerable flock of rotten sheep, which the rascally owners made me pay as much for, when they found my humour, as if they had been sound ones; an infinite number of young birds, which I was obliged to purchase, or see them devoted to destruction, besides one and twenty old cows, that are past calving.[425]

Handford also rails against Christianity and Methodism—it is abundantly clear that Handford represented Ritson. Yet unfortunately for Handford, his role as saviour of the animal species is counterproductive, for local brutes, realising that Handford will come to the aid of all oppressed creatures, begin to deliberately maim or injure their animals because they know he will buy them. Ritson never passed comment on Holcroft's novel but, due to the fact that Holcroft often lightly ridiculed his friend for his vegetarianism, Ritson probably just laughed at his caricature.

Before proceeding further, let us spare a thought for the Christian bishop. Even three years after Ritson's death, Percy was *still* complaining about the 'injuries' Ritson had done him. All the issues of a given periodical, after they had completed their monthly or weekly print runs, were bound together and sold as books. The *British Critic* for 1804, published in 1805, happened to have very briefly made reference in a footnote to one of Ritson's books. This seems to have incensed Percy, who wrote a note to the editor criticizing Ritson's work and requesting that it be published as the preface to the entire volume. Percy assumed his letter would be published. After all, had not the *British Critic* proved one of Ritson's most formidable foes in former years? Yet Percy was astonished when the editor simply placed his letter at the back of the volume with all the others. In Percy's words, the editor 'threw it into a corner of a page … where it cannot but remain unnoticed'.[426] It seemed as though many in Percy's literary circle could simply not be bothered pandering to the bishop's hurt pride anymore, especially now its object was dead. Joseph Cooper Walker, one of Ritson's friends, had published a paper in an academic journal titled *Transactions of the Royal Irish Academy*, and Walker cited Ritson as an authority on the matter of minstrelsy. The citation occupied but two lines in a footnote: '*Vide*. Ritson's Dissertation on Romance and Minstrelsy prefixed to Ancient English Metrical Romances'—that was literally it. To Percy this simply would not do—how dare Mr Walker reference one of Ritson's works and not Percy's own remarks on the minstrels! Percy complained to one Mr Anderson—who served on the committee of the Royal Irish Academy—about Walker's problematic footnote. Anderson did not respond for an entire year. After this, Percy wrote to him again about the matter. Probably with a sigh, Anderson put pen to paper and responded with a brief note saying that it was unlikely that Cooper Walker ever meant any offence. Joseph Cooper Walker died in 1810. Percy was *still* bitter about the Ritson controversy as late as that year. In fact, the many letters he sent to various people after

OLDBUCK AT BREAKFAST

Illustration of Jonathan Oldbuck from Walter Scott's *The Antiquary* (1816). Oldbuck is a crotchety, middle-aged, single man obsessed with researching obscure historical and philological subjects. One cannot help but wonder if Scott put something of his friend Ritson into the character of Oldbuck.

155

Ritson's death, gloating over the manner of his death, and spitting his dummy out over what was by then a nearly 30-year-old criticism makes the bishop appear rather childish. Had Percy simply responded to Ritson's criticisms through the pages of literary magazines, acknowledging the merits of Ritson's conclusions while also offering counter-arguments, the whole 'controversy' might simply have been treated by everyone as one of the many mildly interesting disputes between scholars on niche subjects that have occurred throughout the ages.[427]

The name of Walter Scott has loomed large in the latter part of this history. In spite of their differing political opinions, Ritson and Scott were good friends. How fitting, then, that Britain's greatest novelist should pay homage to Ritson in his third historical novel, *The Antiquary* (1816). Ritson would have known Scott as a poet and antiquary, not a novelist. It was not until 1814, long after Ritson's death, that Scott embarked upon a career of novel writing with the publication of *Waverley; or, 'tis Sixty Years Since*.[428] *Waverley* was a serious historical novel set during the Jacobite Rebellion whereas *The Antiquary* was a comedy detailing the life of an eccentric antiquary named Jonathan Oldbuck of Monkbarns and the fortunes of his friend Mr Lovel. Like many an antiquary, Oldbuck has a library filled with many rare and valuable books and manuscripts, and a trusty cat who guards them:

> A large old-fashioned oaken table was covered with a profusion of papers, parchments, books, and nondescript trinkets and gewgaws, which seemed to have little to recommend them, besides rust and the antiquity which it indicates. In the midst of this wreck of ancient books and utensils, with a gravity equal to Marius among the ruins of Carthage, sat a large black cat, which, to a superstitious eye, might have presented the *genius loci*, the tutelar demon of the apartment. The floor, as well as the table and chairs, was overflowed by the same mare magnum of miscellaneous trumpery, where it would have been as impossible to find any individual article wanted, as to put it to any use when discovered.[429]

Oldbuck is much like Ritson. A crotchety middle-aged lawyer and a historian, he generally thinks he is right when it comes to most historical and philological matters. Oldbuck also has a like-minded friend, the history buff and medieval manuscript collector Sir Arthur Wardour, with whom he is ever quarrelling about the meaning of a word in an ancient text. When the pair of them get into debates about historical subjects, usually at the dinner table, the exchanges become heated as each of them is prone to invoking the name of some contemporary historian in support of their points:

> "I say the Pikar, Pihar, Piochtar, Piaghter, or Peughtar," vociferated Oldbuck; "they spoke a Gothic dialect" —
> "Genuine Celtic," again asseverated the knight.
> "Gothic! Gothic! I'll go to death upon it!" counter-asseverated the squire.
> "Why, gentlemen," said Lovel, "I conceive that is a dispute which may be easily settled by philologists, if there are any remains of the language."
> "There is but one word," said the Baronet, "but, in spite of Mr. Oldbuck's pertinacity, it is decisive of the question."
> "Yes, in my favour," said Oldbuck: "Mr. Lovel, you shall be judge — I have the learned Pinkerton on my side."
> "I, on mine, the indefatigable and erudite Chalmers."
> "Gordon comes into my opinion."
> "Sir Robert Sibbald holds mine."
> "Innes is with me!" vociferated Oldbuck.
> "Ritson has no doubt!" shouted the Baronet.[430]

This particular literary debate causes Wardour to rise from his seat and storm out of Oldbuck's house in a huff, seemingly never to associate with Oldbuck again, although the pair do make up again later. It is interesting that Ritson is given the final word on the matter in the debate between Oldbuck and Wardour, as though Ritson's opinion on a subject was the most authoritative to which one could appeal.

This was not the only time that Ritson's name was invoked in Scott's novel. Oldbuck and the local vagrant, Edie Ochiltree, visit a peasant woman named Elspeth. She lives in a hut near the coast. As the two men approach, they hear her singing a ballad. Oldbuck is convinced that it is a ballad of the most ancient kind: "It's a historical ballad," said Oldbuck eagerly,—"a genuine fragment of minstrelsy!—Percy would admire its simplicity—Ritson could not impugn its authenticity."[431]

Scott's novels sold well. The hitherto anonymous 'Author of *Waverley*' became a celebrity not only in Britain but also in the United States and continental Europe, where translations of his works appeared in French, Spanish, and German. Scott followed up *The Antiquary* with two shorter novels set in eighteenth-century Scotland which formed part of his *Tales of My Landlord* series: *The Black Dwarf* (1816) and *A Tale of Old Mortality* (1817). Another full-length, three volume novel was published in the latter part of 1817 titled *Rob Roy*, in which the famous outlaw Robert Roy MacGregor featured. Of course, Ritson's legacy to the modern world comes chiefly from his work on Robin Hood and his friendship with Scott. It was Scott's youthful love of old outlaw tales, along with his having read Ritson's *Robin Hood*, which inspired him to write his most successful novel, *Ivanhoe* (1819) (Scott possessed two copies of Ritson's *Robin Hood*, which can be seen to this day on the shelf in the Abbotsford library where Scott left them).[432]

The framing narrative of *Ivanhoe* reflects Scott's antiquarian interests. The preface purports to be a letter sent from a fictional antiquary, Laurence Templeton, to another make-believe antiquary, Rev. Dr. Dryasdust. The story of *Ivanhoe*, Templeton says, is taken from an ancient manuscript in the possession of Sir Arthur Wardour—the same Arthur Wardour who appeared in *The Antiquary*.[433] The rest of the novel is set during the 1190s, and England is in a parlous state, divided between the Normans and the Anglo-Saxons:

> A circumstance which tended greatly to enhance the tyranny of the nobility, and the sufferings of the inferior classes, arose from the consequences of the Conquest by William Duke of Normandy. Four generations had not sufficed to blend the hostile blood of the Normans and Anglo-Saxons, or to unite, by common language and mutual interests, two hostile races, one of which still felt the elation of triumph, while the other groaned under all the consequences of defeat.[434]

The divisions between the Anglo-Saxons and the Normans come to a head while Richard I is captured by Leopold of Austria, and his brother John rules as Regent. John taxes the people heavily to pay King Richard's ransom but in reality is hoarding the money for himself, hoping to raise an army to overthrow the few remaining barons who support Richard. Unbeknownst to John and his henchmen, Richard has returned to England in disguise. Recognising the parlous state of the country, Robin of Locksley and his outlaws team up with Ivanhoe and King Richard so that the true king can regain control of his kingdom and unite the nation. Added into this plot are vividly exciting scenes; jousting tournaments, archery tournaments, damsels in distress, and epic sieges and battles. It is a piece of pure medieval spectacle.

Scott completely invented the idea that Robin Hood was an Anglo-Saxon freedom fighter. He had a message for nineteenth-century readers: if all classes in society worked together, they could overcome their differences.[435] Medieval feudalism, where each class owed loyalty to the other and produced a harmonious society, could, Scott argued, be adapted for the nineteenth century. The novel was timely: England in 1819 was a divided society. The end of the French Revolutionary and Napoleonic Wars brought in their wake a financial depression and high unemployment. The working and middle classes were clamouring for political reform and universal suffrage. Luddites were busy sabotaging machines; armed uprisings occurred in 1816 and 1817 in London; and the government, in an event now known as the Peterloo Massacre, brutally put down a peaceful crowd of pro-democracy demonstrators at St Peter's Fields in Manchester in August 1819. Scott was horrified by this event and his novel was his own small way of attempting to heal the social and political divisions of nineteenth-century England by creating a shared sense of history around which all people could come together.

Thomas Love Peacock, the author of *Maid Marian* (1822) which was inspired by Ritson's *Robin Hood*.

A different approach from the one Ritson would have advocated, certainly, but in *Ivanhoe* we see people from all classes working together for the good of the nation.[436] Ritson had argued that Robin Hood was not so much an outlaw but a freedom fighter; Scott took the freedom fighter aspect from Ritson's *Robin Hood*, but being a Tory, Scott placed his outlaw on the side of the true king.

The early nineteenth century was a good time if you were a fan of Robin Hood, and all new interpretations of the legend were based upon their author's reading of Ritson's *Robin Hood*. A now-forgotten Robin Hood novel titled *Robin Hood: A Tale of the Olden Time* was published a few months before the release of Scott's novel. Ritson's influence can be felt here because the first part of the novel is set in the nineteenth century at a dinner party where men and women are conversing on the subject of ancient ballads. The next book published was Thomas Love Peacock's *Maid Marian* (1822). Peacock's novel begins with the nuptials of Robert, Earl of Huntingdon, and his lady Matilda. The wedding is interrupted by the sheriff's men who seek to arrest him for 'forest treason'. Robin fights of the sheriff's men and then takes to the woods, despoiling the sheriff and his men of all their goods whenever they can. After resisting the advances of Prince John, Matilda joins Robin in Sherwood Forest and assumes the name of Maid Marian. Together, Robin and Marian effectively rule as King and Queen in the forest, maintaining what Ritson would call an 'independent sovereignty':

> Administering natural justice according to Robin's ideas of rectifying the inequalities of the human condition: raising genial dews from the bags of the rich and idle, and returning them in fertilising showers on the poor and industrious; an operation which more enlightened statesmen have happily reversed.[437]

Maid Marian is the undisputed hero of the novel. She is headstrong and unafraid to defy her father when she expresses her desire to go to live like an outlaw with Robin Hood in the forest.[438] With its rapacious barons and prelates, the novel was clearly very close in spirit to Ritson's *Robin Hood*, a fact recognised by contemporary reviewers:

It is evident, however, that the author of *Maid Marian* was induced to take the adventures of that 'bold yeman' [yeoman] Robin Hood for the subject of his story, by the perusal of the collection of ballads and other poetical remains relating to that celebrated greenwood hero, made by the noted antiquary Joseph Ritson, and published by him in two small 8vo. volumes, in 1795. This curious book, which, when Maid Marian was written, was *extremely* scarce, has since been reprinted with a few alterations. On looking into that pleasant volume, we find that most of the incidents and many good ideas in Maid Marian have been borrowed from it: but the skill and ability with which they have been worked into the narrative are the author's own. The characters of the merry foresters are very well painted, and after the true old model. Perhaps, however, Marian might have been represented somewhat less masculine and warlike in her taste, though we acknowledge the historical correctness of that picture.[439]

The reviewer admired Ritson, but clearly thought that Peacock's proto-feminist Maid Marian was at odds with how they thought a medieval woman should be portrayed, which presumably was as a typical damsel in distress. While there was actually an outlaw named Robin Hood, who is listed as 'fugitive' in the York Assize Rolls for the years 1225–26,[440] Maid Marian is a completely fictional character, a fact recognised by Ritson who observed, 'who or whatever this lady was ... no mention of her occurs either in the *Lytell Geste of Robyn Hode*, or in any other poem or song concerning him, except a comparatively modern one of no merit'.[441]

Just as Ritson had satirised his old acquaintances from Stockton-on-Tees in *The Stockton Jubilee*, a satire of Ritson appeared in a little poem written by Walter Scott entitled 'The Bannatyne Club' which appeared in 1823. Scott lightly mocks many of the now-dead antiquaries and poets who flourished in the previous century. These are his remarks about Ritson:

> As bitter as gall and as sharp as a razor,
> And feeding on herbs like a Nebuchadnezzar,

His diet too acid his temper too sour,
Little Ritson came out with his two volumes more.
But one volume more, my friends, one volume more,
We'll dine on roast beef and print one volume more.[442]

The Bannatyne Club was founded by the printer George Bannatyne in 1822 and was dedicated to reprinting new editions of medieval Scottish texts, many of which had first been identified by the likes of Ritson, Percy, and Pinkerton. Had he been alive when Scott's little poem was printed, Ritson would have probably laughed at this because Scott could almost do no wrong in his eyes.

By the 1820s Frank was busy arranging the publication of 'one volume more' of his uncle's unpublished works. Ritson's *Life of King Arthur* appeared for publication in 1825.[443] This was a serious, scholarly investigation which attempted to untangle the facts from the fiction on all matters relating to the legendary British king. This was no easy task, as Ritson acknowledged in his preface:

> The difficulty of the subject may be partly estimated from doubts having been actually entertained by the author, during his early researches, as to the identity of his hero, and fears lest the real Arthur might not, after all, be found:
> "So many of his shadows" had he "met,
> And not the very King."[444]

Ritson assumed that King Arthur was a historical person but that the only records bequeathed to posterity by various writers since the medieval era were so full of fanciful tales as to effectively make the legendary king a completely fictional character.[445] True to form, Ritson took a snipe at the shoddy scholarship of some of his contemporary antiquaries, and true to form he takes aim at John Pinkerton who assumed that King Arthur was a Romano-British general named Aurelius Ambrosius: 'that Arthur was Aurelius Ambrosius is … an assertion just as true as that Alexander the Great was Julius Caesar, or Merlin the prophet, John Pinkerton.'[446] (The Pinkerton falsehood has been peddled as recently as 2004 by filmmakers where, in the *King Arthur* movie of that year, the same origin story is given for the legendary king of the Britons). Ritson's *Memoirs of the Celts or Gauls* finally appeared in 1827.[447]

This was not the end of Frank's efforts either. His uncle's unpublished *Fairy Tales* appeared in 1831. This was not attempt to prove that fairies were real but an account of their appearance in literature throughout the centuries and a study of the etymology of 'fairy':

> The word *Fairy*, as used in our own language, is a mere blunder; the proper name of the French Fairy is *Faée* or *Fée*, or in the English *Fay*; *Faerie*, or *Féerie*, which we apply to the person being, in fact, the *country*, or *kingdom*, of the *Fays*, which we call *Fairy-land*.[448]

While the book went into great detail on the history of these mythical, magical beings, the stories reproduced by Ritson were not all strictly about fairies as little winged nymphs. One of the notable tales which he included in *Fairy Tales* was the story of the Pied Piper of Hamelin, which sixteen years after the posthumous publication of Ritson's book would be made famous by the poet Robert Browning (1812–89) in a children's version of the tale.

Publishers were busy issuing second editions of Ritson's works in multivolume sets. The twelve volume edition of *Ritson's Works and Metrical Romances*, sold by H. Bohn, for example, sold at the hefty price of £3 8s.[449] Ritson's work on Scotland's history also received renewed interest. *The Caledonian Muse*, having passed through various hands, was finally printed in 1821 by Robert Triphook. *Annals of the Caledonians, Picts, and Scots* appeared in two volumes in 1828. The first batch of Ritson's unpublished letters was published in 1829 by the Edinburgh publisher John Stevenson—a slim volume containing all of the letters Ritson sent to his friend George Paton. Although only 100 copies of this book were published, it was a project to which some of the big names in the literary world were attached: the editor was James Maidment, a famous antiquary at the time, and the letters were prefaced with an essay by Ritson's sometime rival John Pinkerton. Copies of the 'George Paton' letters were quickly snapped up and it was probably the success of this book which convinced Ritson's nephew Joseph Frank to begin collecting, editing, and eventually publishing his uncle's letters. *The Letters of Joseph Ritson, Esq.* was finally published in 1833 with a brief biographical preface, or 'Memoir of Joseph Ritson', written by Sir Nicholas Harris.

An antiquary, Harris enjoyed a fairly successful career, having written several biographies of notable medieval and early modern English literary figures as well as some niche, although important, transcriptions of medieval legal texts. With the help of Nelson's daughter Horatia, Harris also published *Dispatches and Letters of Lord Nelson* (1844–1846).

Frank had two aims when he published his uncle's letters in the 1830s. The first was that of securing his uncle's place in history as a 'great man of letters'. Frank also wanted to reveal his uncle's true temper and dispel the public image of him as having been misanthropic and un-social.[450] Frank may have been largely correct, of course, if a little biased, in his estimation of his uncle's good nature. Yet one does wonder whether Ritson did write some rather nasty letters and whether some of those more mean-spirited letters to associates were left out of the published collection. Whether any 'selective editing' went on while Frank was collating all of his uncle's manuscripts, is something that we will never know.

None of Ritson's posthumous publications had the impact that *Robin Hood* had. Scott's *Ivanhoe* was informed by his Tory politics and Peacock's *Maid Marian*, while it had anti-establishment sentiments, was hardly radical. A return to Robin Hood's radical 'Ritsonian' roots appeared in the Victorian era with Pierce Egan the Younger's serialised penny novel entitled *Robin Hood and Little John; or, The Merry Men of Sherwood Forest* (1838–40). It was published just as the campaign for universal male suffrage or 'Chartism' was beginning in earnest.[451] Egan acknowledged his debt to Ritson, calling him a 'gentleman' whose scholarly opinion on the subject of Robin Hood, 'from his very close research into the subject, is unquestionable'.[452] Egan even gave Ritson a role in his novel. The first characters who readers meet are two people travelling through the thickest part of Sherwood Forest on a dark and stormy night. It is a lord and his servant, who is named Ritson (Ritzon in the first edition). The servant is carrying a baby who will grow up to be none other than Robin Hood. In this novel, it is Ritson who gives the world Robin Hood. This was a fitting tribute to Ritson, especially as Egan's Robin Hood grows up to be a Saxon freedom fighter. While Egan's novel depicts the medieval period as one of unremitting political oppression of the Saxon workers by the Normans, Robin Hood's Sherwood Forest society has a democratic constitution: Robin has to be

Title page to Pierce Egan the Younger's *Robin Hood and Little John; or, The Merry Men of Sherwood Forest* (1838–40).

elected to the position of leader. In a scene which looks almost like an electoral hustings, Robin says:

> Friends and brother Saxons—This is a proud and joyous moment for me, that you should so unanimously and cheerfully, at the instigation of Little John, elect me as the head of your community; warmly and earnestly I thank you for it … All I have to speak upon the fact of my being your leader, is of the duties which will be imposed on me by my post, and of the constant endeavours I will make to perform them to your satisfaction.[453]

Robin's election is based on merit rather than his 'noble' birth. The forest society of Sherwood is egalitarian; when Robin's love interest, Matilda, of aristocratic birth, goes to live in the forest with Robin and the outlaws, she asks that people refer to her as 'Maid Marian' so that the others dwelling in the forest might not think her either above or below the other inhabitants. In a move that would surely have pleased the republican Ritson, Egan's outlaws pay little regard to rank. When Little John first meets Friar Tuck, known as the Clerk of Copmanhurst, he says,

> "Understand me, Sir Clerk of Copmanhurst, if that be thy title, which your boisterous bawling taught me to be it, that you are stopped by him who would stop anyone from whom he wanted an answer, and one who is beneath thee only so much as thy nag gives thee in height."[454]

While Ritson hesitantly acknowledged that Robin might have been a lord in the latter part of his life, Egan skirted smoothly around this issue. Once Robin learns of his birth-right, although he does attempt to reclaim it through legal means, he realises that the possibilities of reclaiming it are slim and thereafter ceases to try. At the end of Egan's novel, Robin is still dispossessed. Although King Richard orders that restitution of his estates be made to Robin, the lying, scheming monks refuse to give up the Huntingdon estates. In the true style of Ritson's Robin Hood, Egan's outlaw is a 'man of the people' unto the end. Moreover, Robin never lives among the upper classes: 'he had mixed with no society above the class in which Gilbert Hood [Robin's adoptive yeoman forester father] was placed'.[455] Egan's casting of Robin as the Earl of Huntingdon stems from the fact that Egan wanted to be 'historically accurate'. Robin Hood's alleged nobility had become a historical 'fact' because of its tentative inclusion in Ritson's book.

Ritson's *Robin Hood* was reprinted fifteen times throughout the nineteenth century.[456] Other antiquaries came after Ritson who published more comprehensive and scholarly collections of Robin Hood ballads, notably John Mathew Gutch who published *A Lytell Geste of Robin Hode* in 1847 (see appendix three). This followed the same format as Ritson's book. It was published in two volumes and contained a new 'Life of Robin Hood' written by Gutch, an abridged version of Ritson's 'Life of Robin Hood', in addition to every ballad and poem which had been discovered until that time.[457] Each of the ballads included in Gutch's collection were accompanied by frontispieces and end-pieces, drawn by F.W. Fairholt, and they were of a similar character to those which Bewick created for Ritson's anthology. Gutch's book was only for a middle-class academic audience.[458] This was in contrast to Ritson whose work was written for the general reader. It certainly was not as commercially successful as Ritson's and only went through two editions.[459]

The 'gentrification' of the Robin Hood tradition seemed to have well and truly taken hold of the legend after the publication of Pierce Egan's radical novel, when a number of conservative children's books retelling the legend were published. These books often referenced Ritson's ballads as an inspiration but took the radicalism out of the story. However, a new radical movement emerged in late-Victorian Britain whose aim was to create a classless and democratic society: socialism. It was socialist writers such as William Morris (1834–96) who were Ritson's heirs and we find Ritson's outlaw make fleeting but noteworthy appearances in Morris's works.

In his early days Morris was associated with the Pre-Raphaelites—a group of artists who, thinking that art had become too stale and formalised, sought to return to a more medieval style of art which flourished before Raphael. It was a desire to 'return to the medieval' which led Morris to become associated with the Arts and Crafts movement. The movement's adherents feared that traditional, specialist craft skills were being lost due to the rise of 'ugly' mass-produced items. As Morris explained in 'How I Became a Socialist' (1894), modern civilisation, with its factory system, had 'destroyed art, the one certain solace of labour'.[460]

WHEN ADAM DELVED AND EVE SPAN
WHO WAS THEN THE GENTLEMAN?

Frontispiece to William Morris's *A Dream of John Ball* (1888).

To remedy this, Morris, along with Edward Burne-Jones, founded
Morris and Company to produce traditionally made everyday items that
would look beautiful in even modest homes.

While Morris was running a thriving design business he also found
time to write several epic poems which drew upon both classical and
medieval literature, the most notable being *The Earthly Paradise* (1868),

The Defence of Guenevere (1858) and *The Life and Death of Jason* (1867). While Morris was living he was lauded by one biographer as

> one of the most original poets of the nineteenth century ...
> he belongs to a brotherhood dear to all ages and to all
> lands; which owns for members the Greek rhapsodists; the
> singers of King Arthur and his knights; the Eastern reciters
> of Aladdin; and the minstrel rehearsers of the exploits of
> Robin Hood.[461]

Although Morris's medievalism predated his conversion to socialism, a reading of Henry Hyndman's *The Historical Basis of Socialism in England* (1883) convinced Morris that England had an indigenous tradition of socialism from the fourteenth century onwards.[462] The tales of Robin Hood were part of this tradition, that had existed since the medieval era, as Morris and his colleague E. Belfort Bax explained in 'Socialism from the Root Up':

> In England what may be called the chronic rebellion of the
> Foresters ... produced such an impression on the minds of
> the people that it has given birth to the ballad epic known
> by the name of its mythical hero, Robin Hood. Resistance
> to authority and contempt of the 'Rights of Property' are the
> leading ideas in this rough but noble poetry.[463]

However, Ritson's presence can be felt most strongly in Morris's novel *A Dream of John Ball* which began its serialization in the socialist newspaper *Commonweal* on 13 November 1886 and was published as a single volume in 1888.

A Dream of John Ball was, in the opinion of the famous socialist writer Robert Blatchford, 'the best of William Morris's prose romances'.[464] It tells the story of a time traveller from the Victorian era who wakes up in Kent on the eve of the Peasants' Revolt of 1381, a time when the people of southern England revolted against the poll tax and the onerous conditions of serfdom. They were led by Wat Tyler, the proto-socialist radical preacher, John Ball, and Jack Straw. For a socialist such as William Morris, who had always been a student of medieval history, a tale of rebels rising up against the ruling class seemed ripe for retelling.

He depicted a revolutionary Ritsonian Robin Hood as figuratively preparing the way forward for the ideology of the radical preacher John Ball and the Peasants' Revolt, an event, so Morris thought, that marked the first appearance of socialist ideology in England.[465]

Morris's time-traveller finds himself in a tavern in which one villager requests another to sing 'a stave of Robin Hood; maybe that shall hasten the coming of one I wot of.'[466] The song relates 'the struggle against tyranny for the freedom of life'.[467] The idea that the songs of Robin Hood were stories of 'the struggle against tyranny' chime with Ritson's interpretation of the outlaw's legend, who said that he was a man who 'displayed a spirit of freedom and independence' in opposing what he saw as the tyrannical rule of medieval English kings. It is a rousing Robin Hood ballad that Morris's fourteenth-century rebels hear on that day, for the time traveller says,

> My heart rose high as I heard him, for it was concerning the struggle against tyranny for the freedom of life, how that the wildwood and the heath, despite of wind and weather, were better for a free man than the court and the cheaping-town; of the life of a man doing his own will and not the will of another man commanding him for the commandment's sake.[468]

In the *Commonweal* version of *A Dream of John Ball*, the wording is slightly different: he says that 'the wild wood and the heath weather were better than … the existence of machines'.[469]

The vision of the outlaws' way of life Morris gives in his Robin Hood ballad resembles the description of it given by Ritson:

> The deer with which the royal forests then abounded … would afford our hero and his companions an ample supply of food throughout the year; and of fuel, for dressing their venison, or for the other purposes of life, they could evidently be in no want. The rest of their necessaries would be easyly [sic] procured, partly by taking what they had an occasion for from the wealthy passenger, who traversed or approached their territories.[470]

The outlaws depicted in Ritson's text were truly free men; the forests provide them with everything they require. Occasionally they steal, but Ritson says that they only ever stole from the rich and gave to the poor. In Ritson's *Robin Hood*, there was no mention of the town and the court. But upon reading the next part of the book which contains 'A Gest of Robyn Hode', Morris would have encountered the 'Eighth Fytte' of the tale. Robin Hood, having been pardoned by the King, is invited to enter the King's service and join his court. Robin Hood finds the world of the Royal Court unpalatable, and after having dwelt among the nobles for fifteen months, he desires to go back to Barnsdale forest. The King grants Robin Hood permission to return to the greenwood for seven days. In what must be one of the earliest literary portrayals of recidivism, Robin Hood becomes an outlaw again and decides to stay another twenty-two years, thereby risking the wrath of the King. Clearly for the freedom-loving outlaws in Ritson's and Morris's texts, 'the wildwood and the heath, despite of wind and weather, were better for a free man than the court and the cheaping-town' and they prefer 'doing [their] own will and not the will of another man'.[471]

The reader is not given the text of the first ballad which the traveller hears and Morris only describes it as relating the idea of freedom from tyranny. A second villager continues by singing another ballad, or 'more of a song than a story ballad', praising resistance to a corrupt sheriff and abuses of kingly authority.[472] The medieval justice system presided over by the sheriff, as Morris imagined it, was corrupt and the cause of the downfall of many a good man. In spite of the sheriff's gold and superior strength, however, the outlaws ensure that the sheriff never encroaches on their domain, a place where 'the king's writ' never shall know. Here again there were resonances with the sentiments found in Ritson's biography in which the outlaw defies corrupt authority and establishes 'an independent sovereignty' in the forests of Barnsdale and Sherwood.[473] Yet there was also a warning for the outlaws and, by extension, the villagers assembled in Morris's fourteenth-century tavern:

> Now yeomen walk ye wearily,
> And heed the houses where you go,
> For as fair and as fine as they may be,
> Lest behind your heels the doors clap to.[474]

Most late-Victorian Robin Hood novels such as Edward Gilliat's *In Lincoln Green* (1897) or Escott Lynn's *When Lionheart was King* (1908)—and truly to read one of these Robin Hood children's novels is to read them all—depict the local population as having been nothing but friendly towards the outlaws. But in Ritson's text, outside the forest 'his hand was against every man, and every mans [sic] against him'; it was only the forest which was 'free from the alarms, or apprehensions, to which our foresters, one would suppose, must have been too frequently subject.'[475] It was a brave act to resist authority, as Robin and the merry men do in both Ritson's and Morris's texts, and to do so often came at a price. The forest was the only place where 'the Sheriff's word is nought of worth'.[476]

After the 'stave of Robin Hood' has been heard by the assembled villagers, the men gathered in the tavern hear the church bells begin to ring and they make their way outside. The ballad singer approaches the time-traveller and asks, 'was it not sooth that I said, brother, that Robin Hood should bring us John Ball?'[477] John Ball has arrived in the village and is about to deliver a sermon to the inhabitants on the importance of 'fellowship' and of a future world when there will be no masters; men will work for themselves and 'shall not lack for the fields ye have tilled, nor the houses ye have built, nor the cloth ye have woven'.[478] The sermon is a vision of a future time when 'all things will be held in common'. In Morris's novel, in a literal sense, Robin Hood 'brings us John Ball' because a song of Robin Hood is heard before the preacher's arrival. In a figurative sense, Ritson's radical Robin Hood prepares the way for the arrival of John Ball the proto-socialist preacher. Robin Hood fought for freedom against tyranny before the fourteenth century, although it is Ball who brings an egalitarian ideology to the struggle against medieval tyranny by preaching of a time when 'those that labour become strong and stronger ... and have the goods of the earth without money and without price'.[479]

The relationship between Ritson's radical Robin Hood and Morris's proto-socialist John Ball mirrored how nineteenth-century socialists saw themselves: heirs to a radical tradition. This tradition, while not strictly socialist, laid the groundwork for the emergence of socialism. Eighteenth- and early nineteenth-century radical thought were a part of the 'roots' of socialism.[480] There was also a weekly section in *Commonweal* entitled 'Revolutionary Calendar' that sought to educate adherents of the late nineteenth-century socialist cause by making them aware of their radical heritage through commemorations of various radicals' births and deaths, including Thomas Paine, who Ritson so admired. In effect, Morris was paying his and many other contemporary socialists a debt to the spirit of Robin Hood and, by extension, early radicals such as Ritson.[482]

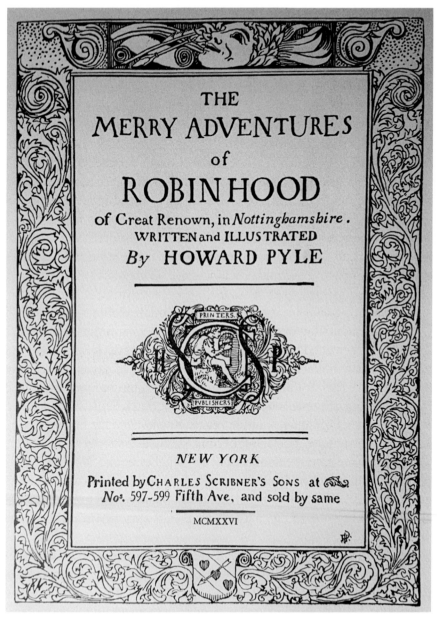

Howard Pyle's *Merry Adventures of Robin Hood* (1883).

The American children's book by Howard Pyle, *The Merry Adventures of Robin Hood* (1883), was credited by Paul Buhle as having influenced Morris's references to the Robin Hood of *A Dream of John Ball*.[483] This is unlikely because neither Morris's letters nor the catalogue of the books in his personal library contain any evidence that he owned or even read Pyle's *Robin Hood*. There *is* evidence from the catalogue of William Morris's library catalogue that he was acquainted with Ritson's *Robin Hood*. The edition of Ritson's *Robin Hood* which Morris owned was the Bell and Daldy version printed in 1862. It contained the full text of the 1795 edition, including Ritson's biography and lengthy footnotes.[484] Morris did not like children's novels and was more interested in what might be called 'Bibles': the foundational documents of a civilization—the Bible is one such 'Bible' of course, but into this category belong the Indian, Greek, Persian, and Anglo-Saxon epics, as well as the Norse *Edda*. These works were 'in no sense the work of individuals but have grown up from the very hearts of the people'.[485] Leading cultural critics who preceded Morris looked upon the poems and ballads of Robin Hood as being in the same class as these epics, as Thomas Carlyle noted in *Past and Present* (1843):

> The great *Iliad* in Greece, and the small *Robin Hood's Garland* in England, are each, as I understand, the well-edited select beauties of an immeasurable waste imbroglio of Heroic Ballads in their respective centuries and countries. Think what strumming of the seven-stringed heroic lyre, torturing of the less heroic fiddle-catgut, in Hellenic Kings' Courts, and English wayside Public Houses; and the beating of the studious poetic brain, and gasping here too in the semi-articulate windpipe of Poetic men, before the Wrath of a Divine Achilles, the Prowess of a Will Scarlet or Wakefield Pinder, could be adequately sung! Honour to you, ye nameless great and greatest ones, ye long-forgotten brave![486]

Morris would have been drawn to Ritson's *Robin Hood* because it was a collection of such 'Biblical' tales; the 'rough yet noble' poetry of the people in times gone by.

Ritson's book of Robin Hood may have influenced Victorian writers, but after Pierce Egan's text, Ritson virtually ceases to be credited by name in popular literary texts written about the famous outlaw. It seems, furthermore, that after the establishment of the Historical Manuscripts Commission in the 1860s, along with the professionalization of historical studies within academia, Ritson's work was, in spite of its importance, increasingly forgotten. Folklorists in late nineteenth-century Britain such as Cecil Sharpe had also been active in republishing more comprehensive editions of folk songs and ballads. Some of Ritson's antiquarian work had been superseded by that of Francis James Child, who published an edition of *English and Scottish Popular Ballads* in 1860, and a revised version and more comprehensive five volume edition between 1882 and 1898. Where Ritson found radical, anti-establishment sentiments in early Robin Hood poems, Child maintained that Robin Hood 'has no sort of political character'.[487]

It was not until the early twentieth century that academics based in the United States began to re-examine Ritson's texts with fresh eyes and thereby 'rediscovered' Ritson's importance in literary and folklore studies. The beginning of academic studies into Ritson's life and research was marked by the appearance in *The Sewanee Review* of H.S.V. Jones's article entitled 'Joseph Ritson: Romantic Antiquarian'. Jones remarked,

> The permanent value of [Ritson's] unremitting campaign against elegant imposture and amiable inaccuracy is hard to overestimate. If it is true, according to a writer in the *Gentleman's Magazine*, that there was at this time 'a prevailing maxim that no author is to be told of his faults plainly, but we must use a kind of polite literary periphrasis,' an exception to the rule was furnished by Ritson's sharp decision of manner.[488]

Further investigations followed: Henry Alfred Burd completed his PhD dissertation on Ritson's research at the University of Illinois in 1916. Burd's dissertation was then published as *Joseph Ritson: A Critical Biography* in August of the same year. A reviewer in *Modern Philology*, Tom Peete Cross, made the following remarks upon Burd's book:

> Ritson was disregarded by most of his contemporaries and by posterity has been well-nigh forgot; but, thanks to Dr. Burd, he is at last revealed as a scholar and critic who,

by his passion for accuracy and his tremendous grasp of fact, rebuked an age of intellectual dishonesty, and who, by an acumen at times little short of inspiration, enunciated theories to which the scholarly world has finally returned.[489]

Burd's biography was soon replaced with a larger two volume work published in 1938 entitled *Joseph Ritson: Scholar-at-Arms* by B.H. Bronson, a professor of English literature at the University of California, Berkeley. Bronson was one of Ritson's main cheerleaders in fact: not only in his 1938 book but in the many subsequent books he wrote on folk tales and popular ballads he repeatedly praised Ritson's accuracy in transcribing old texts. Much of Ritson's early research formed the basis of Bronson's *The Singing Tradition of Child's Popular Ballads*, where Bronson reprinted the texts of many of the ballads first collected by Ritson.[490] Bronson also republished a large part of Joseph Ritson's unpublished 'Bibliographia Scotia', intended by him to recount, like the *Bibliographia Poetica*, short accounts of the lives of famous poets.

Scholarship on Robin Hood has continued apace. We have already given credit to Genevieve McNutt's fantastic PhD thesis. In the twentieth and twenty-first century there are now Robin Hood scholars all around the world, all of whom have, at some point in their works, drawn upon Ritson's pioneering 1795 book. Like Percy and Ritson, it should be noted that disputes and catty remarks are made by Robin Hood scholars about each other's works even in our modern day: Stephen Knight, who holds Robin Hood to be a mythic personage, sneered at the 'empricism which runs rampant' through various historians' works; R.B. Dobson and J. Taylor likewise made a little snipe at John Bellamy whose ideas about Robin Hood were so abstract and 'of a kind so esoteric that it has successfully defied detection throughout the centuries until Professor Bellamy has at last brought it to light.' I myself have in recent years defended the existence of a historical Robin Hood and, in a previous book, *Robin Hood: The Life and Legend of an Outlaw* (2019), criticised those who have attempted to argue that 'the name of Robin Hood is the product of orgies which apparently occurred in England's woodlands in some far off point in time'. These scholars, including myself, often stick to our guns.[491]

Of course, the twentieth century is when film and television superseded text as the main vehicle of transmission of Robin Hood stories. The presence of Ritson's *Robin Hood* can be felt in practically

Right and below: Images from *The Adventures of Robin Hood* (1938) starring Errol Flynn in the title role. The presence of Ritson's freedom fighting outlaw can be felt in this movie as well as countless other portrayals of the Robin Hood story in the twentieth and twenty-first centuries.

" ' I'VE CALLED YOU HERE AS FREE-BORN ENGLISHMEN.' "

177

every one of them ever produced which cast Robin as a freedom fighter. In Errol Flynn's incarnation of the outlaw in *The Adventures of Robin Hood* (1938)—which takes its inspiration from Ritson via Walter Scott—Robin makes the outlaws recite the Forest Outlaws' Oath:

> I've called you here as freeborn Englishmen, loyal to our king. While he reigned over us, we lived in peace. But since Prince John has seized the regency, Guy of Gisbourne and the rest of his traitors have murdered and pillaged. You've all suffered from their cruelty: the ear loppings, the beatings, the blindings with hot irons, the burning of our farms and homes, the mistreatment of our women. It's time to put an end to this! Now, this forest is wide. It can shelter and clothe and feed a band of good, determined men, good swordsmen, good archers, good fighters. Men, if you're willing to fight for our people, I want you! Are you with me? … That you, the freemen of this forest, swear to despoil the rich only to give to the poor, to shelter the old and the helpless, to protect all women rich or poor, Norman or Saxon. Swear to fight for a free England. To protect her loyally until the return of our King and sovereign Richard the Lion Heart. And swear to fight to the death against our oppressors![492]

Just as Ritson's *Robin Hood* was published to criticise the political and social problems of the 1790s, Flynn's movie was, in part, a criticism of *laissez-faire* capitalism and a promotion of Franklin D. Roosevelt's New Deal in the wake of the Great Depression in 1930s America.

The portrayal of a 'Ritsonian' Robin Hood, in fact, seems to be one of the deciding factors in whether a particular Robin Hood movie is commercially successful. While hardly a hit with film critics, the box office takings and popularity of movies such as *Robin Hood: Prince of Thieves* (1991) starring Kevin Costner, *Robin Hood* (2010), with Russell Crowe playing the outlaw, and *Robin Hood* (2018) starring Taron Egerton, far outstripped the so-called 'mock busters' of those Robin Hood films which did not feature an outlaw-freedom fighter. Ritson would probably have given a nod of approval—while simultaneously lambasting their historical inaccuracies—to the Crowe and Egerton movies. In Russell Crowe's version, Robin Hood helps to repel a French invasion of England and also campaigns for the establishment of a Charter of Rights. The movie has resonances with an earlier novel by Thomas Miller titled *Royston Gower; or, The Days of King John* (1838), in which Robin's exploits take place against the backdrop of the Barons' War of 1215–17 and the fight for Magna Carta. Miller's novel was, just like previous Robin Hood novels, inspired by youthful readings of the ballads in Ritson's book. The Taron Egerton movie sees Robin Hood become something of a Wat Tyler figure by leading a peasants' revolt in Nottingham (coincidentally the first edition of Ritson's *Robin Hood* was printed by one T. Egerton). The less successful Robin Hood movies tend not to follow Ritson's model. Among the more dismal straight-to-DVD/ TV portrayals of the Robin Hood legend in recent years, for example, we have the gloriously bad *Ghosts of Sherwood*. This is a bizarre and cheaply made romp in which Robin is turned into a zombie and endeavours to feast on Marian and Tuck's flesh, complete with Cosplay standard costumes. Another is *Beyond Sherwood Forest*, a low-budget monstrosity in which Robin fights a dragon. There are many more dire interpretations of the Robin Hood legend on film but they belong in the dustbin of history and it is not necessary to dredge them up here.

It is the freedom fighting outlaw who audiences love. If every author throughout history was given due credit for their labours, then every Robin Hood book, play, movie, and television show would credit Joseph Ritson. It was Ritson, the poor lad from Stockton-on-Tees, who first laid down the vision of a noble and inspiring outlaw and freedom fighter dedicated to the cause of liberty and ameliorating the condition of the poor. Ritson 'invented', we might say, the modern image of Robin Hood. The continuing popularity of the outlaw's legend is Ritson's legacy to the world. Without Ritson, the story of Robin Hood might have gone the way of Adam Bell, Clim of the Clough, William Cloudesley, Eustace the Monk, and Hereward the Wake. All of these were outlaws whose deeds were once celebrated in verse and song—yet among the general public their stories have faded into obscurity! It is thanks to Ritson's diligent research in the late eighteenth century that we can agree with the Elizabethan poet Michael Drayton, who, speaking of the Robin Hood legend, declared:

> In this our spacious isle I think there is not one
> But he hath heard some talk of him and little John;

And to the end of time the tales shall ne'er be done,
Of Scarlock, George-a-Green, and Much the miller's son,
Of Tuck the merry friar, which many a sermon made
In praise of Robin Hood, his outlaws and their trade.[493]

Appendix 1

Joseph Ritson's
'Life of Robin Hood' (1795)

It will scarcely be expected that one should be able to offer an authentic narrative of the life and transactions of this extraordinary personage. The times in which he lived, the mode of life he adopted, and the silence or loss of contemporary writers, are circumstances sufficiently favourable, indeed, to romance, but altogether inimical to historical truth. The reader must, therefore, be contented with such a detail, however scanty or imperfect, as a zealous pursuit of the subject enables one to give; and which, though it may fail to satisfy, may possibly serve to amuse.

No assistance has been derived from the labours of his professed biographers; and even the industrious Sir John Hawkins, from whom the public might have expected ample gratification upon the subject, acknowledges that "the history of this popular hero is but little known, and all the scattered fragments concerning him, could they be brought together, would fall far short of satisfying such an inquirer as none but real and authenticated facts will content. "We must," he says, "take his story as we find it." He accordingly gives us nothing but two or three trite and trivial extracts, with which every one at all curious about the subject was as well acquainted as himself. It is not, at the same time, pretended, that the present attempt promises more than to bring together the scattered fragments to which the learned historian alludes.

This, however, has been done, according to the best of the compiler's information and abilities; and the result is, with a due sense of the deficiency of both, submitted to the reader's candour.

***

ROBIN HOOD was born at Locksley, in the county of Nottingham, in the reign of King Henry the Second, and about the year of Christ 1160. His extraction was noble, and his true name ROBERT FITZOOTH, which vulgar pronunciation easily corrupted into ROBIN HOOD. He is frequently styled, and commonly reputed to have been, EARL OF HUNTINGDON; a title to which, in the latter part of his life, at least, he actually appears to have had some sort of pretension. In his youth he is reported to have been of a wild and extravagant disposition; insomuch that, his inheritance being consumed or forfeited by his excesses, and his person outlawed for debt, either from necessity or choice, he sought an asylum in the woods and forests, with which immense tracts, especially in the northern parts of the kingdom, were at that time covered. Of these, he chiefly affected Barnsdale, in Yorkshire, Sherwood, in Nottinghamshire, and, according to some, Plompton Park, in Cumberland. Here he either found, or was afterward joined by, a number of persons in similar circumstances—

> "Such as the fury of ungovern'd youth
> Thrust from the company of awful men,"

who appear to have considered and obeyed him as their chief or leader, and of whom his principal favourites, or those in whose courage and fidelity he most confided, were Little John (whose surname is said to have been Nailor), William Scadlock (Scathelock or Scarlet), George a Green, pinder (or pound-keeper) of Wakefield, Much, a miller's son, and a certain monk or frier named Tuck. He is likewise said to have been accompanied in his retreat by a female, of whom he was enamoured, and whose real or adopted name was Marian.

His company, in process of time, consisted of a hundred archers; men, says Major, most skilful in battle, whom four times that number of the boldest fellows durst not attack. His manner of recruiting was somewhat singular; for, in the words of an old writer, "whersoever he hard of any that were of unusual strength and 'hardines,' he would desgyse himselfe, and, rather then fayle, go lyke a begger to become acquaynted with them; and, after he had tryed them with fyghting, never give them over tyl he had used means to drawe [them] to lyve after his fashion": a practice of which numerous instances are recorded in the more common and popular songs, where, indeed, he seldom fails to receive a sound beating. In shooting with the long bow, which they chiefly practised, "they excelled all the men of the land; though, as occasion required, they had also other weapons".

In those forests, and with this company, he for many years reigned like an independent sovereign; at perpetual war, indeed, with the King of England, and all his subjects, with an exception, however, of the poor and needy, and such as were "desolate and oppressed," or stood in need of his protection. When molested, by a superior force in one place, he retired to another, still defying the power of what was called law and government, and making his enemies pay dearly, as well for their open attacks, as for their clandestine treachery. It is not, at the same time, to be concluded that he must, in this opposition, have been guilty of manifest treason or rebellion; as he most certainly can be justly charged with neither. An outlaw, in those times, being deprived of protection, owed no allegiance: "his hand was against every man, and every man's hand against him". These forests, in short, were his territories; those who accompanied and adhered to him his subjects:

"The world was not his friend, nor the world's law:"

and what better title King Richard could pretend to the territory and people of England than Robin Hood had to the dominion of Barnsdale or Sherwood is a question humbly submitted to the consideration of the political philosopher.

The deer with which the royal forests then abounded (every Norman tyrant being, like Nimrod, "a mighty hunter before the Lord") would afford our hero and his companions an ample supply of food throughout the year; and of fuel, for dressing their vension, or for the other purposes of life, they could evidently be in no want. The rest of their necessaries would be easily procured, partly by taking what they had occasion for from the wealthy passenger who traversed or approached their territories, and partly by commerce with the neighbouring villages or great towns.

It may be readily imagined that such a life, during great part of the year, at least, and while it continued free from the alarms or apprehensions to which our foresters, one would suppose, must have been too frequently subject, might be sufficiently pleasant and desirable, and even deserve the compliment which is paid to it by Shakespeare in his comedy of *As you like it* (act i. scene 1), where, on Oliver's asking, "Where will the old duke live?" Charles answers, "They say he is already in the forest of Arden, and a many merry men with him; and there they live like the OLD ROBIN HOOD OF ENGLAND ... and fleet the time carelessly as they did in the golden world." Their gallant chief, indeed, may be presumed to have frequently exclaimed with the banished Valentine, in another play of the same author:

> "How use doth breed a habit in a man!
> This shadowy desert, unfrequented woods,
> I better brook than flourishing peopled towns:
> Here can I sit alone, unseen of any,
> And, to the nightingale's complaining notes,
> Tune my distresses and record my woes."
> He would doubtless, too, often find occasion to add:
> "What hallooing and what stir is this to-day?
> These are my mates, that make their wills their law,
> Have some unhappy passenger in chace:
> They love me well; yet I have much to do,
> To keep them from uncivil outrages."
> But, on the other hand, it will be at once difficult and painful
>   to conceive,
> "When they did hear
> The rain and wind beat dark December, how,
> In that their pinching cave, they could discourse
> The freezing hours away!"

Their mode of life, in short, and domestic economy, of which no authentic particulars have been even traditionally preserved, are more easily to be guessed at than described. They have, nevertheless, been elegantly sketched by the animating pencil of an excellent though neglected poet:—

184

"The merry pranks he play'd, would ask an age to tell,
And the adventures strange that Robin Hood befell,
When Mansfield many a time for Robin hath been laid,
How he hath cousen'd them, that him would have betray'd;
How often he hath come to Nottingham disguis'd,
And cunningly escap'd, being set to be surpriz'd.
In this our spacious isle, I think there is not one,
But he hath heard some talk of him and Little John;
And to the end of time, the tales shall ne'er be done,
Of Scarlock, George a Green, and Much the miller's son,
Of Tuck the merry frier, which many a sermon made
In praise of Robin Hood, his outlaws, and their trade.
An hundred valiant men had this brave Robin Hood,
Still ready at his call, that bowmen were right good,
All clad in Lincoln green, with caps of red and blue,
His fellow's winded horn not one of them but knew,
When setting to their lips their little beugles shrill,
The warbling ecchos wak'd from every dale and hill.
Their bauldricks set with studs, athwart their shoulders cast,
To which under their arms their sheafs were buckled fast,
A short sword at their belt, a buckler scarce a span,
Who struck below the knee, not counted then a man:
All made of Spanish yew, their bows were wondrous strong;
They not an arrow drew, but was a cloth-yard long.
Of archery they had the very perfect craft,
With broad-arrow, or but, or prick, or roving shaft,
At marks full forty score, they us'd to prick, and rove,
Yet higher than the breast, for compass never strove;
Yet at the farthest mark a foot could hardly win:
At long-outs, short, and hoyles, each one could cleave the pin:
Their arrows finely pair'd, for timber, and for feather,
With birch and brazil piec'd to fly in any weather;
And shot they with the round, the square, or forked pile,
The loose gave such a twang, as might be heard a mile.
And of these archers brave, there was not any one,
But he could kill a deer his swiftest speed upon,
Which they did boil and roast, in many a mighty wood,
Sharp hunger the fine sauce to their more kingly food.

Then taking them to rest, his merry men and he
Slept many a summer's night under the greenwood tree.
From wealthy abbots' chests, and churls' abundant store,
What oftentimes he took, he shar'd amongst the poor:
No lordly bishop came in lusty Robin's way,
To him before he went, but for his pass must pay:
The widow in distress he graciously reliev'd,
And remedied the wrongs of many a virgin griev'd:
He from the husband's bed no married woman wan,
But to his mistress dear, his loved Marian,
Was ever constant known, which wheresoe'er she came,
Was sovereign of the woods; chief lady of the game:
Her clothes tuck'd to the knee, and dainty braided hair,
With bow and quiver arm'd, she wander'd here and there,
Amongst the forests wild; Diana never knew
Such pleasures, nor such harts as Mariana slew."

That our hero and his companions, while they lived in the woods, had recourse to robbery for their better support is neither to be concealed nor to be denied. Testimonies to this purpose, indeed, would be equally endless and unnecessary. Fordun, in the fourteenth century, calls him "*ille famosissimus siccarius*," that most celebrated robber, and Major terms him and Little John "*famatissimi latrones*." But it is to be remembered, according to the confession of the latter historian, that, in these exertions of power, he took away the goods of rich men only; never killing any person, unless he was attacked or resisted: that he would not suffer a woman to be maltreated; nor ever took anything from the poor, but charitably fed them with the wealth he drew from the abbots. I disapprove, says he, of the rapine of the man: but he was the most humane and the prince of all robbers. In allusion, no doubt, to this irregular and predatory course of life, he has had the honour to be compared to the illustrious Wallace, the champion and deliverer of his country; and that, it is not a little remarkable, in the latter's own time.

Our hero, indeed, seems to have held bishops, abbots, priests, and monks, in a word, all the clergy, regular or secular, in decided aversion.

"These byshoppes and thyse archebyshoppes,
Ye shall them bete and bynde,"

was an injunction carefully impressed upon his followers. The Abbot of Saint Mary's, in York, from some unknown cause, appears to have been distinguished by particular animosity; and the Sheriff of Nottinghamshire, who may have been too active and officious in his endeavours to apprehend him, was the unremitted object of his vengeance.

Notwithstanding, however, the aversion in which he appears to have held the clergy of every denomination, he was a man of exemplary piety, according to the notions of that age, and retained a domestic chaplain (Frier Tuck, no doubt) for the diurnal celebration of the divine mysteries. This we learn from an anecdote preserved by Fordun, as an instance of those actions which the historian allows to deserve commendation. One day, as he heard mass, which he was most devoutly accustomed to do (nor would he, in whatever necessity, suffer the office to be interrupted,) he was espied by a certain sheriff and officers belonging to the king, who had frequently before molested him in that most secret recess of the wood where he was at mass. Some of his people, who perceived what was going forward, advised him to fly with all speed, which, out of reverence to the sacrament, which he was then most devoutly worshipping, he absolutely refused to do. But the rest of his men having fled for fear of death, Robin, confiding solely in Him whom he reverently worshipped, with a very few, who by chance were present, set upon his enemies, whom he easily vanquished; and, being enriched with their spoils and ransom, he always held the ministers of the Church and masses in greater veneration ever after, mindful of what is vulgarly said:

> "Him God does surely hear
> Who oft to th' mass gives ear."

Having, for a long series of years, maintained a sort of independent sovereignty, and set kings, judges, and magistrates at defiance, a proclamation was published offering a considerable reward for bringing him in either dead or alive; which, however, seems to have been productive of no greater success than former attempts for that purpose. At length, the infirmities of old age increasing upon him, and desirous to be relieved, in a fit of sickness, by being let blood, he applied for that purpose to the Prioress of Kirkleys nunnery in Yorkshire, his relation (women, and particularly religious women, being, in those times, somewhat better skilled in surgery than the sex is at present), by whom he was treacherously suffered to bleed to death. This event happened on the 18th of November 1247, being the 31st year of King Henry III, and (if the date assigned to his birth be correct) about the 87th of his age. He was interred under some trees, at a short distance from the house; a stone being placed over his grave, with an inscription to his memory.

Such was the end of Robin Hood: a man who, in a barbarous age, and under a complicated tyranny, displayed a spirit of freedom and independence which has endeared him to the common people, whose cause he maintained (for all opposition to tyranny is the cause of the people), and, in spite of the malicious endeavours of pitiful monks, by whom history was consecrated to the crimes and follies of titled ruffians and sainted idiots, to suppress all record of his patriotic exertions and virtuous acts, will render his name immortal.

With respect to his personal character: it is sufficiently evident that he was active, brave, prudent, patient; possessed of uncommon bodily strength and considerable military skill; just, generous, benevolent, faithful, and beloved or revered by his followers or adherents for his excellent and amiable qualities. Fordun, a priest, extols his piety, Major (as we have seen) pronounces him the most humane and the prince of all robbers; and Camden, whose testimony is of some weight, calls him "*prædonem mitissimum*," the gentlest of thieves. As proofs of his universal and singular popularity: his story and exploits have been made the subject as well of various dramatic exhibitions, as of innumerable poems, rimes, songs and ballads: he has given rise to divers proverbs; and to swear by him, or some of his companions, appears to have been a usual practice: his songs have been chanted on the most solemn occasions; his service sometimes preferred to the Word of God: he may be regarded as the patron of archery; and, though not actually canonised (a situation to which the miracles wrought in his favour, as well in his lifetime as after his death, and the supernatural powers he is, in some parts, supposed to have possessed, give him an indisputable claim), he obtained the principal distinction of sainthood, in having a festival allotted to him, and solemn games instituted in honour of his memory, which were celebrated till the latter end of the sixteenth century; not by the populace only, but by kings or princes and grave magistrates; and that as well in Scotland as in England; being considered, in the former country, of the highest political importance, and essential to the civil and religious liberties of the people, the efforts of government to suppress them frequently producing tumult and insurrection. His bow, and one of his arrows, his chair, his cap, and one of his slippers, were preserved, with peculiar veneration, till within the present century; and not only places which afforded him security or amusement, but even the well at which he quenched his thirst, still retain his name: a name which, in the middle of the present century, was conferred as a singular distinction upon the prime minister to the king of Madagascar.

After his death his company was dispersed. History is silent in particulars: all that we can, therefore, learn is, that the honour of Little John's death and burial is contended for by rival nations; that his grave continued long "celebrous for the yielding of excellent whetstones;" and that some of his descendents, of the name of Nailor, which he himself bore, and they from him, were in being so late as the last century.

Appendix 2

Ritson's 'Versees Addressed to the Ladies of Stockton' (1772)

First Printed in the Newcastle Miscellany,
MDCCLXXII.

——PROGREDITUR NYMPHARUM SPLENDIDUS ORDO,
ANTE ALIOS UNUS ARRIPUIT, TENUITQUE MORANTES,
ARDENTESQUE OCULOS.

The women came, as custom wills they pass'd,
On one (oh! That distinguished one) I cast
The favourit glance: O yet my mind retains
This fond begging of my infant pains.——*Prior*.

Accept, ye fair, the tribute of my praise,
And deign a smile upon my humble lays;
For your applause i strike the tuneless lyre,
And strive to raise within the poets fire:
In hobbleing verse your charms attempt to sing;
Your charms adorn'd with ever blooming spring.

Ye female critics, read, sans spleen, my song,
Nor deem it or too languid, or too long;
For your applause i write, your frowns I fear;
Hence, fellows! Hence! Your judgment's nothing here.
Let not harsh censure my poor rhimes asperse,
But with the subject dignify the verse
Where Tees in sweet meanders slowly glides,

And gentlely murmuring rolls his easy tides,
There stands a town, with peace and plenty crown'd,
For wit, for wealth, and loyal sons renown'd;
Far famed for dames, wife, charitable, chaste,
And first in beautys annals ever place'd.

In every age has STOCKTON been revere'd,
Her sons have always been belove'd and fear'd.
When, 'gainst the hardy legions of the North,
Brave Percy led his youthful warriors forth,
Her valiant deeds let history proclaim,
And Cheviot hills record the fatal name.
Her nymphs, erst wont to trip the verdant groves,
Seem'd sisters to the Gracees and the Loves

Leave these, my muse, and sing, in careless rhimes,
The special beauties of her modern times;
Let them alone engage thy every care,
Speak but the truth, and paint them as they are.

With thee, TITANIA, does the muse advance,
The leader thou in this uncouple'd dance;
Thy prudent maxims, and thy manners sage,
To us seem wonderous, far above thine age;
Thy infant buds, like bees about thee swarm,
Thyself their empress, shielding them from harm;
Of treacherous man warn'd in each dayly task,
Though, spite of thee, he'll soon be all they ask,
To thee the riseing generation bows,
Accept our homage, nor our praise refuse.

From grandsire magistrates OLIVIA springs;
How pleasantly she looks! How sweet she sings!
To her though Venus have not deign'd her aid,
Nor do her charms adorn the wity maid,
Yet with their want who cannot but dispense,
Where such goodnature joins with such good sense?

When unbecomeing wildness rules the fair,
Let her of slanders evil tongue beware;
Lost fame, says Prior, ne'er can be regain'd;
A character that's once, is always, stain'd:
Mark youthful CELIA! Though that evil tongue
Have hardly yet had power to do thee wrong,
From light behaviour drawn, hints vile and dark
The pureest fame eternally may mark.

Fair DAPHNE! Tears bedew the musees eyes,
And heaves of pity in her bosom rise;
In sorrow silent, she but breathes thy name,
Nor good, nor ill, of thee commits to fame.

View haughty CHLOE! Sneaking even in state,
How few who love her! And how few who hate!—
Beneath the last, from most:—long may live,
Adorn'd with all the graces pride can give.
Her affectation, spleen, ridic'lous ease,
Show what you can be, fair ones, when you please.

In malice laughing, of her laughter vain,
See cookmaid Phillis, envious, spiteful, plain.

The LEARNED SISTERS next demand my lays;
Few outward charms they boast to speak their praise,
But by their mental they shall lovers thrall,
And, with goodnature, make them bless'd in all.

Let not THE WIDOW miss her share of fame,
Nor uninserted here let pass her name:
A Stockton toast, wit, critic, lo! She stands;
Beaus, bucks and fribbles press to kiss her hands;
To all at home;—sh' 'as felt the marriage chain,
Nor would be grieve'd to have it on again.

Nor thee, fair ANNA, shall the muse pass by,
Nor 'mongst these charmers thee a place deny;

192

Remote from Stocktons hospitable doors,
Thou, like ELVIRA, pass'd'st thy natal hours;
And, honour'd by her friendship, e'er shalt share,
The utmost praise my suckeling muse can spare:
Goodnature, sense, and modesty are join'd,
Equally fair to make thy face and mind.

Though last in number, yet in beauty first,
Among Strenshelians happy people Nurse'd,
Hail, my ELVIRA! Graceful, debonair;
Among the fairest thou alone art fair:
In vain i bid the muse attempt thy praise;
In vain the muse to sing thy charms essays;
To sing thy charms—alone the heavenly quires
Should raise their Halleluias,—strike their lyres;
The theme but worthy them:—yet gracious deign
To pardon my sincere, though lowly, strain;
All i dare ask:—Adieu, my Fair, though thou
Nor grant a smile, nor an unclouded brow,—
Thy bard, thy slave i'll be—and, with the thought
My bosom cheer, although my chance be nought.

Appendix 3

List of Joseph Ritson's Works

Archival Material

'Four letters to George Chalmers, 1792-1803', Beinecke Rare Book and Manuscript Library Repository, New Haven, Yale University, GEN MSS 76

'Letter to George Ellis., 1803', Beinecke Rare Book and Manuscript Library Repository, New Haven, Yale University, GEN MSS 76

————, 'Transcripts of letters to Joseph Cooper Walker., 1789-1801', Beinecke Rare Book and Manuscript Library Repository, New Haven, Yale University, GEN MSS 76

————, 'Transcript of letter to William Laing., 1793', Beinecke Rare Book and Manuscript Library Repository, New Haven, Yale University, GEN MSS 76

Minutes of the Parish Vestries, 9 October 1789. London, Westminster Archives Centre. London Lives [online], 'St Clements Danes Parish: Minutes of Parish Vestries CD/MV 13 July 1787–6 August 1795. Available at www.londonlives.org.

'Receipt signed by Ritson as bailiff., 1791', Beinecke Rare Book and Manuscript Library Repository, New Haven, Yale University, GEN MSS 76

Books

Ancient Engleish Metrical Romanceës, 3 vols (London: W. Blumer, 1802)

Ancient Songs from the Time of King Henry the Third to the Revolution (London: J. Johnson, 1790)

Ancient Songs from the Time of King Henry the Third to the Revolution, 2 vols (London: Payne and Foss, 1790)

Annals of the Caledonians, Picts, and Scots, 2 vols (Edinburgh: W.D. Laing, 1828)

'Bibliographia Scotica', *PMLA*, 52: 1 (1937), 122–59

The Bishoprick Garland; or, Durham Minstrel (Stockton: 1784)

The Caledonian Muse (London: Robert Triphook, 1804)

Cursory Criticisms on the Edition of Shakespeare Published by Edmond Malone (London: Hookham and Carpenter, 1792)

Dido: A Tragedy (London, 1792)

The English Anthology, 3 vols (London: T. and J. Egerton, 1793)

A Digest of the Proceedings of the Court Leet (London: Printed in the Year 1789)

An Essay on Abstinence from Animal Food as a Moral Duty (London: Printed for Richard Phillips, 1802)

Fairy Tales (London: Payne and Foss, 1831).

Gammer Gurton's Garland; or, The Nursery Parnassus (Stockton: Christopher and Jennet, 1784)

Law Tracts by Joseph Ritson, Esq. (London: Printed in the Year 1794)

Letters from Joseph Ritson Esq. to Mr George Paton, ed. by James Maidment (Edinburgh: John Stevenson, 1829)

The Letters of Joseph Ritson, ed. by Joseph Frank, 2 vols (London: William Pickering, 1833)

Life of King Arthur (London: Payne and Foss, 1825)

Modes of Trying Peers (London, 1776)

The North Country Chorister (Durham, 1792)

Northern Garlands (London: R. Triphook, 1810)

Observations on the Three First Volumes of the History of English Poetry. In a familiar letter to the author, T.W. (London: J. Stockdale, 1782)

The Office of Constable: Being an Entirely New Compendium of the Law Concerning that Ancient Minister for the Conservation of the Peace, 2nd edn (London: W. Clarke, 1815)

The Office of Liberty of a Bailiff (London: A. Strahan, 1811)

Poems on Interesting Events in the Reign of King Edward III (London, 1795)

Practical Points; or, Maxims in Conveyancing (London: W. Clarke, 1804)

Pieces of Ancient Popular Poetry, rev. Edmund Goldsmid, 2 vols (Edinburgh: privately printed, 1884)

Pieces of Ancient Popular Poetry (London: William Pickering, 1833)

The Quip Modest; a Few Words by Way of Supplement to Remarks, Critical and Illustrative, on the Text and Notes of the Last Edition of

Shakespeare; Occasioned by a Republication of that Edition (London: J. Johnson, 1788)

Remarks, Critical and Illustrative, on the Text and Notes of the Last Edition of Shakespeare (London: J. Johnson, 1783)

Robin Hood: A Collection of All the Ancient Poems, Songs, and Ballads, Now Extant, Relative to that Celebrated English Outlaw: To which are Prefixed Historical Anecdotes of his Life, 2 vols (London: T. Egerton, 1795)

Robin Hood: A Collection of all the Ancient Poems, Songs, and Ballads, Now Extant, Relative to that Celebrated English Outlaw 2nd edn (London: Longman, 1820)

Robin Hood: A Collection of all the Ancient Poems, Songs, and Ballads, Now Extant, Relative to that Celebrated English Outlaw, 3rd edn (London: C. Stocking, 1823)

Scotish Song, 2 vols (London: J. Johnson and J. Egerton, 1794)

A Select Collection of English Songs, 2nd edn, 3 vols (London: F.C. and J. Rivington, 1813)

The Spartan Manual (London: C. Dilley, 1785)

The Stockton Jubilee (Newcastle, 1781)

The Yorkshire Garland (York, 1782)

Magazine Articles and Broadsides

'Elegy to the Late Mrs Todd of Stockton', *The Literary Register*, 2 (1770), 78.

'Letter Signed Anti-Scot', *The Gentleman's Magazine*, November 1784, 812-14

'My Cousin's Tale', *The Literary Register*, 3 (1771), 252-3

Tables Shewing the Descent of the Crown of England (London: privately printed, 1778)

Versees Addressed to the Ladies of Stockton (Newcastle: privately printed, 1782)

Part-Published and Unpublished Works

This list is taken from *A Catalogue of the Entire and Curious Library and Manuscripts of the Late J. Ritson* (London: Leigh Sotheby, 1803),

Henry Alfred Burd, *Joseph Ritson: A Critical Biography* (1916), and B.H. Bronson, *Joseph Ritson: Scholar-at-Arms* (1938)

'Antient and Modern Deeds, Charters, Grants, Surveys, and other Instruments, Writings, Extracts, &c., relating to the Manor, Borough, Township, Chapelry, and Parish of Stockton, in County Durham' [not dated]

'Bibliographia Scotia' [see published version by Bronson]

'Catalogues of Old Ballads' [not dated]

'The Comedy of Errors' (1787) [two sheets printed]

'Description of the North-East Part of Cleveland, with notes' [not dated]

'The Disobedient Child'

'Dissertation on the use of Self' [not dated]

'Ancient Poetry' [not dated]

'An English Dictionary' [not dated]

'An Enquiry into the Connection between the Families of Bailiol and Comyn in the thirteenth century' [not dated]

'Extracts of Entries (chiefly of songs and ballads) in the Stationers' books, from a transcript by the late W. Herbert' [not dated]

'Fabularum Romanensium Bibliotheca' (c. 1782) [two sheets printed]

'The Famous Tragedy of the Rich Jew of Malta' [not dated]

'Gleanings of English Grammar, chiefly with a view to illustrate and establish a just system of Orthography, upon etymological principles' [not dated]

A Glossary of obsolete or difficult Words occurring in the Charters granted to the Duchy of Lancaster [not dated]

'The Institution, Authority, Acts and Proceedings of Burgesses of the Savoy — Repertory of Evidences in the Duchey Office relating to Manor and Liberty of the Savoy — and other papers relative to the Hospital, with the Views and Plans, framed and glazed, of the Savoy' [not dated]

'A List of River Names in Great Britain and Ireland, with a few etymological notes on them' [MS. Douce 340, Bodleian.] [not dated]

'Magnyfycence, a goodly interlude and a mery devysed and made by Mayster Skelton' [not dated]

'The Massacre of Paris' [not dated]

'Nature, a good interlude of Nature compyled by Mayster Henry Medwall' [not dated]

'A New Enterlude, never before this tyme imprinted entreating of the Life and Repentance of Marie Magdalene' [not dated]

'Notes and corrections on Shakspeare, prepared for the press', 3 vols [not dated]

'Notes for a life of Philip, Duke of Wharton' [not dated]

'Notes on Shakspeare, and Various Readings' [not dated]

'Old Riddles' [not dated]

'On Cardinal Wolsey's dissolving the Convocation of St Paul's' [not dated]

'Poems' [not dated]

'The Poetical Works of Mr. George Knight, formerly of Stockton, Shoemaker of facecious memory' [not dated]

'The Poetical Works of William Dunbar' [not dated]

'Precedents by Mr. Bradley' [not dated]

'The Privileges of the Duchy of Lancaster, by Charter, Statute, and Judicial Determination' [not dated]

'Scotish Ballads' [not dated]

'Select Scotish Poems' [not dated]

Topographical Rines [not dated]

'Treatise on Conveyancing' [not dated]

'Villare Dunelmesne, the names of all the towns, villages, hamlets, castles, sea-houses, halls, granges, and other houses and buildings, having any appellation within the Bishopricks or county palatine of Durham' [not dated]

'Vita Merlini Caledonii, metrice composite Galfrico Monumetensi' [not dated]

'Wills drawn by the late Ralph Bradley, Esq., of Stockton in the County of Durham', 2 vols. [not dated]

Appendix 4

A Brief Account of the Life and Work of J.M. Gutch (1776–1861): Joseph Ritson's Scholarly Successor

The materials for writing a biography of Joseph Ritson are scant indeed, but even rarer are materials relating to the life and work of Ritson's successor in the scholarly study of Robin Hood ballads and poems, J.M. Gutch. The following brief note is based on a paper I was supposed to have read at the Leeds International Medieval Congress in 2020, and originally written with the purpose of expanding upon the brief entry on him in *The Oxford Dictionary of National Biography*. Ritson and Gutch, although they were both Robin Hood scholars, could not have been more different politically.

John Mathew Gutch was born in Oxford in 1776. His father, the Reverend John Gutch, a medieval scholar in his own right, was the Registrar of the University of Oxford and Chaplain of All Souls College—a position which he held until 1824.[495] The younger Gutch's early life followed a pattern which was usual for the sons of the Victorian middle classes: educated at Christ's Hospital, he forged a friendship with two very famous future literary men, Samuel Taylor Coleridge and Charles Lamb. During his school years he published a few lines of bad poetry in *The Gentleman's Magazine*, entitled 'Magdalena; written at Godstowe, Oxfordshire, the Retreat of Fair Rosamund'.[496] Gutch did not attend university, however, but was sent by his family to Bristol where he was apprenticed as a law stationer—a seller of, as the name implies, stationary specifically for members of the legal profession. From there he swiftly moved into the newspaper business and purchased a proprietary share in *Felix Farley's Bristol Journal* in the early 1800s. Through the columns that he wrote on commerce and local politics under the pseudonym 'Cosmo', he soon became one of the most popular journalists in the city. Much of his popularity, it is said by his biographer in the *Gentleman's Magazine*, is due to the fact that he apparently 'invented' the concept of the leading newspaper article—the lead usually being his own articles.[497] A series of other less successful ventures followed after a brief move to the capital—an associate named Mr Alexander convinced Gutch to establish a new newspaper, *The London Morning Journal*, in which Gutch eventually invested a significant part of his fortune from *Felix Farley's Bristol Journal*.

The London Morning Journal soon ran into trouble because one of its authors wrote a libellous article calling the Duke of Wellington and Lord Lyndhurst 'traitors' because of their promotion of Catholic relief.[498] Gutch was an Anglican, very anti-Catholic, and despised atheists. He strongly objected to the passage of the Catholic Emancipation Bill in 1829, and in one column for *Felix Farley's Bristol Journal* he accused all Irish Catholics of being guilty of treason solely because of their religion.[499] Part of the reason that he felt the need to compile his own Robin Hood ballad anthology in the 1840s was because he was annoyed at the anti-clerical and anti-Christian tone of Ritson's biography of the outlaw.[500]

Gutch was a conservative and highly patriotic. He was 'disgusted' with the fact that British generals and army officials, having spent a long time in France, had allowed some French words to seep into their dispatches. He concluded in a letter to *The Gentleman's Magazine* in 1814 that, because the French had, during the French Revolution and Napoleonic Wars, committed 'unparalleled atrocities', then it was the duty of all patriotic Englishmen to keep their letters pure of 'French manners and principles'.[501] His overt anti-French Revolutionary sentiments place Gutch as the direct antithesis of everything that Ritson had stood for: in the latter's biography of Robin Hood the outlaw's actions are infused with pro-French radical sentiments. Gutch's peculiarly English patriotism would have an effect on his scholarship, for over the course of his life he amassed a large collection of rare books for his personal library. The principal subjects were old English ballads and tales, chapbooks, broadside ballads, early editions of Shakespeare, the unpublished works of Thomas Chatterton, a Bible once owned by King James I, and of course many Robin Hood books, to name just a few of the items in his collection.[502] These were all English; it is striking, in fact, that at his death, when his library was catalogued, there were virtually no works by foreign authors, in contrast to his forebear Ritson, who devoured several foreign-language works and was one of London's principal dealers in early modern Italian books.

While Gutch was working as a journalist, he was also editing, like the eighteenth-century antiquaries who had come before him, 'ancient' English poems and ballads and publishing them as books. The first of these was *The Poems of George Wither*, published in 1820 in three volumes—a fourth volume containing a biography of the 'Spenserian' Wither was planned but never materialised. Gutch's first major work was his two-volume collection of Robin Hood ballads: *A Lytell Geste of Robin Hode*, published in 1847. There was a nationalist element to Gutch's desire to publish a new book of Robin Hood's life and ballads—his purpose was, as he says, 'to throw some new light on the life and actions of this celebrated hero of the English serfs, the poor and obscure of the Anglo-Saxon race'.[503] Gutch wanted to establish his superiority over radical Ritson:

A Lytell Geste of Robin Hode
With Other Ancient and Modern Ballads and Songs
Relating to this Celebrated Yeoman to Which is Prefixed
His History and Character Grounded Upon Other
Documents than those Made Use of by His Former
Biographer "Mister" Ritson.

The use of scare quotes around 'mister' was telling—he was even doubting Ritson's claims to being a gentleman. The first thing which Gutch wanted to do was to 'controvert the noble lineage which Mr Ritson ... ascribed to [Robin Hood].'[504] Had Gutch read Ritson's *Robin Hood* properly, he would have seen that Ritson only gave hesitant acceptance to the theory that Robin Hood was of noble birth. Ritson had stated that it was 'in the latter part of his life, at least' that Robin Hood had pretension to an earldom.[505] Gutch should have realised that the Anglo-Saxon connection to Robin Hood had absolutely nothing to do with the pre-nineteenth-century tradition—the idea that Robin Hood was a Saxon first having first appeared, of course, in Scott's *Ivanhoe*.

Although Gutch claimed to give readers a new biography of Robin Hood, most of the preface in *A Lytell Geste of Robin Hode* was concerned with pointing out some of Ritson's errors rather than writing a completely new biography. Most of the first volume after the 'biography' of Robin Hood was concerned with miscellaneous essays on Morris dancing, as well as extracts of various articles on Robin Hood from various Victorian literary magazines. Two versions of 'A Gest of Robyn Hode' were reprinted in Gutch's book—one was in the original Middle English, printed in Gothic typeface, and there was a modern English translation. This latter was composed by Gutch's friend the Reverend John Eagles, 'an old and highly valued friend' who thought that the early Robin Hood poem 'ought not to remain in its antiquated form and language'.[506] Gutch's second volume was impressive too for it included all of the medieval and early modern poems of Robin Hood, including the 1465 poem 'Robin Hood and the Monk' as well as every single Robin Hood ballad and poem he could find from the seventeenth and eighteenth centuries.

Gutch was a member of the British Archaeological Association, and his interests encompassed more than just Robin Hood studies. His activities with the B.A.A. mirror the practices of modern academics. Gutch read several papers at conferences held by this society, the first apparently on 14 August 1848. It was here that he delivered a paper on the history of the Clothier's Company of Worcester in the Middle Ages.[507] It was clear that Gutch's first interest was Robin Hood however, and shortly after the publication of his own book there was a new development in the tradition. Joseph Hunter had discovered a man named Robin Hood in fourteenth-century archival records whose life appeared to match that of the outlaw's as it appeared in the 'Gest of Robyn Hode'. Hunter's findings appeared in a pamphlet titled *The Great Hero of the Ancient Minstrelsy of England, Robin Hood*, published in 1852. At the news of the discovery of the real Robin Hood, Gutch, as the most prominent Robin Hood scholar of the age, was asked by various newspapers to comment on the discovery—much as academics are asked now to comment on various research findings. Gutch was impressed with Hunter's findings:

> The Rev. Joseph Hunter … establishes beyond a reasonable doubt that Robin Hood,—"The Great Hero of the Ancient Minstrelsy of England," was a real personage, and not a mere poetical creation.[508]

He supported Hunter's thesis on several occasions—there was a large meeting of the B.A.A. members in Nottingham in August 1852, attended by such luminaries as the Duke of Newcastle. The meeting was widely reported in the press, and here Hunter delivered a paper which argued that Robin Hood was indeed a real person. *The Times* gave a brief synopsis of the paper:

> Mr. Gutch then proceeded to read an elaborate and interesting paper on Robin Hood and the ballads, which he had prepared in consequence of the vicinity of the place of their present meeting to Sherwood Forest, which had been hitherto regarded as the habitation of the celebrated English yeoman Robin Hood. The recent singular discovery by the Rev. J. Hunter, in his researches among the ancient records of the Exchequer, justified him (Mr. Gutch) in asserting the veritable existence of Robin Hood and the county of his residence.[509]

This paper may have been similar in substance to an article that Gutch published shortly before the B.A.A. meeting on 'The Discovery of the Veritable Robin Hood' in *The Gentleman's Magazine*.[510] Interestingly, and much like what happens at the modern International Medieval Congress in Leeds, there appears to have been a panel devoted to Robin Hood matters. Gutch was followed by a Mr Pettigrew, who read out a paper for J.O. Halliwell. Halliwell's paper made a different argument to Gutch, asserting that Robin Hood was a complete myth. After this, Sir F. Dwarris delivered a paper on the Norman Forest Laws.[511] The whole meeting then finished with an 'address', or keynote, on the subject of medieval outlaws.[512]

Gutch published very few scholarly publications after the B.A.A. meeting in 1852. During this time he moved from London to Worcester where he and his wife lived with their father-in-law. He published two further books: *A Garland of Roses from the Poems of the Late Rev. John Eagles* (1857) and *Watson Redivivus* (1860). In 1861 he contributed another article on the identity of the 'real' Robin Hood to a magazine titled *The Reliquary*.[513] He was also at this point compiling a history of Worcester's battlefields for the local history society there, but on 20 September 1861 he passed away. He was survived by his wife and son, and several newspapers and periodicals paid tribute to him at the time of his death, most notably *The Gentleman's Magazine* with whom he had had a long-standing association.[514]

Notes

Introduction

1. Nicholas Harris, 'Memoir of Joseph Ritson', in *The Letters of Joseph Ritson, Esq. Edited Chiefly from Originals in the Possession of his Nephew. To which is Prefixed a Memoir of the Author*, ed. by Joseph Frank, 2 vols (London: William Pickering, 1833), I, p. liv.
2. Ingrid Tieken-Boon van Ostade, 'Eighteenth-Century Letters and Journals as Evidence: Studying Society through the Individual', in *Literature and the New Interdisciplinarity: Poetics, Linguistics, History*, ed. by Roger D. Sell and Peter Verdonk (Atlanta, GA: Rodopi, 1994), pp. 179-92 (p. 179).
3. *The Complete Letter Writer; or, Polite English Secretary* (London: Stanley Crowder, 1772), p. 1.
4. Joseph Ritson, 'To the Editor. 13 March 1783', in *The Letters of Joseph Ritson, Esq. Edited Chiefly from Originals in the Possession of his Nephew. To which is Prefixed a Memoir of the Author*, ed. by Joseph Frank, 2 vols (London: William Pickering, 1833), I, pp. 63-4 (p. 63). Subsequent reference to Ritson's letters will include the title and date of letter and volume, e.g. Ritson, 'To George Allan, 26 August 1786', in *Letters*, I, pp. 1-3.
5. Miriam Dobson, 'Letters', in *Reading Primary Sources: The Interpretation of Texts from Nineteenth- and Twentieth-Century History*, ed. by Miriam Dobson and Benjamin Ziemann (Abingdon and New York: Routledge, 2009), pp. 57-73.
6. Joseph Addison and Richard Steele, 'No. 284: Friday 25 January 1711', in *The Spectator: A New Edition Reproducing the Original Text Both As First Issued and as Corrected by its Authors*, ed. by Henry Morley (London: George Routledge, [c. 1880?]), pp. 407-08 (p. 407).

7. Ritson, 'To Mr Wadeson. 30 November 1783', in *Letters*, I, p. 69.

8. Ritson, 'To Mr Walker. 4 November 1789', in *Letters*, I, p. 149.

9. Ritson, 'To the Editor, 8 October 1799', in *Letters*, II, p. 189.

10. John Britton [online], 'Joseph Ritson, in *Autobiography* (1850)', accessed 7 January 2020. Available at spenserians.cath.vt.edu

11. Joseph Ritson, ed., *Robin Hood: A Collection of All the Ancient Poems, Songs, and Ballads, Now Extant, Relative to that Celebrated English Outlaw: To which are Prefixed Historical Anecdotes of his Life*, 2 vols (London: T. Egerton, 1795), I, p. i.

12. Ritson, *Robin Hood*, I, p. i.

13. Genevieve Theodora McNutt, 'Joseph Ritson and the publication of early English literature' (Unpublished PhD thesis, Edinburgh University, 2018), p. 7.

Chapter One

14. Daniel Defoe, *A Tour Through the Whole Island of Great Britain*, ed. by P.N. Furbank, W.R. Owens and A.J. Coulson (London: Folio Society, 2006), p. 354.

15. *Ibid.*

16. Rodney Hilton, 'Towns in English Society', *Review (Fernand Braudel Center)*, 3: 1 (1979), 3-20 (pp. 5-6).

17. 'Parishes: Stockton on Tees', in *A History of the County of Durham*, ed. by William Page, 3 vols (London: Victoria Country History, 1928), III, pp. 348-65 (p. 349).

18. *Ibid.*, III, p. 351.

19. Benjamin Pye, 'The New Way of Stockton's Commendation', in *Northern Garlands*, ed. by Joseph Ritson (London: R. Triphook, 1810), pp. 20-26.

20. Alexander Pope, *The Guardian*, 2 vols (London: Longman, 1801), I, p. 267 cited in Stephen Basdeo, 'Bred Up a Butcher: The Meat Trade and Its Connection with Criminality in Eighteenth-Century England', in *Food and Feast in Modern Outlaw Tales*, ed. by Alexander Kaufman and Penny Vlagopoulos (Abingdon and New York: Routledge, 2016), pp. 12-26 (p. 14).

21. Peter Raedts, 'Representations of the Middle Ages in Enlightenment Historiography', *The Medieval History Journal*, 5: 1 (2002), 1-20 (p. 1).

22. Ritson, 'To John Russell Rowntree, 19 July 1782', in *Letters*, I, p. 54.

23. B.H. Bronson, *Joseph Ritson: Scholar-at-Arms*, 2 vols (Berkeley, CA: University of California Press, 1938), I, p. 12.

24. Geoffrey Chaucer, 'The General Prologue', in *The Canterbury Tales and the Faerie Queene*, ed. by D. Laing Purves (London: W.P. Nimmo, Hay and Mitchell, 1897), pp. 17-25 (p. 18): Thus we have in Chaucer's *Canterbury Tales* (1387-1400) the story of a knight who has a yeoman in his retinue. The idea that yeomen served knights is perhaps where the military connection with yeomanry comes from—the British sovereign's Yeoman of the Guard being one example.

25. A.J. Pollard, *Imagining Robin Hood: The Late Medieval Stories in Historical Context* (Abingdon and New York: Routledge, 2004), p. 35.

26. Bronson, I, p. 12.

27. J.T. McCullen Jnr., 'Tobacco: A Recurrent Theme in Eighteenth-Century Literature', *The Bulletin of the Rocky Mountain Modern Language Association*, 22: 2 (1968), 30-39 (p. 30).

28. Roy Porter, *English Society in the Eighteenth Century*, rev. ed. (London: Penguin, 1991), p. 23.

29. Rodney Hilton, *Bond Men Made Free: Medieval Peasant Movements and the English Rising of 1381* (New York: Viking, 1973), p. 25.

30. Alice Chandler, 'Sir Walter Scott and the Medieval Revival', *Nineteenth-Century Fiction*, 19: 4 (1965), 315-22 (p. 316).

31. Henry Fielding, *The History of the Adventures of Joseph Andrews* (London: F.C. and J. Rivington, 1820), pp. 323, 393.

32. Porter, p. 31.

33. Bronson, I, p. 10.

34. Bronson, I, p. 11.

35. Porter, p. 13.

36. R.E. Jones, 'Infant Mortality in Rural North Shropshire, 1561-1810', *Population Studies*, 30: 2 (1976), 305-17 (p. 317).

37. Harris, 'Memoir of Joseph Ritson', in *Letters*, I, p. i.

38. Bronson, I, p. 10.

39. George Allen [online], 'Letter to John Nichols, c.1812. Nichols, Literary Anecdotes of the XVIII Century', accessed 7 January 2019. Available at spenserians.cath.vt.edu

40. 'Parishes: Stockton-on-Tees', p. 355.
41. John Wesley, *The Journal of the Rev. John Wesley*, 4 vols. (London: J. Kershaw, 1827), II, p. 125.
42. Ritson, 'To the Editor, 24 February 1785', in *Letters*, I, p. 100.
43. *Ibid*.
44. Ritson, *Robin Hood*, I, p. x.
45. Porter, p. 31.
46. E. Mackenzie and D. Ross, *An Historical, Topographical, and Descriptive View of the County Palatine of Durham*, 2 vols (Newcastle-upon-Tyne: Mackenzie and Dent, 1834), II, p. 31.
47. Ritson, 'To the Same', in *Letters*, I, p. 28.
48. John Skinner, 'Don Quixote in 18th-Century England: A Study in Reader Response', *Cervantes: Bulletin of the Cervantes Society of America*, 7: 1 (1987): 45-57 (pp. 48-9).
49. Jonathan Rose, *The Intellectual Life of the British Working Classes*, 2nd edn (New Haven: Yale UP, 2001), pp. 16-18.
50. Boyd Hilton, *A Mad, Bad, and Dangerous People? England, 1783-1846*, The New Oxford History of England (Oxford Clarendon Press, 2006), p. 25.
51. 'Romance', in *A Dictionary of the English Language*, ed. by Samuel Johnson, rev. ed. (Dublin: W.G. Jones, 1768), n. p.
52. *The Children in the Wood* (Boston: N. Coverly [n.d.]), p. i.
53. Joseph Addison, 'No. 85: Thursday June 7th, 1711', in *The Spectator: A New Edition Reproducing the Original Text Both As First Issued and as Corrected by its Authors*, ed. by Henry Morley (London: George Routledge, [c. 1880?]), p. 136.
54. Ritson, 'To the Editor', in *Letters*, I, p. 20.
55. Ritson, 'To the Same', in *Letters*, I, p. 28
56. Addison, 'No. 70: Monday, May 21st, 1711', in *The Spectator*, p. 114. Addison likewise had much praise for this ballad as one of the best specimens of 'Gothick' writing, and remarked that 'the old song of 'Chevy Chase' is the favourite ballad of the common people of England'.
57. 'Ballad: The Hunting in Chevy Chase', in *Elegant Extracts in Poetry: Selected for the Improvement of Young Persons* (London: F.C. and J. Rivington, 1816), pp. 970-72 (p. 971).
58. Ritson, 'To the Editor', in *Letters*, I, p. 11.

59. Patrick Wallis, 'Apprenticeship and Training in Pre-modern England', *London School of Economics, No. 22/07: Working Papers on The Nature of Evidence: How Well Do 'Facts' Travel?* (London: LSE, 2007), pp. 1-3.

60. Burd, p. 16.

61. Not to be confused with Greatham in Hampshire, UK.

62. Ritson, 'To Ralph Hoar, Esq. New Years Day 1787', in *Letters*, I, p. 120.

63. Simon Atkinson, ed., *Practical points in conveyancing, from the manuscripts of Butler, Preston, and Bradley* (London: S. Sweet, 1829), pp. x-xviii.

64. Bernard Mandeville, *The Fable of The Bees: or, Private Vices, Publick Benefits*, 6th edn (London: J. Tonson, 1729), pp. 131-2.

65. Ritson, 'To the Same, 23 January 1782', in *Letters*, I, p. 41.

66. Henry Fielding, 'The Roast Beef of Old England', in *Tegg's Social Songster and Everlasting Melodist*, ed. by Thomas Tegg (London: T. Tegg [c. 1820?]), p. 293: Fielding's song, originally included in a forgettable play he had written for the Covent Garden Theatre in 1731 entitled *The Grub Street Opera*, enjoyed a musical 'afterlife' as a military march and is still used on occasion in modern times by the British Royal Navy as well as the United States Marine Corps. The famous painter William Hogarth likewise adapted Fielding's theme in a painting, *The Gate of Calais; or, the Roast Beef of Old England* (1748).

67. Thomas Holcroft, *Memoirs of the Late Thomas Holcroft*, 3 vols (London: Longman, 1816), I, p. 13.

68. *Ibid.*

69. Ritson, 'To Mrs Frank, 7 June 1782', in *Letters*, I, p. 49.

70. Ritson, 'To the Same, 27 April 1781', in *Letters*, I, p. 30.

71. Heidi Ledford [Online], 'Rot, drills and inequity: the tangled tale of teeth', *Nature: International Journal of Science*, 22 May 2018. Available at nature.com/articles/d41586-018-05236-4 [Accessed 17 August 2019]: A German visitor to Elizabeth's court in 1598 remarked, 'her lips are narrow and her teeth black, a defect that the English seem subject to, from their great use of sugar.'

72. Rose-Marie Hagen and Rainer Hagen, *What Great Paintings Say*, 2 vols (Cologne: Taschen, 2003), pp. 305-6.

73. Thomas De Quincey, *Confessions of an English Opium-Eater and Selected Essays*, ed. by David Masson (New York: A.L. Burt, 1856), p. 4.

74. Hagen and Hagen, p. 306.

75. Ritson, 'To the Same, 27 April 1781', in *Letters*, I, p. 30.

76. Bronson, I, p. 28.

77. Joseph Ritson, 'Elegy to the Late Mrs Todd of Stockton', *The Literary Register*, 2 (1770), 78.

78. Bronson, I, p. 14. Bronson attributes to Ritson this early poem entitled 'An Elegy to the Memory of the Late Mrs Todd, of Stockton', which appeared in *The Literary Register: Or, Weekly Miscellany*, 5 vols (Newcastle: Printed for the Benefit of Subscribers, 1770), III, p. 78.

79. Richard H. Perkinson, 'The Plot of the Faerie Queene', *PMLA*, 48: 1 (1933), 295-7 (p. 295). It reprinted several times in the Georgian era. In 1715, John Hughes published *The Works of Edmund Spenser*, which was followed by John Upton's edition of *The Faerie Queene* in 1758.

80. Andrew Hadfield, 'William Kent's Illustrations of *The Faerie Queene*', *Spenser Studies*, 14:1 (1999), 1-15 (p. 1).

81. 'My Cousin's Tale', *The Literary Register*, 3 (1771), 252-3.

82. Bronson, I, p. 14.

83. Bronson, I, p. 20n.

84. Joseph Ritson, *Versees Addressed to the Ladies of Stockton* (Stockton: privately printed, 1782), p. 1.

85. Ritson, *Versees*, pp. 1-2.

86. Ritson, *Versees*, p. 3.

87. Shakespeare, 'A Midsummer Night's Dream', in *The New Oxford Shakespeare: Modern Critical Edition: The Complete Works*, ed. by Gary Taylor et al (OUP, 2016), III.4, ll. 288-90.

88. John Kruse, 'Who is Titania?' *British Fairies: A Site Studying and Discussing British Fairy Lore*, 30 September 2018. Available at britishfairies.wordpress.com/2018/09/30/who-is-titania, accessed 4 February 2020.

89. Ritson, *Versees*, pp. 4-5.

90. Sophia, 'To Mr J— R—n of Stockton', *The Literary Register*, 4 (1772), 282.

91. Stephen Basdeo, *Robin Hood: The Life and Legend of an Outlaw* (Barnsley: Pen and Sword, 2019), p. 35.

92. *Old Bailey Proceedings* [online], Old Bailey Proceedings: Accounts of Criminal Trials: 10 October 1722 (t 17221010-17), accessed 9 November 2019. Available at www.londonlives.org

93. *Northumbrian Jacobite Society* [Online], 'Jacobite Support in the North-East', cited 24 August 2019. Available at northumbrianjacobites.org.uk.

94. *Ibid.*

95. Joseph Ritson*, Tables Shewing the Descent of the Crown of England* (London: privately printed, 1778), cited in Bronson, I, p. 57.

96. Ritson, *Tables Shewing the Descent of the Crown of England*, cited in Bronson, I, p. 58.

97. Ritson, 'To Mr Wadeson. 14ᵗʰ January 1782', in *Letters*, I, pp. 38-9.

98. John Wood Sweet, *Bodies Politic: Negotiating Race in the American North, 1730-1830*, 2nd edn (Philadelphia, PA: University of Pennsylvania Press, 2006), p. 189.

99. Patricia Bradley, *Slavery, Propaganda, and the American Revolution* (Jackson, MS: UP of Mississippi, 1998), pp. 67-8.

100. John W. Derry, *Politics in the Age of Fox, Pitt, and Liverpool* (Basingstoke: Palgrave, 2001), pp. 16–18. Samuel Johnson, 'Taxation No Tyranny: An Answer to the Resolutions and Address of the American Congress', in *The Works of Samuel Johnson*, 16 vols (New York: Pafraets and Company, 1913), XIV, pp. 93-144

101. Stephen Basdeo, *Heroes and Villains of the British Empire* (Barnsley: Pen and Sword, 2020), p. 65.

102. Ritson, 'To Ralph Hoar, 1 January 1787', in *Letters*, I, p. 117.

103. Walter Scott, *Chronicles of the Canongate*, 2 vols (Edinburgh: Cadell, 1827), II, p. 146.

104. Ritson, 'To Ralph Hoar, 1 January 1787', in *Letters*, I, pp. 123-4.

105. Ritson, 'To the Same, 17 March 1792', in *Letters*, I, pp. 212-13.

106. 'Despairing Beside a Clear Stream', in Joseph Ritson, ed., *A Select Collection of English Songs*, 2nd edn, 3 vols (London: F.C. and J. Rivington, 1813), III, pp. 31-2.

107. Nicholas Rowe [online], 'Colin's Complaint', *English Poetry, 1579-1830: Spenser and the Tradition*, accessed 9 November 2019. Available at spenserians.cath.vt.edu.

108. 'Notices', *Newcastle Chronicle*, 18 June 1774, 2.

109. Bronson, I, pp. 50-51.
110. Ritson, 'To Ralph Hoar, 1 January 1787', in *Letters*, I, p. 120.

Chapter Two

111. Ritson, 'To Mr Harrison, 11 October 1788', in *Letters*, I, p. 138.
112. *Digital Panopticon* [online]. 'Digital Panopticon: London, 1780-1900', cited 11 October 2019. Available at digitalpanopticon. org
113. Emily Cockayne, *Hubbub: Filth, Noise and Stench in England* (New Haven: Yale UP, 2007), p. 9.
114. Martin Charles Burney, ed., *General Index to the Journals of the House of Commons: Commencing with the First Parliament of the United Kingdom of Great Britain and Ireland Vol. LVI. A.D. 1801 and Ending with Vol. LXXV. A.D. 1820* (London: Luke Hansard and Sons, 1825), p. 718.
115. Cockayne, pp. 190-91.
116. Ritson, 'To Mr Joseph Ritson, Sen., 3 March 1777', in *Letters*, I, p. 4.
117. Burd, p. 26.
118. Porter, p. 32.
119. This place is now South Square, Gray's Inn, and the place where the Honourable Society of Gray's Inn hold private banquets for their own society as well as corporate guests.
120. Hilton, *A Mad, Bad, and Dangerous People*, p. 146.
121. Ritson, 'To Mr Wadeson, 27 June 1782', in *Letters*, I, p. 52.
122. Joseph Ritson, *The Stockton Jubilee* (Newcastle, 1781) cited in Bronson, pp. 62-3.
123. Boswell cited in Bronson, I, p. 62.
124. Ritson, 'To Mr Wadeson, 14 January 1782', in *Letters*, I, pp. 37-8.
125. John Cawdell, *The Miscellaneous Poems of John Cawdell* (Sunderland, 1785), pp. 154-5 cited in Bronson, p. 64.
126. Robert E. Burns, 'The Catholic Relief Act in Ireland, 1778', *Church History*, 32: 2 (1963), 181-206 (p. 183).
127. Eugene Charlton Black, 'The Tumultuous Petitioners: The Protestant Association in Scotland, 1778-1780', *The Review of Politics*, 25: 2 (1963), 183-211 (p. 184).
128. Ritson, 'To the Same. June 7th, 1780', in *Letters*, I, pp. 14-15.
129. *Ibid.*
130. Ritson, 'To the Same. 14th June 1780', in *Letters*, I, pp. 17-18.

131. *Ibid.*, p. 18.

132. Ritson, 'To Mrs Frank, 25th November 1780', in *Letters*, I, p. 19.

133. Bronson, I, p. 11.

134. Burd, p. 42.

135. Ritson, 'To Mr Wadeson, 15th March 1783', in *Letters*, I, p. 66.

136. *Ibid.*

137. Ritson, 'To Mr Rowntree, 23rd June 1790', in *Letters*, I, p. 166.

138. *Ibid.*

139. Burd, p. 28.

140. Robert Robson, *The Attorney in Eighteenth-Century England* (CUP, 1959), p. 49.

141. Ritson, 'To Mr Rowntree, 4th December 1786', in *Letters*, I, p. 113.

142. Hilton, *A Mad, Bad, and Dangerous People*, p. 144.

143. *Alcester Court Leet* [online], 'History of the Court Leet', cited 13 October 2019. Available at alcestercourtleet.co.uk/history/court-leet-history

144. John Harland, ed. *A Volume of Court Leet Records of the Manor of Manchester in the Sixteenth Century* (Manchester: Chetham Society, 1844), p. 18: Bailiff (ballivus) from the French bailiff, that is *praefectus provinciae*. There are in England several kinds of bailiffs. Bailiffs of liberties are those bailiffs who are appointed by every lord within his liberty, to execute processes and do such offices therein, as the bailiff errant doth at large in the country. Bailiffs of liberties and franchises are to be sworn to take distresses, truly impanel jurors, make returns by indenture between them and the sheriffs, &c.

145. Joseph Ritson, *The Office of Bailiff of a Liberty* (London: A. Strahan, 1811), p. 1.

146. 'Receipt, Joseph Ritson', Beinecke Library, Yale University GEN MSS 76 Box 1.10.

147. Ritson, *The Office of Liberty of a Bailiff*, p. 51.

148. Edward Coke, *The Third Part of the Institutes of the Laws of England Concerning High Treason and Other Pleas of the Crown and Criminal Causes*, rev. ed. (London: E.R. Brooke, 1792), p. 197: 'Against Roberdsmen: It is an English proverb, that many men talk of Robin Hood, that never shot his bow: and because the statutes and records hereafter mentioned cannot well be understood, unless it be known what this Robin Hoode was that hath raised a name to these kinde of men called Roberdsmen, his followers.'

149. Cockayne, p. 10.
150. Joseph Ritson, 'To the Governors, 4 August 1789', cited in Bronson, II, p. 657.
151. Minutes of Parish Vestries, 9 October 1789. London, Westminster Archives Centre. *London Lives* [Online], 'St Clement Danes Parish: Minutes of Parish Vestries CD | MV 13th July 1787-6th August 1795', cited 13 October 2019. Available at londonlives.org
152. Joseph Ritson, *A Digest of the proceedings of the Court Leet of the Manor and Liberty of the Savoy* (London: printed in the year 1789), p. i.
153. Ritson, *A Digest of the Proceedings of the Court Leet*, p. 13.
154. *Ibid*, p. 14.
155. Ritson, *Ibid*, p. 18.
156. Lincoln B. Faller, *Turned to Account: The Forms and Functions of Criminal Biography in Late Seventeenth- and Early Eighteenth-Century England* (CUP, 1987), p. x.
157. James A. Sharpe, *Crime in Early Modern England 1550-1750* (London and New York: Routledge, 1984), pp. 119-20.
158. Henry Fielding, *An Enquiry into the Causes of the Late Increase of Robbers* (Dublin: G. Faulkner, 1751), p. 1
159. Robert Shoemaker, 'The Street Robber and the Gentleman Highwayman: Changing Representations and Perceptions of Robbery in London, 1690-1800', *Cultural and Social History*, 3: 4 (2006), 381-405 (p. 383).
160. *The New Newgate Calendar; or, The Malefactor's Bloody Register*, 5 vols (London: A. Hogg, 1795), II, p. i: on the title page: 'The crimes related here art great and true,/The subjects vary, and the work is new,/By reading, learn the ways of sin to shun,/Be timely taught, and you'll not be undone.'
161. Peter Wagner, 'Trial Reports as a Genre of Eighteenth-Century Erotica', *Journal for Eighteenth-Century Studies*, 5: 1 (1982), pp. 117-21. We have only to look at a passage in Charles Johnson's *General and True History of the Most Notorious Pyrates* (1724): 'she … carelessly [showed] her breasts, which were very white. The young fellow, who was made of flesh and blood, had his curiosity raised by this sight … Now begins the scene of love.'
162. Ritson, 'To the Same, 5 January 1790', in *Letters*, I, p. 155.
163. Ritson, 'To the Same, 14 May 1790', in *Letters*, I, pp. 160-1.

164. Henry Fielding, *The History of the Life and Death of the Late Jonathan Wild the Great* (London: J. Bell, 1775), p. 3.

165. Ritson, 'To Mr Walker, 8 March 1794', in *Letters*, II, p. 49.

166. Ritson, *A Digest of the Proceedings of the Court Leet*, pp. 8-9.

167. Joseph Ritson, *The Office of Constable: Being an Entirely New Compendium of the Law Concerning that Ancient Minister for the Conservation of the Peace*, 2nd edn (London: W. Clarke, 1815), p. 1.

168. Ritson, *The Office of Constable*, p. 7.

169. Marco Sampaolo et al., [online], 'constable', in *Encyclopædia Britannica* cited 15 October 2019. Available at britannica.com/topic/constable

170. Ritson, *The Office of Constable*, p. 44.

171. *Ibid.*

172. Joseph Ritson, *Law Tracts* (London, 1794), p. 48.

173. Philo R—, 'Letters', *St James's Chronicle*, 13 November 1792 cited in Bronson, I, p. 142.

174. Burd, p. 333. Previous biographers have also attributed an earlier 'law tract' to Ritson: the anonymously published *Modes of Trying Peers* (1776), although no copies of this seem to have survived.

175. Burd, p. 213

176. Ritson, 'To the Editor, 7 April 1784', in *Letters*, I, pp. 86-7.

177. Ritson, 'To the Editor, 31 January 1781', in *Letters*, I, p. 21.

178. Paul Langford, 'The Uses of Eighteenth-Century Politeness', *Transactions of the Royal Historical Society*, 12 (2002), 311-31 (p. 311).

179. Ritson, 'To the Editor, 27 April 1781', in *Letters*, I, p. 29.

180. Paul Langford, *A Polite and Commercial People* (OUP, 1989), p. 4.

181. Richard Steele, 'The Tatler, 12 April 1709', in Joseph Addison and Richard Steele, *The Tatler and the Guardian Complete in One Volume* (Edinburgh: W.P. Nimmo, 1880), pp. 1-2:

182. Addison, 'No. 119: Thursday 17 July 1711', in *The Spectator*, pp. 181-2.

183. Ritson, 'To Mr Harrison, 20 October 1789', in *Letters*, I, p. 149.

184. Ritson, 'To the Editor, 7 April 1784', in *Letters*, I, pp. 86-7

185. Ritson, 'To the Editor, 15 March 1780', in *Letters*, I, p. 10; Ritson, 'To the Editor, 8 November 1782', in *Letters*, I, pp. 61-2.

186. Ritson, 'To the Editor, 29 November 1793', in *Letters*, II, p. 33.

187. Ritson, 'To the Editor, 27 April 1781', in *Letters*, I, p. 27.

188. Ritson, 'To the Editor, 27 April 1781', in *Letters*, I, pp. 27-31.

189. Langford, *A Polite and Commercial People*, p. 1.

Chapter Three

190. Joseph Addison [online], 'An Account of the Greatest English Poets. To Mr. H. S. Ap. 3d. 1694', accessed 6 January 2019. Available at spenserians.cath.vt.edu

191. *Ibid.*

192. Kenneth Clark, *The Gothic Revival: An Essay in the History of Taste*, rev. ed. (London: John Murray, 1995), p. 72.

193. Rosemary Mitchell, *Picturing the Past: English History in Text and Image, 1830-1870* (OUP, 2000), p. 9

194. John Dryden, *King Arthur; or, The British Worthy* (London: J. Tonson, 1731), p. i: the frontispiece to Dryden's play depicts King Arthur as a Roman centurion. John Winstanley, *Poems Written Occasionally, Interspersed with Many Others by Several Ingenious Hands* (London, 1742), 210-21: Winstanley's poem sees Robin Hood dining with Apollo, the messenger of the gods.

195. Abbey Coykendall, 'Gothic Genealogies, the Family Romance, and Clara Reeve's The Old English Baron', *Eighteenth-Century Fiction*, 17: 3 (2005), 443-80 (p. 443).

196. Nick Groom, *The Making of Percy's Reliques* (OUP, 1999), p. 25.

197. Langford, *A Polite and Commercial People*, p. 473.

198. Thomas Percy, ed., *Reliques of Ancient English Poetry*, 3 vols (London: J. Dodsley, 1765), I, p. ix.

199. Stephen Basdeo, 'The Once and Future Viking: The Popularity of Ragnar Lodbrok in the 18th Century', in *Vikings and the Vikings: Essays on Television's History Channel Series*, ed. by Paul Hardwick and Kate Lister (Jefferson, NC: MacFarland, 2019), pp. 7-20 (p. 7).

200. Bruce E. Graver, 'The Reception of Chaucer from Dryden to Wordsworth', in *Geoffrey Chaucer in Context*, ed. by Ian Johnson (CUP, 2019), pp. 403-19.

201. Brown, *Romanticism*, p. 203, 317.

202. Bronson, I, p. 47.

203. Ritson, 'To the Editor, 31 January 1781', in *Letters*, I, p. 20.

204. Ritson, 'To Mr Harrison, 11 October 1788', in Letters, I, p. 138; Ritson, 'To Mr Harrison, 12 March 1789', in Letters, I, p. 140; Ritson, 'To Mr Walker, 1 April 1800', in Letters, II, p. 207; Joseph Ritson, 'To Mr George Paton, 15 November 1792', in *Letters from Joseph Ritson, Esq.*, to Mr. George Paton, ed. by James Maidment (Edinburgh: John Stevenson, 1829), p. 1.

205. Joseph Ritson, *Observations on the Three First Volumes of the History of English Poetry. In a familiar letter to the author, T.W.* (London: J. Stockdale, 1782), p. i-ii.

206. Thomas Warton, *The History Of English Poetry*, ed. by Richard Price, 3 vols (London: Thomas Tegg, 1840), I, pp. 6-7.

207. Ritson, *Observations on the Three First Volumes of the History of English Poetry*, pp. 3-4.

208. Samuel Parr (attr.), *A Familiar Address to the Curious in English Poetry* (London, 1784) cited in Bronson, I, p. 79.

209. J.T. Gilbert, ed. *The Manuscripts and Correspondence of James, First Earl of Charlemont*, 2 vols (London: HMSO, 1891-94), I, p. 423.

210. Thomas Warton, *The History Of English Poetry*, rev. ed., 4 vols (London: Thomas Tegg, 1825), I, p. 23.

211. Bronson, I, p. 75.

212. Ritson, 'To Mr Harrison, 8 October 1782', in *Letters*, I, p. 61.

213. Victoria Joynes [online], 'Into the 18th Century: Shakespeare in Performance', accessed 14 November 2019. Available at shakespeare.org.uk

214. Porter, p. 10.

215. David Wiles, *The Early Plays of Robin Hood* (Cambridge: D.S. Brewer, 1981), pp. 71-9.

216. David Blayney Brown, *Romanticism*, Art and Ideas (London: Phaidon, 2001), p. 205.

217. *Harlequin Student; or, The Fall of Pantomime and the Restoration of Drama* (London, 1741) cited in Brewer, p. 331.

218. Joseph Ritson, *Remarks, Critical and Illustrative, on the Text and Notes of the Last Edition of Shakespeare* (London: J. Johnson, 1783), p. iii-iv.

219. Steven Lynn, 'Johnson's Critical Reception', in *The Cambridge Companion to Samuel Johnson*, ed. by Greg Clingham (CUP, 1997), pp. 240-53 (p. 251).

220. Ritson, *Remarks, Critical and Illustrative*, p. 81.

221. Joseph Ritson, *The Quip Modest; a Few Words by Way of Supplement to Remarks, Critical and Illustrative, on the Text and Notes of the Last Edition of Shakespeare; Occasioned by a Republication of that Edition* (London: J. Johnson, 1788), p. iii.

222. Edmund G.C. King, 'Fragmenting Authorship in the Eighteenth-Century Shakespeare Edition', *Shakespeare*, 6: 1 (2010), 1-19 (p. 16).

223. Joseph Ritson, *Cursory Criticisms on the Edition of Shakespeare Published by Edmond Malone* (London: Hookham and Carpenter, 1792), p. vii.

224. Ritson, 'To Mr Walker, 25 June 1790', in *Letters*, I, p. 167.

225. Michael Lort [online], 'To Thomas Percy, 15 January 1783. Illustrations of the Literary History of the XVIII Century', accessed 7 January 2020. Available at spenserians.cath.vt.edu

226. Percy, *Reliques of Ancient English Poetry*, I, p. ix.

227. Joseph Ritson, ed., *Ancient Songs from the Time of King Henry the Third to the Revolution* (London: J. Johnson, 1790), p. i.

228. The appearance of the *Reliques* was hardly innovative when it was first published in 1765. Multivolume collections of ballads had existed since the seventeenth century, although they were mainly filled with songs that were still thought of as a part of the 'current' in popular culture at the time. Famous among these early ballad collections was Thomas D'Urfey's *Pills to Purge Melancholy*, published in several volumes between 1698 and 1720. D'Urfey did not have any scholarly pretensions however: his work was for people to enjoy rather than study.

229. M.L. McKenzie, 'The Great Ballad Collectors: Percy, Herd, and Ritson', *Studies in Scottish Literature*, 2: 4 (1965), 213-33 (p. 219).

230. 'Robin Hood and Guy of Gisborne', in *Reliques of Ancient English Poetry*, ed. by Thomas Percy, 3 vols (London: J. Dodsley, 1765), I, p. 86.

231. Joseph Ritson, *Pieces of Ancient Popular Poetry*, rev. Edmund Goldsmid, 2 vols (Edinburgh: privately printed, 1884), I, p. i.

232. Joseph Ritson, ed., *A Select Collection of English Songs*, 2nd edn, 3 vols (London: F.C. and J. Rivington, 1813), I, p. lxxvi.

233. Anon. 'George Barnwell', in *Reliques of Ancient English Poetry*, ed. by Thomas Percy, 3 vols (London: J. Dodsley, 1765), III, pp. 225-33.

234. Ritson, *A Select Collection of English Songs*, I, p. lxviii.
235. *Ibid.*, I, p. lxxvi.
236. Burd, p. 159.
237. Burd, p. 161.
238. Anon. 'The Pythagorean Critick', *St. James's Chronicle*, 3 June 1783 cited in Burd, p. 192.
239. Ritson, 'To the Same, 6 January 1785', in *Letters*, I, p. 96.
240. 'Parishes: Norton', in *A History of the County of Durham*, ed. by William Page, 3 vols (London: Victoria County History, 1928), III, pp. 304-15 (p. 312): 'The Grammar school at Norton is supposed to have been founded about 1600, but the circumstances are unknown. The bishops were accustomed to demise certain trust lands on lease to the vicar, who was to pay the proceeds to a schoolmaster for the free education of six boys nominated by the vicar. The demise included two ovens or bake-houses, one of which had fallen into decay by 1828, the toft where the Lady Kiln had stood, the Kiln Close or Lady Close in Portrack Lane with an acre appurtenant thereto, and the Hermitage garth. At an inclosure in 1673 more land was given to the school. A scheme for the use of the endowment was made in 1898; scholarships are provided by it for boys of the parish tenable at a secondary or technical school approved by the governors. A school board was formed in 1872.'
241. Ritson, 'To Joseph Frank, 17 June 1784', in *Letters*, I, p. 91.
242. Ritson, 'To Mr Wadeson, 30 November 1784', in *Letters*, I, p. 69.
243. Ritson, 'To the Same, 16 August 1803', in *Letters*, II, p. 247.
244. Joseph Ritson, *The Spartan Manual; or, Tablet of Morality* (London: C. Dillington, 1785), p. viii-ix.
245. Stephen Bygrave, *Uses of Education: Readings in Enlightenment in England* (Lewisburg: Bucknell UP, 2009), p. 123.
246. Lawrence Stone, *The Family, Sex and Marriage in England 1500-1800* (New York: Harper & Row, 1979), p. 294.
247. H. Cunningham, *Children and Childhood in Western Society since 1500* (Harlow: Longman, 1995), p. 64.
248. J.H. Plumb, 'The New World of Children in Eighteenth-Century England', *Past and Present*, 67: 1 (1975), 64-95 (p. 80).
249. Ritson, *The Spartan Manual*, p. 7.
250. Ritson, 'To the Editor, 24 February 1785', in *Letters*, I, p. 101.

251. Ritson, 'To the Editor, 6 January 1785', in *Letters*, I, p. 97.
252. Ritson, 'To the Editor, 30 July 1785', in *Letters*, I, p. 103.
253. Ritson, *The Spartan Manual*, p. 30.
254. Ritson, 'To the Same, 30 July 1785', in *Letters*, I, pp. 104-05.
255. Ritson, 'To Mr Harrison, 3 October 1786', in *Letters*, I, p. 110.
256. Ritson, *Northern Garlands*, p. vii.
257. Ritson, 'To Mr Walker, 4 November 1789', in *Letters*, I, p. 149.
258. Ritson, 'To Mr Harrison, 22 June 1780', in *Letters*, I, p. 162.
259. Ritson, *Ancient Songs*, p. i.
260. Ritson, *Ancient Songs*, p. xxi.
261. 'Review: Scotish Songs, 2 vols. 12mo. 10s. boards. Johnson, 1794', *Critical Review*, January 1795, 49.
262. William Godwin, 'To Joseph Ritson, March 1801', cited in Harris, 'Memoir of Joseph Ritson', in *Letters*, I, p. lxxviii.
263. Patrick O'Flaherty, *Scotland's Pariah: The Life and Work of John Pinkerton, 1758-1826* (Toronto, ON: Toronto UP, 2015), p. 70.
264. Ritson, 'To the Editor, 20 April 1796', in *Letters*, p. 122.
265. Joseph Ritson, ed. *Pieces of Ancient Popular Poetry* (London: William Pickering, 1833), p. xi.
266. Alexander Chalmers [online], 'Life of Warton; Works of the English Poets (1810)', accessed 7 January 2020. Available at spenserians.cath.vt.edu
267. Brewer, p. 85.
268. Jenny Uglow, 'Fielding, Grub Street, and Canary Wharf', in *Grub Street and the Ivory Tower: Literary Journalism and Literary Scholarship from Fielding to the Internet*, ed. by Jeremy Treglown, Bridget Bennett (Oxford: Clarendon Press, 1998), pp. 1-21 (p. 7).
269. Carly Watson [online], 'Verse Miscellanies in the Eighteenth Century', *Oxford Handbooks*, accessed 23 November 2019. Available at 10.1093/oxfordhb/9780199935338.013.114
270. Dorothy Wordsworth, *Journals of Dorothy Wordsworth*, ed. by Helen Darbishire (OUP, 1958), p. 32 cited in Abigail Williams, *The Social Life of Books* (New Haven: Yale UP, 2017), p. 7.
271. Joseph Ritson, ed., *The English Anthology*, 3 vols (London: T. and J. Egerton, 1793), I, p. vi.
272. Ritson, 'To Mr Walker, 4 November 1789', in *Letters*, I, p. 152.
273. Burd, pp. 139-40.

274. Ritson, 'To Mr Walker, 25 June 1790', in *Letters*, I, p. 167.

275. Joseph Ritson, ed., *Scotish Song*, 2 vols (London: J. Johnson and J. Edgerton, 1794), I, p. i.

276. Ritson, *Scotish Song*, I, p. lxxxi.

Chapter Four

277. Jonathan Swift, cited in J.A. Downie, *A Political Biography of Henry Fielding* (London: Chatto and Windus, 2009), p. 9.

278. Ritson, 'To Mr Wadeson. March 1782', in *Letters*, I, pp. 45-6.

279. Ritson, 'To Mr Rowntree. 23 May 1784', in *Letters*, I, p. 88.

280. This constituency existed from 1675 until the Reform Act was passed in 1832 (this act significantly extended the franchise to people who owned *or* leased property worth over 40s, whereas in Ritson's day the qualification was based upon the ownership of freehold property).

281. Ritson, 'To Mr Rowntree, 23 June 1790', in *Letters*, I, pp. 165-6.

282. Ritson, 'To Mr. Walker', in *Letters*, I, p. 169.

283. Ritson, 'To Mr Rowntree, 25 June 1790', in *Letters*, I, p. 167.

284. John A. Phillips, *Electoral Behavior in Unreformed England: Plumpers, Splitters, and Straights* (Princeton, NJ: Princeton UP, 1982), p. 20.

285. Ritson, 'To Mr Rowntree, 28 November 1789', in *Letters*, I, p. 154.

286. Ritson, 'To Mr Harrison, 3 August 1791', in *Letters*, I, p. 198.

287. Ritson, 'To the Same, 17 March 1792', in *Letters*, I, pp. 211-12.

288. Thomas Paine [online], 'Common Sense (1776)', accessed 8 January 2020. Available at oll.libertyfund.org

289. Charles James Fox cited in Mark Philip, 'Introduction', in *The French Revolution and British Popular Politics*, ed. by Mark Philip (CUP, 1991), p. 3.

290. Timothy Michael, *British Romanticism and the Critique of Political Reason* (Baltimore: Johns Hopkins UP, 2016), p. 41.

291. Mackenzie and Ross, II, p. 37: only this source attests that Shield accompanied Ritson to Paris, while Ritson's letters are silent on the matter. There does not appear to be any reason to doubt the claim, for Mackenzie and Ross probably spoke to those who had been acquainted with Ritson.

292. Harris, 'Memoir of Joseph Ritson', p. xli.

293. Ritson, 'To Mr Harrison. 9 June 1791', in *Letters*, I, p. 192.

294. Ruth Mather [online], 'The impact of the French Revolution in Britain', accessed 4 January 2020. Available at bl.uk/romantics-and-victorians

295. *Ibid.*

296. William Wordsworth, *The Complete Poetical Works of William Wordsworth*, 10 vols (New York: Cosimo Classics, 2008), IV, p. 317.

297. Charles II le Chauve, a king of France whose reign lasted from 843-877.

298. Ritson, 'To Mr Harrison. 26 November 1791', in *Letters*, I, pp. 203-4.

299. Philip M. Taylor, *Munitions of the Mind: A History of Propaganda*, 3rd edn (Manchester UP, 2013), p. 147

300. Edmund Burke, *Reflections on the Revolution in France*, 3rd edn (London: J. Dodsley, 1790), p. 45.

301. Thomas Paine, *The Rights of Man in Two Parts* (New York: G. Vale, 1848), p. 111.

302. Mark Philp [online], 'Paine, Thomas (1737-1809)', *Oxford Dictionary of National Biography*, accessed 8 January 2020. Available at oxforddnb.com

303. Ritson, 'To the Editor. 29 November 1793', in *Letters*, II, p. 35.

304. Ritson, 'To the Editor, 30 January 1794', in *Letters*, II, p. 39.

305. Ritson, 'To the Editor. 18 Germinal, 2', in *Letters*, II, p. 12.

306. Ritson, *Ancient Songs*, p. 229.

307. Ritson, 'To Mr Wadeson, 20 April 1793', in *Letters*, II, p. 12.

308. Bronson, I, p. 39.

309. Ritson, 'To the Editor, 23 April 1793', in *Letters*, II, pp. 14-15.

310. Ritson, 'To the Editor, 2 May 1793', in *Letters*, II, p. 16.

311. Ritson, 'To Mr Harrison, 19 June 1793', in *Letters*, II, p. 18.

312. Ritson, 'To the Editor, 9 August 1793', in *Letters*, II, p. 24.

313. Roger Paden, 'Marx's Critique of the Utopian Socialists', *Utopian Studies*, 13: 2 (2002), 67-91 (p. 67).

314. V.I. Lenin [online], 'Meeting of the All-Russia Central Executive Committee, 4 November 1917', accessed 21 January 2020. Available at marxists.org

315. Bronson, I, p. 151.

316. Ritson, 'To the Editor, 9 August 1793', in *Letters*, II, p. 24.
317. Ritson, 'To the Editor. 29 November 1793', in *Letters*, II, p. 34.
318. Richard Gough Thomas, *William Godwin: A Political Life* (London: Pluto Press, 2019), p. 19.
319. Ritson, 'To the Editor. 18 Germinal, 2', in *Letters*, II, p. 12.
320. Ritson, 'To the Editor. 5 Vendemaire, 3', in *Letters*, II, pp. 57-8.
321. Ritson, 'To Mr Walker, 8 March 1794', in *Letters*, II, pp. 51-2.
322. Ritson, 'To the Editor, 23 March 1795', in *Letters*, II, p. 69.
323. *Ibid.*
324. Ritson, 'To the Editor, 14 July 1795', in *Letters*, II, p. 89.
325. Ritson, 'To Mr Wadeson. 16 January 1793', in *Letters*, II, p. 8.
326. Ritson, 'To Mr Laing. 5 March 1794', in *Letters*, II, p. 47.
327. Ritson, 'To Mr Harrison, 26 December 1792', in *Letters*, I, p. 223.
328. Ritson, 'To the Same, 26 February 1796', in *Letters*, II, p. 117.
329. Edward P. Thompson, *The Making of the English Working Class*, rev. ed. (New York: Vintage, 1966), p. 179.
330. Eric J. Evans, *William Pitt the Younger* (London: Routledge, 1999), p. 58.
331. *Ibid.*, p. 59.
332. Ritson, 'To Mr Walker, 25 June 1790', in *Letters*, I, p. 170.
333. Cecil Thelwall, *The Life of John Thelwall*, 2 vols (London: John Macrone, 1837), I, pp. 140-1.
334. John Mee, *Print, Publicity, and Radicalism in the 1790s: The Laurel of Liberty* (CUP, 2016), p. 181.
335. Bronson, I, p. 147.
336. Robert Reed, *The Peterloo Massacre*, 2nd edn (London: Windmill Books, 2018), p. 38.
337. Ritson, 'To the Editor, 12 October 1795', in *Letters*, II, pp. 102-3.
338. Ritson, 'To the Editor, 9 August 1793', in *Letters*, I, p. 22.
339. Ritson, 'To Mr Wadeson, 26 February 1794', in *Letters*, II, p. 42.
340. *Ibid.*
341. *Ibid.*
342. Ritson, 'To Mr Wadeson. 15 December 1791', in *Letters*, I, pp. 208-9.
343. McNutt, p. 115.
344. Ritson, *Pieces of Ancient Popular Poetry*, p. 3.
345. Ritson, 'To J.R. Rowntree, 19 July 1782', in *Letters*, I, p. 54.

346. There is some debate among scholars as to the dating of *Robin Hood and Guy of Gisborne*: a similar story survives in a play that can be dated to the late fifteenth century, but the poem itself can be dated to the seventeenth century.

347. Ritson, *Robin Hood*, I, p. xiv.

348. *Ibid.*, I, p. xiv.

349. Johnson, *History of the Highwaymen* (London: T. Tegg, 1834), p. 70, 423.

350. *Ibid.*, I, p. xi.

351. *Ibid*, I, p. xii.

352. *Ibid.*, 1: xi-xii.

353. *Ibid.,* I, pp. xi-xii.

354. Matthew McCormack, *The Independent Man: Citizenship and Gender Politics in Georgian England* (Manchester: Manchester UP, 2005), pp. 1-15, 63.

355. *Ibid*, I, p. v.

356. *Ibid*, 1: ix.

357. *Ibid*, I, p. vi.

358. *Ibid*, I, p. x.

359. Paine, *Common Sense*, op cit.

360. Ritson, *Robin Hood*, I, p. x. Emphasis added.

361. Stephen Knight, *Robin Hood: A Mythic Biography* (Ithaca: Cornell UP, 2003), p. 97.

362. Ritson, *Robin Hood*, I, p. iv. Emphasis added.

363. *Ibid*, I, pp. 71-80.

364. *Ibid*, I, p. xxii, lxvi.

365. *Ibid.*, I, p. lxiv.

366. 'This day is published', *The Morning Chronicle*, 14 December 1795, 2.

367. This look appears to have been a trend for depictions of Robin Hood, for he is depicted in a similar manner in William Blake's 1783 print *Robin Hood and Clorinda* or John Raphael Smith's 1787 illustration of Mr Bowden as Robin Hood in Leonard MacNally's play *Robin Hood, or Sherwood Forest*.

368. Katey Castellano, *The Ecology of British Romantic Conservatism, 1790-1837* (Basingstoke: Palgrave, 2013), p. 81.

369. 'Robin Hood', *The Critical Review or Annals of Literature*, 23 (1798), 229.

Chapter Five

370. Ritson, 'To Mr Walker, 14 December 1790', in *Letters*, II, p. 176.

371. Ritson, 'To Mr Harrison, 22 June 1790', in *Letters*, II, p. 162.

372. Heather R. Beattie, *Nervous Disease in Late Eighteenth-Century Britain: The Reality of a Fashionable Disorder* (Abingdon: Routledge, 2016), p. 1.

373. Beattie, p. 4.

374. Jane Austen, *Pride and Prejudice* (London: Bentley, 1853), p. 3.

375. Ritson, 'To the Same, 5 April 1798', in *Letters*, II, p. 166.

376. Joseph Ritson, *Ancient Engleish Metrical Romanceës*, 3 vols (London: W. Bulmer and Company, 1802), I, p. ii.

377. *Ibid.*, I, pp. iii-iv.

378. Bronson, II, p. 568.

379. Monica Santini, *The Impetus of Amateur Scholarship: Discussing and Editing Medieval Romances in Late-Eighteenth and Nineteenth-Century Britain* (Bern: Peter Lang, 2009), p. 108.

380. Ritson, 'To Mr Walker, 18 October 1799', in *Letters*, II, p. 190.

381. Robert Southey, 'Harold; or, The Castle of Morford', Bodleian MS Misc. Eng. e.21. An edition of this will be published by myself and Mark Truesdale in due course.

382. Ritson, *Ancient Engleish Metrical Romanceës*, I, p. 3.

383. Bronson, I, p. 135.

384. *Ibid.*, I, p. 136.

385. Joseph Ritson, *Bibliographia Poetica: A Catalogue of Engleish Poets of the Twelfth, Thirteenth, Fourteenth, Fifteenth, and Sixteenth Centuries, with a Short Account of Their Works* (London: C. Roworth, 1802), p. i.

386. *Ibid.*

387. Ritson, *Bibliogaphia Poetica*, p. 93.

388. *Ibid.*

389. 'Robyn Hode and the Munke', in *Popular Ballads and Songs: From Tradition, Manuscripts, and Scarce Editions*, ed. by Robert Jamieson, 2 vols (Edinburgh: Archibald Constable, 1806), II, pp. 54-72. To take one example of modern historians and literary critics crediting Jamieson and not Ritson for the poem's discovery, see the following: Thomas Ohlgren, *Robin Hood: The Early Poems, 1465-1560 — Texts, Contexts, and Ideology* (Cranbury, NJ: Associated University Presses, 2010), pp. 28-9.

390. Alistair Johnson [Online], 'Sir Walter Scott in Kevock, Lasswade', *Bonnyrigg and Lasswade Local History Society*, cited 31 August 2019. Available at bonnyrigglasswadelocalhistory.org

391. A.H.C. Ratcliffe [Online], 'The Short Leg in Poliomyelitis', *The Journal of Bone and Joint Surgery*, 41b: 1 (1959), cited 31 August 2019. Available at online.boneandjoint.org.uk

392. Walter Scott [Online], 'To Robert Surtees', in *The Letters of Sir Walter Scott*, ed. by Sir Herbert Grierson and Takero Sato, 12 vols (London: Constable, 1932-37), I, pp. 355-6, cited 31 August 2019. Available at walterscott.lib.ed.ac.uk

393. Joseph Ritson, 'Letter Signed Anti-Scot', *The Gentleman's Magazine*, November 1784, 812-14.

394. Joseph Ritson, 'To Mr Scott. 2 July 1803', in *Letters*, II, p. 237.

395. Timothy Morton, 'Joseph Ritson, Percy Shelley, and the Making of Romantic Vegetarianism', *Romanticism* 12.1 (2006), 52-61 (p. 52).

396. Joseph Ritson, *An Essay on Abstinence from Animal Food as a Moral Duty* (London, 1802), p. 229.

397. *Ibid.*, pp. 13-14.

398. Peter J. Bowler, *Evolution: The History of an Idea*, 3rd edn (Berkeley, CA: University of California Press, 2003), p. 70.

399. *Ibid.*

400. Ritson, 'To the Same, 23 January 1782', in *Letters*, I, p. 41.

401. Hilton, *A Mad, Bad, and Dangerous People*, p. 132.

402. Florin Aftalion, *The French Revolution: An Economic Interpretation*, Trans. Martin Thom (CUP, 1990), p. 187.

403. Ritson, 'To Mr Wadeson, 15 December 1791', in *Letters*, I, p. 209.

404. Karl A. Roider Jr., *Baron Thugut and Austria's Response to the French Revolution* (Princeton, NJ: Princeton UP, 1987), p. 67.

405. Michael Duffy, 'Contested Empires, 1756-1815', in *The Eighteenth Century, 1688-1815*, ed. by Paul Langford (OUP, 2002), pp. 213-44 (p. 222).

406. Ritson, 'To Mrs Mary Ritson, 23 May 1803', in *Letters*, II, p. 236.

407. Ritson, 'To the Editor, 11 August 1803', in *Letters*, II, p. 245.

408. Ritson, 'To Mr Harrison, 1 February 1802', in *Letters*, II, p. 216.

409. Ritson, 'To the Same, 28 February 1803', in *Letters*, II, p. 229.

410. Ritson, 'To the Editor, 11 August 1803', in *Letters*, II, p. 246.

411. H.C. Selby, 'Narrative of Ritson's Last Days' cited in Burd, p. 202.

412. Ritson, 'To the Same, 16 August 1803', in *Letters*, I, p. 248.
413. Selby, p. 200.
414. *Ibid.*, p. 201.
415. *Ibid.*, p. 202.
416. Burd, p. 194.
417. *Ibid.*
418. Ritson, 'To Mrs Frank, 30 November 1784', in *Letters*, I, p. 95.
419. '[Review] Essay on Abstinence from Animal Food', *British Critic*, 22 (1803), 488-9.
420. Richard Nares [online], 'Letter to Thomas Percy, April 1803. Nichols, Illustrations of the Literary History of the XVIII Century', accessed 7 January 2020. Available at spenserians.cath.vt.edu
421. George Steevens [online], 'Letter to Thomas Percy, 11 January 1788. Nichols, Illustrations of the Literary History of the XVIII Century', accessed 7 January 2020. Available at spenserians.cath.vt.edu
422. Bronson, II, p. 293. How much of Percy's opposition to Ritson was mere intellectual snobbery is difficult to say. Ritson was a self-educated expert who went up against a grammar school and later Oxford educated member of the literary elite. That Ritson praised him publicly in further publications meant nothing to him.
423. Bronson, II, p. 296.
424. Morton, p. 53.

Chapter Six

425. Thomas Holcroft, *Alwyn; or, The Gentleman Comedian*, 2 vols (London: printed for Fielding and Walker, 1780), II, p. 155.
426. Thomas Percy, 'To Mr Malone, 26 February 1806', Bodleian MS Malone 39, fols. 182-3.
427. Bronson, I, p. 307.
428. Chris Worth, 'Ivanhoe and the Making of Britain', *Links and Letters*, 2 (1995), 63-76 (p. 64): The Author of *Waverley* was known as 'The Great Unknown' initially, although news and rumour that the celebrated *Waverley* author was in fact Walter Scott soon found its way into public knowledge. It tells the story of Edward Waverley, who gets caught up in the events of the Jacobite Rising of 1745. Scott's grand aim in writing his first novels was to depict Scottish life at certain points during the eighteenth century. His second novel,

Guy Mannering; or, The Astrologer (1815), recounts the story of Harry Bertram who is kidnapped at a young age by smugglers after witnessing the murder of an excise officer. Bertram has to make his way in the world in the quite lawless coastal regions of mid-eighteenth-century Scotland, when piracy was rife.

429. Walter Scott, *The Antiquary*, 3 vols (Edinburgh and London: Archibald Constable and Longman, Rees, Orme and Brown, 1816), I, pp. 52-3.

430. Scott, *The Antiquary*, I, pp. 130-1.

431. *Ibid.*, II, pp. 221-2.

432. The tour guide at Abbotsford assured me that it was their policy to keep the books in the order that Scott had originally arranged them.

433. Walter Scott, *Ivanhoe: A Romance*, ed. by Andrew Lang (London: MacMillan, 1910), p. xliii.

434. *Ibid.*, p. 3.

435. Chandler, 'Sir Walter Scott and the Medieval Revival', p. 324.

436. W.E. Simeone, 'The Robin Hood of Ivanhoe', *Journal of American Folklore*, 74: 293 (1961), 230-4 (p. 236).

437. Thomas Love Peacock, *Maid Marian and Crochet Castle*, ed. by G. Saintsbury (London: MacMillan, 1895), p. 126.

438. *Ibid.*, p. 28.

439. 'Maid Marian [Review]', *Monthly Review* (2nd Series), April 1822, 443-4 (p. 443).

440. I am aware that there is controversy over this issue. However, it should be noted that this Robin Hood is most likely *the* Robin Hood, and that his life gave rise to the legends about our famous outlaw. The 1225 Robin Hood was pursued by Eustace of Lowdham, the High Sheriff of York, who in his previous occupation was High Sheriff of Nottingham.

441. Ritson, *Robin Hood*, I, p. xxx.

442. Walter Scott, 'The Bannatyne Club', in *The Songs and Ballads of Sir Walter Scott with his Life*, ed. by Rufus W. Griswald (Philadelphia: Uriah Hunt, 1845), pp. 42-3.

443. Annette B. Hopkins, 'Ritson's 'Life of King Arthur', *PMLA*, 43: 1 (1928), 251-87 (p. 251).

444. Joseph Ritson, *The Life of King Arthur* (London: Payne and Foss, 1825), p. i.

445. Hopkins, 'Ritson's Life of King Arthur', p. 255.

446. Ritson, *Life of King Arthur*, p. xlin.

447. Ritson, 'To Mr Harrison, 22 August 1795', in *Letters*, II, p. 99; Ritson, 'To the Same, 16 August 1803', in *Letters*, II, p. 248.

448. Joseph Ritson, *Fairy Tales* (London: Payne and Foss, 1831), p. 12.

449. *A Select Catalogue of New Books at Reduced Prices* (London: Henry G. Bohn, 1846), p. 19.

450. Joseph Frank, 'Advertisement', in *The Letters of Joseph Ritson, Esq. Edited Chiefly from Originals in the Possession of his Nephew. To which is Prefixed a Memoir of the Author*, ed. by Joseph Frank, 2 vols (London: William Pickering, 1833), I, p. i.

451. A version of this section on Egan appeared originally appeared as a working paper (now out of print) but the original citation is as follows: Stephen Basdeo, 'Radical Medievalism: Pierce Egan the Younger's Robin Hood, Wat Tyler, and Adam Bell', in *Imagining the Victorians*, ed. by Stephen Basdeo and Lauren Padgett, Leeds Working Papers in Victorian Studies, 15 (Leeds: LCVS, 2016), pp. 49-65

452. Pierce Egan, *Robin Hood and Little John; or, the Merry Men of Sherwood Forest* (London: W.S. Johnson, 1850), p. ii.

453. *Ibid.*, p. 146.

454. *Ibid*, p. 107.

455. *Ibid*, p. 8.

456. R.B. Dobson and J. Taylor, *Rymes of Robyn Hood: An Introduction to the English Outlaw*, 3rd edn (Stoud: Sutton, 1982), p. 54

457. The 'Whood' is not a typographical error but its actual title.

458. E. David Gregory, *Victorian Songhunters* (London: Scarecrow Press, 2006), p. 142.

459. E. Baigent, [online], 'Gutch, John Mathew (1776-1861)', in *The Oxford Dictionary of National Biography*, accessed 22 January 2015, oxforddnb.com/view/article/11780.

460. William Morris, 'How I Became a Socialist', in *News from Nowhere and Other Writings*, ed. by Clive Wilmer, 3rd edn (London: Penguin, 2004), pp. 379-83 (p. 381).

461. 'William Morris', in *Treasury of Modern Biography*, ed. by Robert Cochrane (Edinburgh: William P. Nimmo, 1878), p. 529.

462. David A. Kopp, 'Two Williams of one medieval mind: reading the Socialist William Morris through the lens of the Radical William Cobbett', *Journal of William Morris Studies*, 20: 3 (2013), 31-46 (p. 31).

463. E. Belfort Bax and William Morris, 'Socialism from the Root Up', *Commonweal*, 22 May 1886, 61.

464. Robert Blatchford, *My Favourite Books* (London: The Clarion Office, 1900), p. 106.

465. A version of the section on Joseph Ritson and William Morris originally appeared as: Stephen Basdeo, 'That Robin Hood should bring us John Ball: William Morris's References to the Outlaw in A Dream of John Ball (1888)', *Journal of William Morris Studies*, 23: 2 (2019), 52-63.

466. William Morris, *A Dream of John Ball* (London: Longman, 1912), p. 20.

467. *Ibid*, p. 20.

468. *Ibid*.

469. William Morris, 'A Dream of John Ball', *Commonweal*, 20 November 1886, 266-7 (p. 267).

470. Ritson, *Robin Hood*, I, p. vi.

471. Morris, *A Dream of John Ball*, p. 20.

472. *Ibid*, p. 20.

473. Ritson, *Robin Hood*, I, p. v.

474. Morris, *A Dream of John Ball*, p. 22.

475. Ritson, *Robin Hood*, I, p. vi.

476. Morris, *A Dream of John Ball*, p. 22.

477. *Ibid*, p. 23.

478. *Ibid*, p. 47.

479. *Ibid*, p. 116.

480. 'E. Belfort Bax and William Morris, 'Socialism from the Root Up', *Commonweal*, 28 August 1886, 170-1.

481. 'Revolutionary Calendar', *Commonweal*, 2 June 1888, 175.

482. Ashton Nichols, 'Liberationist Sexuality and Nonviolent Resistance: The Legacy of Blake and Shelley in Morris's News from Nowhere', *Journal of William Morris Studies*, 10: 4 (1994), 20-27 (p. 20).

483. Paul Buhle, *Robin Hood: People's Outlaw and Forest Hero* (Oakland, CA: PM Press, 2011), pp. 17-20. This book was Howard Pyle's lavishly illustrated *Merry Adventures of Robin Hood* (1883). Yet Buhle's supposition seems highly unlikely for various reasons: while many works examining Pyle's life and works state that Pyle won praise from Morris for the illustrations in Pyle's *Robin Hood*, there are few references to him actually owning it. Buhle does not provide a supporting citation for his suppositions either.

484. Morris may have praised Pyle's illustrations but he appears to have said little about Pyle's actual text which Morris owned. In his personal library, Morris also possessed Francis James Child's *English and Scottish Popular Ballads* (1882-98). However, Child's text is unlikely to have been a factor in Morris's inclusion of Robin Hood in *A Dream of John Ball*; the third volume of Child's anthology, which contains all of the Robin Hood ballads, was not published until 1888, almost one year after *A Dream of John Ball* finished its initial serialisation in *Commonweal*.

485. Clive Wilmer, 'Introduction', in *William Morris: News from Nowhere and Other Writings*, ed. by Clive Wilmer, 3rd edn (London: Penguin, 2004), pp. ix-xlii.

486. Thomas Carlyle, *Past and Present*, 3rd edn (New York: William H. Colyer, 1844), pp. 93-4.

487. Francis J. Child, ed., *The English and Scottish Popular Ballads*, 5 vols (London: Houghton, 1882-1898; repr. New York: Dover, 2003), III, p. 43.

488. H.S.V. Jones, 'Joseph Ritson: A Romantic Antiquarian', *The Sewanee Review*, 22: 3 (1914), 341-50 (p. 344).

489. Tom Peete Cross, 'Reviews and Notices', *Modern Philology*, 17: 4 (1919), 233-8 (p. 238).

490. Bertrand H. Bronson, *The Ballad as Song* (Berkley, CA: University of California Press, 1969), p. 2, 66, 76, 321. See also Bertrand H. Bronson, ed. *The Singing Tradition of Child's Popular Ballads* (Princeton, NJ: Princeton UP, 1976).

491. Bertrand H. Bronson, 'Ritson's Bibliographia Scotica', *PMLA*, 52: 1 (1937), 122-59. For the modern disagreements between Robin Hood scholars see: Knight, *Robin Hood: A Mythic Biography*, p. 197; Dobson and Taylor, p. xx; Basdeo, *Robin Hood: The Life and Legend of an Outlaw*, p. xvi.

492. Norman Reilly Rane [online], 'The Adventures of Robin Hood, Robin Hood', in *The Monologue Database*, accessed 2 November 2019. Available at monologuedb.com

493. Michael Drayton, 'Sherwood Forest: Robin Hood. From "Poly-Olbion"', in *Poems of Places: An Anthology*, ed. by Henry Wadsworth Longfellow, 31 vols (Boston: James R. Osgood, 1876-79), I, p. 411.

494. This version of Ritson's 'Life of Robin Hood' is taken from the original 1795 edition published by T. Egerton. Later editions after 1820 cut out some parts of this.

Appendix Three

495. 'Memoir of the Reverend John Gutch', *The Gentleman's Magazine*, September (1831), 201-03.

496. J.M. Gutch, 'Magdalena; written at Godstowe, Oxfordshire, the Retreat of Fair Rosamund', *The Gentleman's Magazine*, August (1797), 693.

497. 'John Mathew Gutch, Esq.', *The Gentleman's Magazine*, December (1861), 682-6.

498. 'J.M. Gutch', *The London Review*, 12 October 1861, 463.

499. 'To Mr J.M. Gutch', *Bristol Mercury*, 12 February 1827, 3.

500. J.M. Gutch, 'Preface', in *A Lytell Geste of Robin Hode*, ed. by J.M. Gutch, 2 vols (London: Longman, 1847), I, p. xxvi.

501. J.M. Gutch, 'Letter', *The Gentleman's Magazine*, June (1814), 531-4 (p. 532).

502. 'The Library of Mr John Gutch', *The Athenaeum*, 3 April 1858, 436.

503. Gutch, *A Lytell Geste of Robin Hode*, I, p. iii.

504. *Ibid.*, I, p. i.

505. Joseph Ritson, *Robin Hood: A Collection of All the Ancient Poems, Songs, and Ballads* (London: Longman, 1820), p. iv.

506. Gutch, *A Lytell Geste of Robin Hode*, I, p. 222.

507. 'Antiquarian Researches', *The Gentleman's Magazine*, October (1848), 405.

508. 'Literary Notices', *Berrow's Worcestor Journal*, 5 August 1852, 3.

509. 'British Archaeological Association', *The Times*, 18 August 1852, 6.

510. J.M. Gutch, 'The Discovery of the Veritable Robin Hood', *The Gentleman's Magazine*, August 1852, 160-62.

511. 'British Archaeological Association', *Caledonian Mercury*, 23 August 1852, 5.

512. 'British Archaeological Association', *Nottinghamshire Guardian*, 19 August 1852, 3. This also gives a fuller account of Gutch's paper.

513. J.M. Gutch, 'The Ballad Hero Robin Hood', *The Reliquary*, January (1861), 128-43.

514. 'John Mathew Gutch', *The Gentleman's Magazine*, December (1861), 682-6.

Select Bibliography

This bibliography lists relevant scholarship on Robin Hood and eighteenth-century social and cultural history, Romanticism, and antiquarianism. For further references please see individual chapter notes.

Barczewski, Stephanie, *Myth and National Identity in Nineteenth-Century Britain: The Legends of King Arthur and Robin Hood* (Oxford: Clarendon Press, 2000)

Basdeo, Stephen, 'The Changing Faces of Robin Hood: Rethinking Gentrification in the Post-Medieval Tradition (Unpublished PhD thesis, University of Leeds, 2017)

———— [online], *Here Begynneth a Lytell Geste of Robin Hood*, accessed 22 March 2020. Available at: www.gesteofrobinhood.com.

————, *Robin Hood: The Life and Legend of an Outlaw* (Barnsley: Pen and Sword, 2019)

————, 'That Robin Hood should bring us John Ball: William Morris's References to the Outlaw in A Dream of John Ball (1888)', *Journal of William Morris Studies*, 23: 2 (2019), 52-63

Brewer, John, *The Pleasures of the Imagination: English Culture in the Eighteenth Century* (Abingdon: Routledge, 2013)

Bronson, B.H., *Joseph Ritson: Scholar-at-Arms*, 2 vols (Berkeley, CA: University of California Press, 1938)

Burd, Henry A., *Joseph Ritson: A Critical Biography*, University of Illinois Studies in Language and Literature, II: 3 (Urbana: University of Illinois, 1916)

Derry, John W., *Politics in the Age of Fox, Pitt, and Liverpool* (Basingstoke: Palgrave, 2001)

Groom, Nick, *The Making of Percy's Reliques* (OUP, 1999)

Holt, James C., *Robin Hood*, 2nd edn. (London: Thames and Hudson, 1989)

Hopkins, Annette B., 'Ritson's 'Life of King Arthur', *PMLA*, 43: 1 (1928), 251-87

Knight, Stephen, *Reading Robin Hood: Content, Form and Reception in Outlaw Myth* (Manchester: Manchester UP, 2015)

———, *Robin Hood: A Mythic Biography* (Ithaca: Cornell UP, 2003)

Langford, Paul, ed., *The Eighteenth Century, 1688-1815* (OUP, 2002)

———, *A Polite and Commercial People* (OUP, 1989)

McAuley, Karen, *Our Ancient National Airs: Scottish Song Collecting from the Enlightenment to the Romantic Era*, 2nd edn (Abingdon: Routledge, 2013)

McNutt, Genevieve Theodora, 'Joseph Ritson and the publication of early English literature' (Unpublished PhD thesis, Edinburgh University, 2018)

Mitchell, Rosemary, *Picturing the Past; English History in Text and Image, 1830-1870* (OUP, 2000)

Ohlgren, Thomas, *Robin Hood: The Early Poems, 1465-1560—Texts, Contexts, and Ideology* (Cranbury, NJ: Associated University Presses, 2010)

Santini, Monica, *The Impetus of Amateur Scholarship: Discussing and Editing Medieval Romances in Late-Eighteenth and Nineteenth-Century Britain* (Bern: Peter Lang, 2010)

Sweet, Rosemary, *Antiquaries: The Discovery of the Past in Eighteenth-Century Britain* (Basingstoke: Palgrave, 2004)

Tattersfield, Nigel, *Thomas Bewick: Graphic Worlds* (London: British Museum Press, 2014)

Uglow, Jenny, *Nature's Engraver: A Life of Thomas Bewick* (London: Faber, 2006)

Index